Best Beach Vacations

THE MID-ATLANTIC

By Donald D. Groff

A Beachscape Publishing, Inc. production for
MACMILLAN TRAVEL • U.S.A.

Frommer's Best Beach Vacations: The Mid-Atlantic

Publishers *Gary Stoller and Bruce Bolger*
Editor *Lauren Bernstein*
Design Director/Macmillan USA *Michele Laseau*
Art Director *Sun Design/Lauri Marks*
Beach Consultant *Dr. Stephen Leatherman*
Senior Editor *Marita Begley*
Research Editor *Betty Villaume*
Map Designer *John Grimwade*
Cartographer *Joyce Pendola*

Frommer's Best Beach Vacations: The Mid-Atlantic is produced for Frommer's by Beachscape Publishing, Inc. Please address any comments or corrections to Beachscape at 145 Palisade St., Suite 397, Dobbs Ferry, N.Y. 10522; tel. 914-674-9283, fax 914-674-9285.

Macmillan Travel

A Simon & Schuster Macmillan Company
1633 Broadway, New York, NY 10019-6785
Copyright 1996 by Beachscape Publishing, Inc.

The Library of Congress Cataloging-in-Publication Data is available from the Library of Congress.

ISBN 0-02-860662-0

Manufactured in the United States of America

10 9 8 7 6 5 4 3 2 1

First Edition

Also Available:

Special Sales

A word from the author

For Katherine, Bob, Mary Sue, David, Sherry, David Lee, Rondee, and Bonnie Lee, who have shined on me.

About the author

Donald D. Groff's travel columns appear regularly in *The Philadelphia Inquirer*, *The Boston Globe*, and other publications. A winner of the Lowell Thomas Award for travel news investigative reporting, he contributes to *Condé Nast Traveler* and *Endless Vacation* magazines. He lives in Narbeth, Pennsylvania, and holds an M.A. in journalism and public affairs from the American University in Washington.

Table of Contents

Introduction

Beach Locator Maps

New York

New Jersey

Delaware

Maryland & Virginia

The Best Beach Vacations Rating System

Going to the beach is a great American pastime. Whether for a vacation or just a day, Americans flock to the nation's shores in search of the inexplicable pleasure that comes with a stay by the water. That's about all we have in common regarding our love of beaches, since each person has his or her own special tastes. Some come for serenity, others for action, and there are a hundred variations in between. *Best Beach Vacations* is designed to help you find the beach experience that's right for you, be it for a day, a weekend, or an entire vacation.

Best Beach Vacations uses a unique rating system that systematically evaluates each beach area according to the categories that matter most to beach lovers: **Beauty, Swimming, Sand, Hotels/Inns/B&Bs, House Rentals, Restaurants, Nightlife, Attractions, Shopping, Sports,** and **Nature.** A brief review of the ratings will help you quickly narrow your selection. The overview and service information in each chapter provide everything you'll need to start planning your beach experience.

To select the beaches featured in this book, we began with information gathered by professor Stephen Leatherman, sometimes called Dr. Beach, a coastal geologist and director of the University of Maryland's Laboratory for Coastal Research. For years, Leatherman has collected information on water quality, scenic beauty, sand conditions, surf, temperature, and tourist amenities at beaches around the United States, data he uses to determine an overall rating for each beach. Using that data, along with their own knowledge and input from regional and local sources, the authors visited each beach and combed nearby areas to personally evaluate all of the other important elements that go into a beach experience.

The ratings at the beginning of a chapter summarize the entire area. Within each chapter, individual beaches are listed. Each has its own description, with more specific ratings. It's easy to understand the rating system, because it's based on the A through F scale that's used for report cards; if you see NA (not applicable) in a ratings category, it means that this particular feature does not apply to the beach.

Here are the criteria used to formulate a grade for particular aspects of each beach or beach area. *Beauty:* overall setting, sand, and views offshore.
Swimming: water quality, temperature, and wave conditions.
Sand: texture, color, and cleanliness.
Amenities: rest rooms, food concessions, lifeguards, and sports equipment.

Beauty	A
Swimming	B
Sand	C
Hotels/Inns/B&Bs	E
House rentals	A
Restaurants	E
Nightlife	E
Attractions	E
Shopping	C
Sports	A
Nature	A

The grades for all other categories are based on the quality and quantity of offerings in and around the beach area. The rating for **Attractions**, for example, assesses the quality and quantity of all types of things to do in the area surrounding the beach.

Best Beach Vacations makes every attempt to warn readers of specific safety concerns in each area. However, readers should visit all beaches mindful of the potential dangers posed by water, wave, and sun, and take appropriate precautions.

We hope you have a wonderful beach vacation.

–Gary Stoller and Bruce Bolger

Best Beach Vacations: Overview

What is most astounding about the beaches of the Mid-Atlantic is that there are so many superb ones in a region widely regarded as the paved-over metroplex of America. Somehow, in a relatively small area that embraces one-fifth of the nation's population, much of the shoreline is hallowed ground.

THE MID-ATLANTIC AT A GLANCE

NEW YORK: The South Fork of Long Island is a legendary leisure destination. Near Montauk, some beaches sit beneath sandy bluffs, but usually the beaches rise to dunes that give way to a lowland topography of grass and woodland. Fire Island's 32 miles of beach have a dreamy remoteness; the absence of vehicles combined with wandering deer give it a rare allure. Closer to Manhattan, Robert Moses and Jones Beach state parks are built for the masses.

NEW JERSEY: The coastal resorts offer a choice of honky-tonk, quiet family fun, historic tradition—or a combination. Rich in ocean front and wetlands, Atlantic City boasts the mother of all boardwalks, and towns north and south have erected boardwalks for bikers, hikers, and arcade-hungry teenagers. Spring Lake and Cape May have two of the finest seaside Victorian districts in the country.

DELAWARE: The state's entire Atlantic coast is a tribute to beach conservation; it is public beach, and you can walk nearly all of it without obstacle. At the mouth of Delaware Bay, Cape Henlopen starts the pristine reach southward, with robust surf and high dunes, and gives way to several low-key and distinctive resort communities extending to the state line. Rehoboth Beach offers the most restaurants and hotel rooms.

MARYLAND AND VIRGINIA: Ocean City and Virginia Beach are two of a kind, both vigorously cultivated as big-time resorts. Their broad strips of sand are vast enough to withstand, and delight, huge numbers of visitors. At the same time, both cities have wilder, less commercial beaches within half an hour's drive.

When To Go

Mid-Atlantic resort cities follow the warming pattern of the sun, with tourism-dependent businesses opening on weekends in

March or April, extending hours until they reach a full schedule by late May. The beach season—when lifeguards are on duty—typically runs from Memorial Day through Labor Day, although many communities consider the Fourth of July the start of high season, with hotel rates increasing then. After Labor Day, the trend reverses, with lower rates, reduced schedules, and closings.

Many resort towns extend their season by sponsoring spring and fall events to attract visitors and help keep restaurants and inns open. These periods are often excellent for venturing out. Rates are lower, and the plagues of summer travel—heavy traffic and parking problems—disappear.

Southern destinations stay open longer than northern ones, and if the weather remains warm, many shore towns continue to post lifeguards on weekends in September. The majority of the areas covered in this book have at least some life off-season. Atlantic City and Virginia Beach do a healthy year-round business.

How To Get There

The Mid-Atlantic benefits from the best transportation network in the country, with frequent mass-transit connections in many locations. Air links are also good, with hubs in New York, Baltimore, Washington, and Philadelphia. Amtrak provides frequent rail service to the whole Northeast corridor, and commuter trains reach all of Long Island's shore points.

SERVICE INFORMATION
Hotels/Inns/B&Bs

The Mid-Atlantic region has a full range of lodgings, from basic to luxurious, although some areas have more of one kind than the other. We have selected some of the best choices in each category—from clean and comfortable to elegant. Many properties require a minimum two- or three-day booking in summer; some require a week. Be sure to inquire about cancellation penalties and local taxes. Lodging falls into four price categories, based on double occupancy peak-season nightly rates (before taxes and gratuities):

Very expensive	More than $180
Expensive	$111-$180
Moderate	$76-$110
Inexpensive	$75 or less

House Rentals

Renting a house is a popular way to enjoy an extended vacation. Rates vary considerably, depending on size, amenities, and proximity to the water. In some resort areas, houses can be rented for the season only; in others, weekly rentals are the standard.

Restaurants

For many people, dining out is as much a part of vacationing as the surf and sand, and Mid-Atlantic resorts cater to every culinary taste. While some cities have scores of notable eateries and others have only a few, you're likely to find one or more distinguished restaurants within half an hour's drive, no matter where you go.

Restaurants fall into four price categories, based on the approximate cost of a dinner for one person (including appetizer, main course, and dessert, without drinks, tax, and tip):

Very expensive	More than $50
Expensive	$31-$50
Moderate	$16-$30
Inexpensive	$15 or less

Safety Tips

Any dangers associated with Mid-Atlantic beaches can be minimized through awareness and care. Perhaps the most threatening hazard is surf condition—waves and underwater currents, which can vary greatly depending on the weather. The summer of 1995 was a season of uncommon storm activity in the Atlantic Ocean, resulting in rough water and seaward currents or riptides that closed many beaches and claimed at least eighteen lives. (In a typical season, most of these areas report no drownings at all.) A number of drownings involved people swimming when no lifeguard was on duty, after drinking alcohol, or both. If you have doubts about the safety of a beach ask a lifeguard.

Beach Area Rankings

The author's personal favorites (in order of preference):

1. Southampton, NY (Chapter 3)
2. Chincoteague, VA (24)
3. Lewes/Cape Henlopen, DE (19)
4. Fire Island, NY (6)
5. Westhampton, NY (5)
6. East Hampton, NY (2)
7. Long Beach Island, NJ (12)
8. Hampton Bays, NY (4)
9. Cape May, NJ (18)
10. Montauk, NY (1)
11. Spring Lake, NJ (10)
12. Robert Moses State Park, NY (7)
13. Point Pleasant Beach, NJ (11)
14. Virginia Beach, VA (25)
15. Ocean City, MD (23)
16. Ocean City, NJ (14)
17. Stone Harbor, NJ (16)
18. Sea Isle City, NJ (15)
19. The Wildwoods, NJ (17)
20. Rehoboth Beach, DE (20)
21. Bethany Beach, DE (22)
22. Jones Beach State Park, NY (8)
23. Dewey Beach, DE (21)
24. Atlantic City, NJ (13)
25. Lake George, NY (9)

Best Beaches For . . .

Lodging: Cape May, NJ (Chapter 18)
House Rentals: Stone Harbor, NJ (16)
Restaurants: Southampton, NY (3)
Nightlife: Atlantic City, NJ (13)
Attractions: Virginia Beach, VA (25)
Shopping: Southampton, NY (3), Rehoboth Beach, DE (20)
Fishing: Montauk, NY (1)
Boating: Southampton, NY (3)
Surfing: Dewey Beach, DE (21), Montauk, NY (1)
Diving: Atlantic City , NJ (13)
Bicycling: Virginia Beach, VA (25)
Golf: Ocean City, MD (23)
Nature: Chincoteague, VA (24)

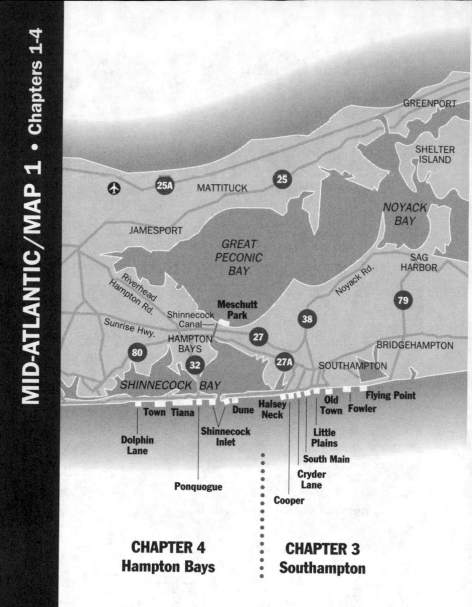

GREENPORT

SHELTER
ISLAND

25A MATTITUCK 25

*NOYACK
BAY*

JAMESPORT

*GREAT
PECONIC
BAY*

SAG
HARBOR

Riverhead
Hampton Rd.

Noyack Rd.

**Meschutt
Park**

Shinnecock
Canal

38

79

Sunrise Hwy.

27

BRIDGEHAMPTON

**HAMPTON
BAYS**

27A

SOUTHAMPTON

80

32

SHINNECOCK BAY

Old
Town Flying Point
Fowler

Town Tiana Dune Halsey
Neck

Shinnecock
Inlet

**Little
Plains**

**Dolphin
Lane**

South Main

**Cryder
Lane**

Ponquogue

Cooper

**CHAPTER 4
Hampton Bays**

**CHAPTER 3
Southampton**

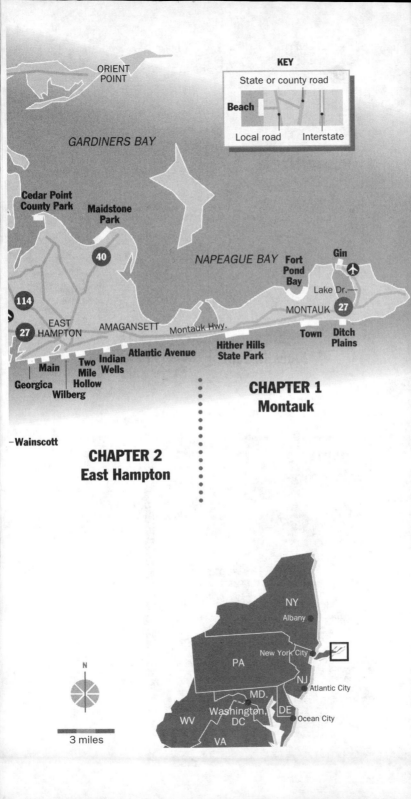

KEY

State or county road

Beach

Local road   Interstate

ORIENT POINT

GARDINERS BAY

Cedar Point County Park

Maidstone Park

40

NAPEAGUE BAY   Fort Pond Bay   Gin

Lake Dr.

114

MONTAUK   27

27 EAST HAMPTON   AMAGANSETT   Montauk Hwy.

Town   Ditch Plains

Atlantic Avenue   Hither Hills State Park

Main   Two Mile Hollow   Indian Wells

Georgica   Wilberg

CHAPTER 1
Montauk

-Wainscott

CHAPTER 2
East Hampton

NY

Albany

New York City

PA

NJ   Atlantic City

MD.

WV   Washington, DC   DE

Ocean City

VA

N

3 miles

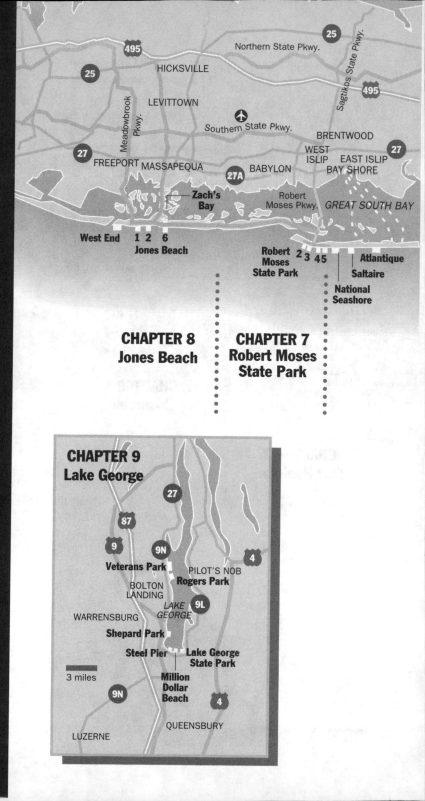

495

25

Northern State Pkwy.

25

Sagtikos State Pkwy.

495

HICKSVILLE

LEVITTOWN

Meadowbrook Pkwy.

Southern State Pkwy.

BRENTWOOD

WEST ISLIP

EAST ISLIP

BAY SHORE

27

FREEPORT   MASSAPEQUA

27A

BABYLON

Zach's Bay

Robert Moses Pkwy.

GREAT SOUTH BAY

West End   1 2 6
Jones Beach

Robert Moses State Park

2 3 45

Atlantique

Saltaire

National Seashore

**CHAPTER 8
Jones Beach**

**CHAPTER 7
Robert Moses
State Park**

**CHAPTER 9
Lake George**

27

87

9

9N

4

Veterans Park

PILOT'S NOB

Rogers Park

BOLTON LANDING

LAKE GEORGE

9L

WARRENSBURG

Shepard Park

Steel Pier   Lake George State Park

3 miles

9N

Million Dollar Beach

4

QUEENSBURY

LUZERNE

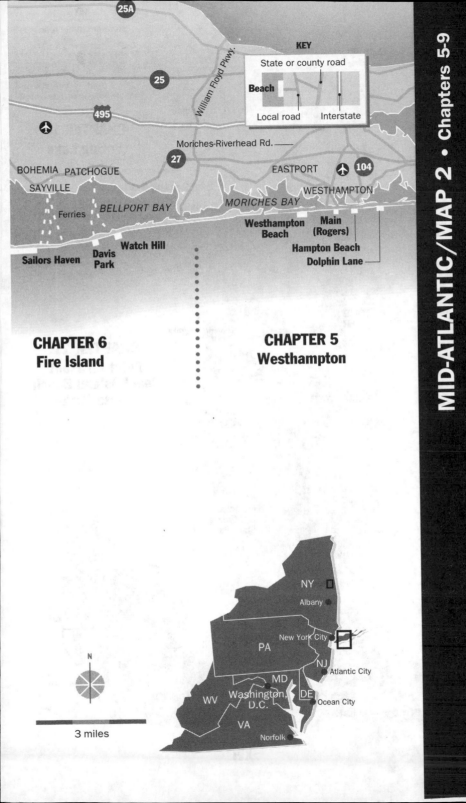

25A

25

495

William Floyd Pkwy.

State or county road

Beach

Local road   Interstate

Moriches-Riverhead Rd.

27

BOHEMIA PATCHOGUE

SAYVILLE

EASTPORT

104

BELLPORT BAY

Ferries

WESTHAMPTON

MORICHES BAY

Watch Hill

Westhampton
Beach

Main
(Rogers)

Sailors Haven

Davis
Park

Hampton Beach

Dolphin Lane

**CHAPTER 6
Fire Island**

**CHAPTER 5
Westhampton**

N

3 miles

NY

Albany

New York City

PA

NJ   Atlantic City

MD

WV   Washington,
D.C.   DE

VA   Ocean City

Norfolk

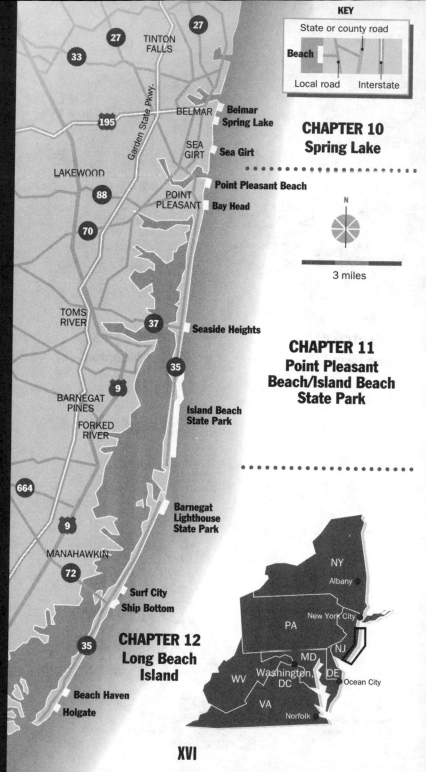

KEY

State or county road

Beach

Local road   Interstate

27

27   TINTON FALLS

33

195

BELMAR   **Belmar**
Spring Lake

SEA GIRT   **Sea Girt**

LAKEWOOD

88

70

POINT PLEASANT   **Point Pleasant Beach**

Bay Head

CHAPTER 10
Spring Lake

N

3 miles

TOMS RIVER

37   **Seaside Heights**

35

BARNEGAT PINES

9

FORKED RIVER

Island Beach State Park

CHAPTER 11
Point Pleasant Beach/Island Beach State Park

664

9

MANAHAWKIN

72

Barnegat Lighthouse State Park

Surf City

Ship Bottom

35

CHAPTER 12
Long Beach Island

Beach Haven

Holgate

NY

Albany

New York City

PA

NJ

MD

DE

Washington, DC

WV

Ocean City

VA

Norfolk

XVI

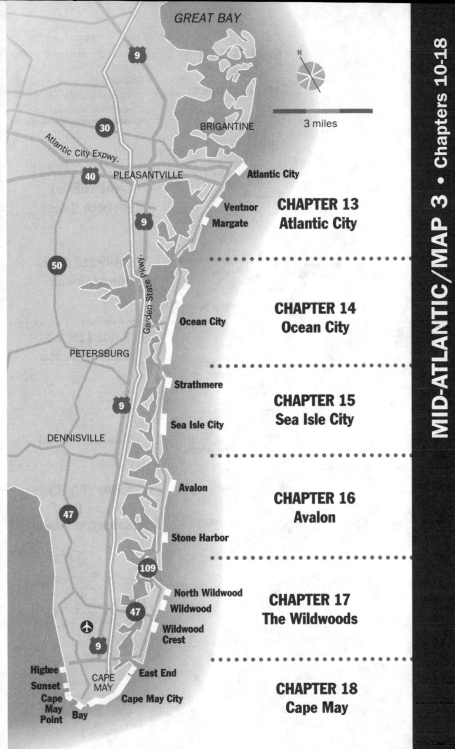

GREAT BAY

N

3 miles

Atlantic City Expwy.

PLEASANTVILLE

BRIGANTINE

Atlantic City

Ventnor
Margate

CHAPTER 13
Atlantic City

Garden State Pkwy.

Ocean City

CHAPTER 14
Ocean City

PETERSBURG

Strathmere

CHAPTER 15
Sea Isle City

Sea Isle City

DENNISVILLE

Avalon

CHAPTER 16
Avalon

Stone Harbor

CHAPTER 17
The Wildwoods

North Wildwood
Wildwood

Wildwood
Crest

Higbee
Sunset
Cape
May
Point   Bay

CAPE
MAY

East End

Cape May City

CHAPTER 18
Cape May

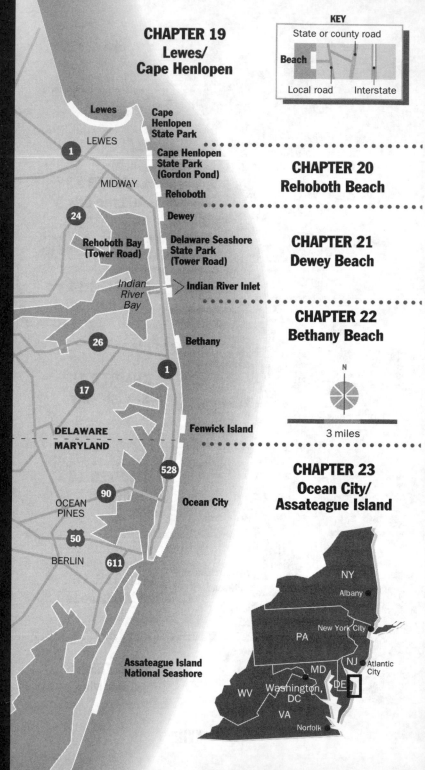

KEY
State or county road
Beach
Local road   Interstate

CHAPTER 19
Lewes/
Cape Henlopen

Lewes
Cape Henlopen State Park
LEWES
Cape Henlopen State Park (Gordon Pond)
MIDWAY
Rehoboth
Dewey

CHAPTER 20
Rehoboth Beach

Rehoboth Bay (Tower Road)
Delaware Seashore State Park (Tower Road)
Indian River Bay
Indian River Inlet

CHAPTER 21
Dewey Beach

Bethany

CHAPTER 22
Bethany Beach

N

Fenwick Island

3 miles

DELAWARE
MARYLAND

CHAPTER 23
Ocean City/
Assateague Island

OCEAN PINES

Ocean City

BERLIN

Assateague Island National Seashore

NY
Albany
New York City
PA
NJ   Atlantic City
MD
WV   Washington, DC   DE
VA
Norfolk

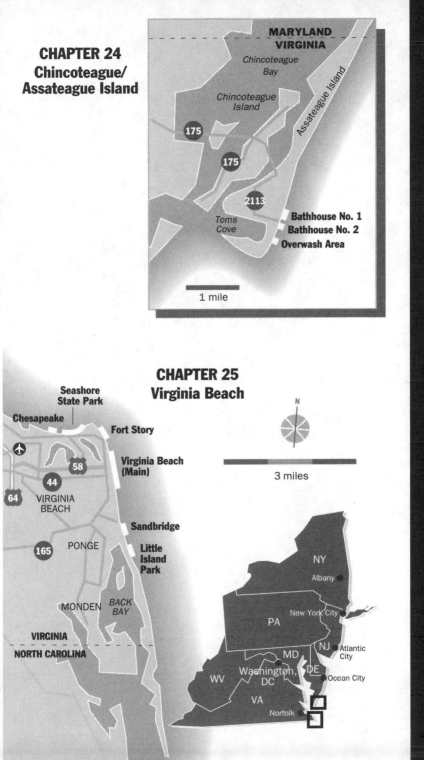

CHAPTER 24
Chincoteague/
Assateague Island

MARYLAND
VIRGINIA

Chincoteague
Bay

Chincoteague
Island

Assateague Island

175

175

2113

Toms
Cove

Bathhouse No. 1
Bathhouse No. 2
Overwash Area

1 mile

CHAPTER 25
Virginia Beach

N

Seashore
State Park

Chesapeake

Fort Story

Virginia Beach
(Main)

3 miles

58

44

64

VIRGINIA
BEACH

Sandbridge

165

PONGE

Little
Island
Park

MONDEN *BACK*
BAY

VIRGINIA

NORTH CAROLINA

NY

Albany

New York City

PA

NJ ● Atlantic
City

MD

WV

Washington,
DC

DE
● Ocean City

VA

Norfolk

CHAPTER 1

Montauk

Beauty	A
Swimming	A
Sand	A
Hotels/Inns/B&Bs	B
House rentals	B
Restaurants	B+
Nightlife	C
Attractions	B
Shopping	C
Sports	B
Nature	A

*P*oised at the eastern tip of Long Island, Montauk Point juts dramatically into the Atlantic Ocean. The historic lighthouse at land's end looks out over fishing boats cutting through heavy surf toward fertile waters. There is no better place to watch the sun rise, but the water near the point is much too rough for swimming. On its southern side, the craggy shore soon gives way to sand and

1

HOW TO GET THERE

◆ The road that carries most Montauk visitors into town, Rte. 27, runs the length of Long Island and goes by several names. It's most commonly known as Rte. 27 or Montauk Hwy., but it also appears as Sunrise Hwy., Montauk Point State Hwy., Main St., Woods Lane, and Pantigo Rd. Try to avoid this road on Fri. and Sun. (and, to a certain extent, on Sat.) in the summer: It virtually becomes a parking lot.

◆ Driving from New York City, take the Long Island Expwy. (Rte. 495) east to Exit 70 (Manorville). Turn right onto Rte. 111 south and continue until it ends, then turn left onto Sunrise Hwy. (Rte. 27). Continue east as it merges into Rte. 39 and becomes Montauk Hwy. In light traffic the trip takes 2-3 hr.

◆ Driving from Philadelphia, take the NJ Tpke. north to I-278 and the Verrazano Bridge; then the Belt Pkwy. to the Southern State Pkwy. Continue east to Rte. 27 and into Montauk. In light traffic the trip takes about 4 hr.

◆ Montauk is the final stop on the Montauk branch of the Long Island Rail Road (LIRR). From Penn Station New York, the trip takes about 3 hr. The Montauk station is about 1 mi. from Town Beach (LIRR schedule and fare information: tel. 718-217-5477).

◆ You can also reach Montauk on the Hampton Jitney, which has regular service from Manhattan (tel. 516-283-4600, 800-936-0440).

more manageable currents and commences the long sweep of Long Island's handsome beach line. The town of Montauk is less than five miles from the point along Route 27, its Main Street shopping area and circular plaza a couple of blocks from a wide stretch of unblemished sand. Most of the town's charter fishing fleet is based a few minutes away in Montauk Harbor, which feeds into Block Island Sound and abuts Lake Montauk, a body that stretches almost from bay to ocean—or three miles across. Montauk also has several smaller lakes, notably Fort Pond, a haven for canoes, rowboats, sailboats, paddle boats, and kayaks. This combination of ocean, bays, and lakes makes Montauk a diverse vacation spot, where you can swim, surf, and boat in tame or tempestuous waters.

Montauk is a hamlet of East Hampton, but unlike the tonier Hamptons, this is a tourist town, not a beach haven for second-home owners. Known as a fishing village and a beach resort for those who steer clear of the Hamptons' priciness and snob appeal, Montauk is a place where you can sleep and eat relatively cheaply, even in summer. But in recent years, it has developed some cachet of its own. Dick Cavett has a home here, as does Paul Simon, whose annual benefit concert at Deep Hollow Ranch features performers such as wife Edie Brickell and James Taylor.

The first of Simon's concerts, in 1990, raised half a million dollars to help preserve the lighthouse, which was nearly 300 feet from the sea when it was completed in 1797. The victim of erosion, it is now just a few dozen feet from the bluff—so close, in fact, that fishermen can cast off the buttressed terrace that fortifies the point against erosion. The effort to stabilize it continues, as do plans to celebrate its bicentennial.

Predating the lighthouse, Deep Hollow Ranch was founded in 1658 and claims the title of first cattle ranch in the country. Montauk County Park was carved from that range, and Deep Hollow riders still meander its wooded trails to the beach. When the ranch needed a new barn in 1992, Amish barn-raisers were hired to construct a historically accurate building. True to style, the barn has a wooden roof and antique-style windows. The project was headed by Elam King, who was an advisor for the movie *Witness*, in which the character played by Harrison

Ford took part in an Amish barn-raising.

Besides the lighthouse, beaches, and harbor, the town's most visible landmark is Montauk Manor, a Tudor-style luxury hotel built in 1927 that sits like a baronial estate atop the highest land in the area. Montauk's most renowned hostelry is the venerable Gurney's Inn Resort & Spa, which is set on the ocean and is the only year-round marino therapeutic spa in the country.

BEACHES

Motels usually provide guests with a beach parking pass. Township parking permits are required for most of the beach lots, and $100 seasonal passes can be purchased in the town clerk's office. Good beach front is within walking distance of many of Montauk's downtown parking spaces.

MONTAUK TOWN BEACH

Just a couple of blocks from Route 27 and the Montauk Plaza lies a delightful stretch of medium-width beach whose uniformly fine sand is mottled with tiny black and gold flecks that give it a golden cast in the low morn-

Beauty	A-
Swimming	A
Sand	A
Amenities	B

ing light. The portion of the beach close to the IGA store is known as Kirk Park Beach. The heavily grassed dunes are high and rolling enough that in some places it's possible to tuck into their edge to get away from the wind.

To the east is a four-block string of beach-front lodgings, and beyond it in the distance are bare dirt bluffs rising from the beach. To the west are more bluffs, these with vegetation. When the beach's central area gets crowded in summer, you can escape to quieter sands in either direction. *To reach Town Beach, go to central Montauk and turn south onto any of several side streets off Rte. 27 (Main St.). There is a wooden boardwalk over the dune at the parking lot near the IGA.*
Swimming: Good swimming in clean water with continuous wave action. Lifeguard on duty on part of the beach.
Sand: Medium-width beach of fine, light brown sand, building to dunes in the areas away from motel frontage.

4

Amenities: Stores and restaurants are a block or two away in the business district. Rest rooms in parking lot.
Sports: Body boarding, fishing.
Parking: The lot near the IGA is $10 a day for nonresidents without a beach parking permit. Limited street parking.

DITCH PLAINS BEACH

This is the area's most often mentioned surfing beach. Just off the parking lot are slabs of broken concrete, and the beach is not particularly attractive, but just to the east, a rocky point near the East Deck Motel offers a good vantage

Beauty	B
Swimming	A
Sand	B
Amenities	D

point for watching surfers. Beyond that, the sand gets better for sunbathing. The water remains very shallow near shore, though, and encrusted rocks make it difficult to wade.

In the opposite direction, west of the parking lot, the beach curves along a dirt bluff rising 20 to 40 feet. It's beautiful, but it has a slightly sea-battered feel. The sand is fine and tan but rock-strewn from the force of the surf, and the bluff shows the erosive wear of sea and wind. Flotsam, such as the odd hay bale, washes up in places.

East of Montauk on Route 27, a pot-holed, one-lane dirt road called Seaside Avenue heads toward the beach and dead-ends, with parking for perhaps half a dozen cars. From there, a path picks its way toward the sea on the scrub-covered bluff overlooking Ditch Plains Beach, offering excellent views and places from which to make your way down to the beach. *From Rte. 27 east of Montauk, follow Ditch Plains Rd. to the parking area.*

HITHER HILL STATE PARK BEACH

This state park beach is splendid, a wide, undulating swath of sand as far as the eye can see, sloping gently seaward to meet rolling waves. The beach is backed by a carefully restored dune that blocks the view of just about everything

Beauty	A
Swimming	A
Sand	A
Amenities	A

except sand, sea, and sky. The dune was rebuilt in 1981, and

20,000 beach grass seedlings were planted in one day. Beachgoers must use a limited number of paths to cross the dune. At the north end of the campground, a stairway winds up a hillside to a picnic area with tables and grills overlooking the beach.

The park is open to day users from 8 a.m. until sunset. On busy summer days when the parking lot fills up, a supplemental lot, near the picnic area, is available. *Hither Hills State Park is west of Montauk along the Old Montauk Hwy.; tel. 516-668-2461.*
Swimming: Fine swimming on a scenic, wave-washed beach. Lifeguard on duty.
Sand: Fine, uniformly tan, building to a grassy dune.
Amenities: Bathhouse, 165-space campground, deli, general store. In summer, camp reservations must be made 90 days in advance.
Sports: Body boarding, fishing.
Parking: Large parking lot for day users, $4 per vehicle.

GIN BEACH

Two parallel jetties form the entrance to Montauk Harbor, and along the east jetty is Gin Beach and the adjacent county park with its long beach. Being on the bay side, the beach gets low waves occasionally kicked up by the

Beauty	B
Swimming	B
Sand	B
Amenities	D

wind. It's a moderately wide, gradually sloping strip of sand eroded in places and backed by a grassy dune. Because the water is tame, Gin Beach is a favorite among families with young children.

Just east of the parking lot, the beach becomes part of Montauk County Park, which, for a steep fee, allows self-contained camping on the beach. But there's no charge if you park at Gin Beach and walk onto the park's beach. On clear days you can see Connecticut and Rhode Island in the distance. *To reach Gin Beach, turn off Rte. 27 onto E. Lake Dr., which winds along Lake Montauk, and follow it to its end.*
Swimming: Swimming in bay water with gentle waves lapping the shore. Lifeguard on duty mid-Jun-early Sep.; no lifeguard in the county park section.

Sand: A narrow strand of fine, tan sand with some shells, pebbles, and dried seaweed.
Amenities: Toilets in the parking lot. Vending from a truck.
Sports: None.
Parking: Parking lot, town permit required.

FORT POND BAY BEACH

This beach stretches for about three-quarters of a mile along Fort Pond Bay and has an off-the-beaten-path feel, with no commercial development—except at the east end, where the Port Royal restaurant and resort are located. The gentle water bare-

Beauty	B
Swimming	B
Sand	C
Amenities	D

ly laps the shore, and it's clear enough to attract snorkelers.

A low, ragged dune separates the beach from the road, and the Long Island Railroad parallels that. It's not an elegant beach, but it does have a soothing character, with its calm water and broad view of the bay, suitable for sunset-watching. The sand is coarse and mixed with pebbles and dried seaweed. *Follow Industrial Rd. along the north edge of Fort Pond to where it meets Second Horse Rd., turning down Shore Rd. toward the railroad tracks. Beyond the tracks is Navy Rd., which runs along the beach.*

HOTELS/INNS/B&BS

Montauk has plenty of low-end lodging (less than $100 a night), even in summer, and a good range of pricier accommodations.

◆ **Beachcomber Resort** (very expensive). This modern complex overlooking the ocean has 88 balconied units in four buildings, including studios, one- and two-bedrooms, and an executive suite with a fireplace. Second-floor rooms in the Ocean East and Ocean West buildings have the best views and are away from the road noise. Getting to the beach means walking across Old Montauk Highway. *727 Old Montauk Hwy., Montauk, NY 11954; tel. 516-668-2894; fax 516-668-3154. Closed Oct. 31-Apr.1. On Old Montauk Hwy. just west of Montauk.*

◆ **Montauk Yacht Club** (very expensive). This posh resort on Star Island has an exclusive setting and amenities to match, including nine tennis courts, a first-rate restaurant and bar, three pools, and a small beach. The 88 rooms in the main complex are tastefully appointed, with walk-in closets and marble-topped desks. Ask for a water-front room. A villa section nearby contains 24 rooms. *Box 5048, Star Island, Montauk, NY 11954; tel. 516-668-3100, 800-777-1700; fax 516-668-3303. Closed early Nov.-Apr. On Star Island Rd. off W. Lake Dr.*

◆ **Surf Club** (very expensive). Tastefully laid out complex of 92 duplex apartments with one or two bedrooms, 32 of them fronting the ocean. Entry level is the living and dining area, with bedrooms on upper levels. Rooms seem somewhat compact, though neatly furnished in light woods and pastels. Complex has its own 550-foot beach front. Dense dune grass provides a lush buffer between beach and buildings. *Box 1174, Montauk, NY 11954; tel. 516-668-3800. Closed mid-Nov.-mid-Apr. North of the Montauk Plaza, turn onto Essex St. toward the beach.*

◆ **Montauk Manor** (expensive). The splendid Tudor exterior of Montauk's palatial landmark has towered over the town since 1927, but its rooms have all been renovated in thoroughly modern fashion. Each unit is individually owned and decorated in this condominium, and about half of the 140 are in the rental program. Request a room with a western exposure (for magnificent sunsets over Block Island Sound) or a first-floor room with large garden terrace. Room 135 has a fireplace. *236 Edgemere St., Montauk, NY 11954; tel. 516-668-4400; fax 516-668-3535. From Flamingo Ave., follow winding Manor Rd. all the way up the hill.*

◆ **Royal Atlantic** (expensive). One of the biggest motels in Montauk, with 152 units, including 46 with beach-front exposures on Kirk Beach. The north building, with 40 one- and two-bedroom suites, is not right on the beach. Rooms have kitchenettes and are basic but tasteful. Royal Atlantic also offers a dozen beach-front condominiums a block away at the Royal Atlantic East—two stories with decks, balconies, and cathedral ceilings. *Box 2247, Montauk, NY 11954; tel. 516-668-5597. Suites and condos open year-round; beach-front building closed late Nov.-mid-Mar. At Edgemere St. and the ocean.*

◆ **Blue Haven Motel** (moderate). Located within walking distance of the harbor, this family-run motel has 30 well-maintained rooms with telephones, TV, pool. *533 W. Lake Dr., Box*

781, Montauk, NY 11954; tel. 516-668-5943, 800-789-5943. Closed mid-Dec.-early Mar.

HOUSE RENTALS

Hundreds of homes are available for rent, usually by the season or, less commonly, by the month. A monthly rental for a two- or three-bedroom house begins in the range of $5,000. Weekly rentals are rare. Wherever the home in Montauk, it won't be far from water.

◆ **Remington Realty.** *649 Montauk Hwy., Montauk, NY 11954; tel. 516-668-4044; fax 516-668-5826. Open daily.*

◆ **Sea & Sun Realty.** *Box 2573, Montauk, NY 11954; tel. 516-668-3223. Open daily.*

RESTAURANTS

◆ **Caswells Restaurant & Bar** (expensive). White-tablecloth elegance in a light and airy setting. The kitchen is renowned for seafood and such innovative dishes as the grilled yellowfin tuna with baby bok choy, adzuki beans, and rice and the crisp roasted Long Island duckling with wild rice flan and raspberry demiglacé. *17 S. Edison St., Montauk, NY 11954; tel. 516-668-0303. Open for dinner nightly. Closed Columbus Day-Memorial Day.*

◆ **Dave's Grill** (expensive). Upscale, comfy bistro with porch, bar, and dining room seating along the wharf. Winning dishes include the fisherman's pasta with local scallops, clams, shrimp, lobster, mussels, calamari, and herbs, the Szechuan-grilled striped bass, and the marinated grilled pork chop with apple chutney and potato-scallion cake. *Box 1491, Montauk, NY 11954; tel. 516-668-9190. Open daily for dinner May-Oct. On Flamingo Rd. at Montauk Harbor.*

◆ **Downtown Grille & Wine Bar** (expensive). From the outside, it looks like a roadside fish house, but inside, the place is classier. Popular dishes are the fisherman's pan roast, marinated organic free-range chicken, and grilled Montauk swordfish. Then there's the pizza with grilled chicken, Maytag blue cheese, and shiitake mushrooms. Dozens of wines. *774 Main St., Montauk Hwy., Montauk, NY 11954; tel. 516-668-4200. Open daily for dinner mid-May-early Sep., Thu.-Sun. in spring and fall.*

◆ **Jolson's** (expensive). Brought to you by the people who own the local landmark Lunch (aka Lobster Roll), Jolson's has the ambience of a stylish speakeasy, with dark-wood trim, quilted bench seats, a piano in the corner, and art reminiscent of the flapper era. It's very inviting and a contrast to all else hereabouts. Favorite dishes include charbroiled tuna and swordfish steaks, crispy coconut shrimp, and filet mignon. *2095 Montauk Hwy., Amagansett, NY 11930; tel. 516-267-6960. Open for lunch and dinner. Closed Oct.-May. Just east of Lobster Roll (Lunch).*

◆ **Shagwong Restaurant** (expensive). Dining here makes you feel like a Montauk insider. Low-lit, chummy, informal atmosphere, complete with anchorlike chandeliers. Seafood, pasta, and steak, with a nightly reduced-fat entrée. *774 Main St., Montauk, NY 11954; tel. 516-668-3050. Open daily for brunch, lunch, and dinner. Food served until midnight. Just north of Montauk Plaza.*

◆ **Cyril's Fish House** (moderate). This roadside hot spot draws raves for its menu *and* its owner, Cyril Fitzsimons, whose personality definitely flavors the atmosphere. You can expect patio furniture and paper plates, but the palate pays this informality no mind. Sample the sesame grilled shrimp or the poached shrimp over linguini with basil cream. The little tile-topped bar out front has the feel of a Caribbean beach café, and no wonder—when Cyril closes for the season, he heads to his other location in Anguilla. *Montauk Hwy., Montauk, NY 11954; tel. 516-267-7993. Open daily for lunch and dinner. Closed Oct.-May. Just east of Napeague Harbor Rd.*

◆ **Gosman's Dock Restaurant** (moderate). Sprawling landmark restaurant known for Montauk lobster and a fabulous sunset vantage point at the harbor entrance. Try the stuffed fillet of sole or the broiled yellowtail flounder; skip the institutional fried clam strips. Dine dockside or indoors. The restaurant's other appendages are the Topside Inlet Cafe and Gosman's Clam Bar. The bar has a floor-to-ceiling whale's rib. *Montauk Wharf, Montauk, NY 11954; tel. 516-668-5330. Open daily for lunch and dinner mid-Apr.-mid-Oct.*

NIGHTLIFE

◆ **Mimosa Beach Cafe.** DJs, with occasional live music. Indoor seating plus beachside deck. *148 S. Edison St., Montauk, NY*

11954; tel. 516-668-3676. Open daily.

◆ **Tipperary Inn.** Irish music with atmosphere: Montauk's Irish work force gathers here. *W. Lake Dr., Montauk, NY 11954; tel. 516-668-2010. Open daily.*

ATTRACTIONS

◆ **Deep Hollow Ranch.** Established in 1658 and billing itself as the oldest cattle ranch in the country, Deep Hollow offers beach and trail rides on 4,000 acres of scenic parkland. *Box 835, Montauk, NY 11954; tel. 516-668-2744. Open daily year-round, weather permitting. Rides hourly 9-6 by reservation only. Admission. Located 3 mi. east of Montauk on the north side of Rte. 27.*

◆ **Montauk Point Lighthouse.** Commissioned by George Washington, it now houses a museum. Visitors can climb the 137 stairs. (Kids must be at least 41 inches tall and cannot be carried.) *Montauk Point, Montauk, NY 11954; tel. 516-668-2544. Open daily 10:30-5 Memorial Day-late Jun., 10:30-6 late Jun.-Labor Day, and 10:30-4:30 Labor Day-Columbus Day. Call for winter and spring schedule. Admission. At the eastern end of Rte. 27.*

SHOPPING

Montauk's shopping areas are Gosman's Dock and the downtown plaza, but serious shoppers head for East Hampton and Southampton or for the outlet stores in Amagansett.

BEST FOOD SHOPS

SANDWICHES: ◆ **Four Oaks General Store & Outdoor Cafe.** *57 Flamingo Ave., Montauk, NY 11954; tel. 516-668-2534. Open Mon.-Sat. 7 a.m.-9 p.m. and Sun. 7-5 May-Nov.; Mon.-Sat. 7-7 and Sun. 7-5 Nov.-May. At W. Lake Dr.*

FRESH PRODUCE: ◆ **Ocean View Farmers Market.** The market also has seafood, meats, bakery, and deli. *805 Main St., Montauk, NY 11954; tel. 516-668-2900. Open daily May-Oct.*

BEVERAGES: ◆ **Montauk Beer & Soda.** *43 Elmwood Ave., Montauk, NY 11954; tel. 516-668-5400. Open Mon.-Thu. 9:30-7, Fri.-Sat. 9:30-9, and Sun. noon-6. Closed Jan.-Feb.*

WINE: ◆ **Whites Liquor Store.** *Montauk Hwy., Montauk, NY 11954; tel. 516-668-2426. Closed Sun. Just west of the Montauk Plaza.*

SPORTS
FISHING
◆ **Star Island Yacht Club & Marina.** Charter boats available, plus tackle, bait, and clothing. *Box 2180, Montauk, NY 11954; tel. 516-668-5052. Open daily. Next to the Coast Guard Station on Star Island Rd.*

BOATING
◆ **Puff 'n Putt.** Sailboat, pedal boat, rowboat, and kayak rentals on Fort Pond. *Box 498, Montauk Hwy., Montauk Village, Montauk, NY 11954; tel. 516-668-4473. Across from the IGA.*

◆ **Uihlein's.** This marina and boat yard offers boat rentals, water-skiing, Jet Skis, scuba gear. *Montauk Harbor, W. Lake Dr. Extension, Montauk, NY 11954; tel. 516-668-3799. Open daily.*

SURFING
Montauk has an active surfing scene, with Ditch Plains Beach one of the most reliable spots.

◆ **Real Surfers Inc.** *S. Etna Ave., Montauk, NY 11954; tel. 516-668-6247. Next to Caswells Restaurant & Bar.*

BICYCLING
◆ **Pfund Hardware.** Mountain bikes, 21-speeds, 7-speeds, and repairs. *725 Montauk Hwy., Montauk, NY 11954; tel. 516-668-2456. Open daily.*

GOLF
◆ **Montauk Downs.** An 18-hole course designed by Robert Trent Jones. Driving range. *Montauk Downs State Park, Box 206A, S. Fairview Ave., Montauk, NY 11954; tel. 516-249-0701, 516-668-5000. Open daily. Admission. The state park is between Lake Montauk and Fort Pond.*

TENNIS
◆ **Montauk Downs State Park.** Six courts, each surrounded by trees. No reservations. *Box 206A, S. Fairview Ave., Montauk, NY 11954; tel. 516-668-5000. Open daily. Admission.*

◆ **Public tennis courts.** Three courts available for hourly rental.

Same-day reservations only at a courtside booth. *Essex St., Montauk, NY 11954. Closed early Sep.-late May. Admission. Just north of Montauk Hwy.*

NATURE

◆ **Hither Hills State Park.** Besides two and a half miles of ocean beach, the park has 165 camping spots and an array of summertime activities, including nature walks, movies, dancing, and sandcastle building. During summer, reservations are for a minimum stay of one-week and should be made 90 days in advance. Reserve by calling 800-456-CAMP. *Old Montauk Hwy., Montauk, NY 11954; tel. 516-668-2461. Open daily. Admission.*

◆ **Montauk Point State Park.** The park has five miles of trails, a picnic area, and stellar views along the coastline. Below the lighthouse are narrow, rocky beaches where water too rough for swimming thunders into the shore. This is a haven for surf casters. *Montauk Point, Montauk, NY 11954; tel. 516-668-3781. Open daily. Parking fee. Admission.*

◆ **Whale Watching.** Available through the Viking Lines fishing fleet. Call for schedule. *Montauk Harbor, Montauk, NY 11954; tel. 516-668-5700. From Rte. 27, take W. Lake Dr. north to the harbor.*

SAFETY TIPS

Montauk is a safe place, but in summer its population of 3,000 swells to about 25,000, and crimes such as pilfering from cars and motel rooms occasionally occur.

TOURIST INFORMATION

◆ **Montauk Chamber of Commerce.** *Box 5029, Montauk, NY 11954; tel. 516-668-2428. Open Mon.-Sat. 10-4 and Sun. 10-3 Memorial Day-Labor Day; Mon.-Fri. 10-4 Labor Day-Memorial Day. On Montauk Hwy., within the Montauk Plaza.*

CHAPTER 2

East Hampton

Beauty	A
Swimming	A
Sand	B-
Hotels/Inns/B&Bs	B
House rentals	B+
Restaurants	B
Nightlife	C
Attractions	B
Shopping	C
Sports	B
Nature	A

riving down Main Street in East Hampton village, you can't help but feel you've come upon the land of milk and honey—or should that be milk and money? The route is a cornucopia of fashionable shops, stylish restaurants, and historic inns with perfect poise. The pedestrians exude prosperity. Then you turn the corner and there, parked in front of one of those chic bistros, is an old pickup truck with a big

14

Doberman chained in the back, nervously guarding its territory, a scene more *Beverly Hillbillies* than *Beverly Hills 90210.*

East Hampton and its environs have their blessedly down-to-earth side, to be sure—there's less commercial, more countrified Amagansett just down the road—but in recent years, it is the show-biz spotlight that has brightly illuminated the area. And while celebrity has never been a stranger to the Hamptons, East Hampton has become known as Hollywood East because so many luminaries and their friends have adopted it as a home or playground.

John F. Kennedy, Jr., Rollerblades in Amagansett. Such notables as Barbra Streisand, Alan Alda, and Katie Couric paddle through. Alexis Stewart (Martha's daughter) owns a spa in the middle of town. Moviemaker Steven Spielberg lives here, on the golden pond of South Fork, better known as Georgica Pond, or the chosen neighborhood.

Like elsewhere in the Hamptons, the summer party and

HOW TO GET THERE

◆ Driving from New York City, take the Long Island Expwy. (Rte. 495) east to Exit 70-Manorville, south to Sunrise Hwy. (Rte. 27), then east on Rte. 27 to E. Hampton. In smooth traffic the trip takes 2 3/4 hr.

◆ From Philadelphia and S. Jersey, take the New Jersey Tpke. north to I-278 and the Verrazano Bridge. Then take the Belt Pkwy. to the Southern State Pkwy. Continue east to Rte. 27 and on to E. Hampton. In smooth traffic, the trip takes almost 4 hr.

◆ E. Hampton is a stop on the Long Island Rail Road. Call for schedule and fare information (tel. 718-217-5477).

◆ Regular bus service from Manhattan to E. Hampton is provided by the Hampton Jitney. Call for information (tel. 800-936-0440).

charity fund-raiser circuit sizzles, as does the dining, and star-gazing is part of the fun. With all of these players, the beach scene may seem only to be stage right. But East Hampton's beaches are many and magnificent. A few miles to the north, the shores along Gardiners Bay are a nice counterpoint to the wave-washed ocean beaches. Just remember that most of the beach lots require a parking permit of one kind or another (sometimes provided by hotels).

Long before parking was tight, land here was valued for what it could grow, not what it would go for. It wasn't until the mid-1800s that the town began to attract the wealthy and artistic. For two centuries prior, East Hampton was an agricultural community, and there are still quite a few vineyards and farms around, which makes this stretch of Montauk Highway down-right bucolic. Some of its history can be revisited today at Main Street locations such as the Town Pond, where cattle once drank, the South End Cemetery, and the Village Green. East Hampton's most prominent landmark is Hook Mill, a big English windmill that sits at the east end, where Montauk Highway becomes Main Street. That's also where two other key arteries, North Main Street and Newtown Lane, converge. The ocean beaches are all within ten minutes of Main Street.

BEACHES
OCEAN BEACHES
Atlantic Avenue Beach, Amagansett

This beach has a rural and remote set-ting and is overlooked by the East Hampton Town Marine Museum on Bluff Road. From the beach, you can see beach houses creeping up the coast to the east; to the west there's scarcely any-

Beauty	A
Swimming	A
Sand	A
Amenities	B

thing in sight except water, sand, and dunes. *From Main St. in Amagansett (Montauk Hwy.), turn south onto Atlantic Ave.*
Swimming: Clean, refreshing surf with waves that on fair days roll in gently without a crash. Lifeguard on duty.
Sand: Light tan and very fine, gently sloping back to a grass-topped dune. The beach is wide, spacious, and uniformly free of

shells, rocks, and other debris.

Amenities: Rest rooms in the parking lot, beach hut for rentals.

Sports: Body boarding.

Parking: Big lot, one of a few available at a daily fee to those without an East Hampton Town resident permit.

Indian Wells Beach, Amagansett

The road to this beach, Indian Well Plain Highway, passes through the Nature Conservancy's Atlantic Double Dunes Preserve. The beach is just west of and similar to Atlantic Avenue Beach, although it undulates slightly. The parking lot requires an East Hampton Town resident permit. *From Main St. in Amagansett (Montauk Hwy.), turn south onto Indian Well Plain Hwy.*

TWO MILE HOLLOW BEACH

This beach is only about three minutes from Montauk Highway but is undeveloped, with just a parking lot and a couple of bike racks. The few beach houses within sight are set back several hundred yards. The scene is very pretty, with the long

Beauty	A
Swimming	A
Sand	B
Amenities	D

view in either direction fading into a swirl of sandy haze on hot days. *From Main St. in E. Hampton, go south on Cross Hwy. to Further Lane. Turn right and then quickly left down Two Mile Hollow Rd.*

Swimming: Clean, refreshing surf with waves that roll in with enough force to kick up sand. No lifeguard.

Sand: Light tan and uniformly fine on a moderately wide beach backed by a low, grassy dune. Erosion scarp comes and goes.

Amenities: None.

Sports: None.

Parking: Lot with nearly 200 spaces requires a village permit.

WILBERG BEACH

Hook Pond is a swan-filled lake near the Maidstone Club and Golf Course. A road called Highway Behind the Pond leads to a nice wide beach. From water's edge, several large homes are visible

Beauty	A
Swimming	A
Sand	A
Amenities	C

behind the low dune, and to the west, Main Beach, with its pavilion, is less than a mile away. *From the east end of Main St., turn south on Egypt Lane. Turn right onto Dunemere Lane, then left onto Hwy. Behind the Pond.*

Swimming: Waves break just offshore, rolling smoothly into the beach. No lifeguard.

Sand: Uniformly fine, light tan, rising very gradually to a fenced dune. Some fading evidence of past storm erosion.

Amenities: None.

Sports: None.

Parking: Lot with about 65 spaces requiring a village permit.

MAIN BEACH

The road to Main Beach winds among sculpted hedges, palatial homes, and vast manicured lawns, ending at a parking lot and a long, low bathhouse. The view west up the beach includes some large shingle-style beach houses that

Beauty	B
Swimming	A
Sand	A
Amenities	B

look like movie props atop the dunes. *From Main St., turn south on Ocean Ave.*

Swimming: Gentle waves break close to shore; backlit by the morning sun, they're a translucent jade. Lifeguard on duty.

Sand: Fine and light tan, rising moderately to meet a grassy dune. Subject to erosive scarps that fade with time.

Amenities: Bathhouse includes changing rooms, rest rooms, and snack bar.

Sports: Volleyball.

Parking: Lot with about 170 spaces. Daily parking fee for those without a village permit.

Georgica Beach

This beach slopes sharply from the parking lot to the water, rolling slightly from left to right. It's backed by medium-high dunes that become the back yards of a dozen large residences. To the west, the beach curves out of sight, then resumes in the distance. *From Main Beach, follow Lily Pond Lane west 1 1/2 mi.*

Swimming: Waves similar to Main Beach. Lifeguard on duty.

Sand: Fine and uniform, light tan with goldish flecks.
Amenities: Rest rooms.
Sports: None.
Parking: About 70 parking spaces requiring a village permit.

BAY BEACH
Cedar Point Park

The beach here is a chore to reach, but it's unlike any in the area—located in the middle of a sandy peninsula connecting a lighthouse and the mainland. The lighthouse was on an island until a 1938 hurricane filled in the gap. After parking, you can walk down a path onto the peninsula; staying on the sandy road in the middle it's a 10- or 15-minute walk to the beach. The narrow spit has calm bay water on both sides. At either end of the beach is dense dune grass with marshy areas along the edge subject to tidal changes. *From Main St., follow Three Mile Harbor Rd. and bear left onto Springy Banks Rd. Then bear right onto Hands Creek Rd. and left onto Ely Brook Rd. Go straight onto Alewive Brook Rd. and turn right at Cedar Point Rd.*
Swimming: Clear, clean, gentle water lapping both edges of the spit. No lifeguard.
Sand: Fine and tan, but mixed with shells, rocks, and other debris, such as seaweed and seagull feathers. Not dirty, but naturally unkempt.
Amenities: Rest rooms, convenience store, and showers in the park.
Sports: None, although duck-blind boxes are embedded in the sand.
Parking: Near the park's showers.

HOTELS/INNS/B&Bs

In summer, less-expensive lodgings can be found on Shelter Island (Chamber of Commerce, tel. 516-749- 0399).

◆ **Mill House Inn B&B** (very expensive). Each of this recently renovated B&B's eight rooms has its own theme and color scheme. The Dominy Mill Room has deep greens, red checks, and floral patterns and looks out on the Hook Mill. The Rose Room has a pale pink rose and lace motif. Three rooms have Jacuzzis; six have hearths. Breakfast is served in the dining room, on the front porch—or in bed. *33 N. Main*

St., E. Hampton, NY 11937; tel. 516-324-9766.

◆ **The Maidstone Arms** (very expensive). This classic inn dating from 1740, with its striped awning and dark shutters, stands across from the Town Pond like a welcoming sentinel. Standard rooms, suites, and cottages are available, all individually and tastefully furnished with antiques, wicker, and period touches. The inn's Maidstone Restaurant is highly regarded, and public spaces are comfortable and inviting. A few minutes' drive from the beach. *207 Main St., E. Hampton, NY 11937; tel. 516-324-5006; fax 516-324-5037.*

◆ **Bluff Cottage** (expensive). Four small but elegant guest rooms are invitingly coordinated in color schemes such as green/plaid and cameo white/blue and charmingly furnished with antiques. Period garden furniture fills the porch, and old pieces like a French dome chair and a carved mahogany English partners desk add refinement in the sitting areas. *266 Bluff Rd., Box 428, Amagansett, NY 11930; tel. 516-267-6172. Closed Nov.-Apr. From Main St. in Amagansett, turn south on Atlantic Ave. to Bluff Rd.*

◆ **East Hampton House** (expensive). This 52-unit property has studios and two-room suites, each privately owned but nearly all available for rental. Decor varies widely, from nicely to minimally furnished. Rooms fronting Montauk Highway have a roadside-motel quality; the majority, around back, are nicer, with grass and trees around. *226 Pantigo Hwy., E. Hampton, NY 11937; tel. 516-324-4300. Less than 1 mi. east of Hook Mill on Pantigo Hwy. (aka Montauk Hwy.).*

HOUSE RENTALS

House rentals are expensive and usually by the month or season. For shorter periods, try local classified ads.

◆ **Braverman, Newbold & Brennan.** *6 Main St., E. Hampton, NY 11937; tel. 516-324-6000. Open daily.*

RESTAURANTS

◆ **Laundry** (expensive). This longtime winner has the spacious feel of a ski chalet, with a soaring ceiling and a long bar. But the real treat is the food. Creatively prepared by chef Dennis MacNeil, it includes tapas and appetizers like spinach and cheese ravioli and sweet potato skins with yogurt, honey, and mint sauce. A good salad selection prefaces such main courses as pan-roasted French-cut breast of chicken with chanterelle and black trumpet mushrooms, white wine, herbs, and a touch of cream. *31 Rice Lane, E. Hampton, NY 11937; tel. 516-324-3199. Open daily for dinner.*

◆ **Nick & Toni's** (expensive). This hot spot for the celeb set has a small bar area in the front, with a walkway leading past the wood-burning oven to the comfortable and open main dining room that's just right for people-watching. A diverse menu includes the likes of wild striped bass with manila clams, sautéed pea shoots, and saffron broth; porcini-crusted sweetbreads with oyster mushrooms; and grilled quail. *136 N. Main St., E. Hampton, NY 11937; tel. 516-324-3550. Open daily for dinner and Sun. for brunch May-Sep. Closed Mon.-Tue. Oct.-Apr.*

◆ **Il Capuccino Ristorante** (moderate). Locals come for reliably prepared, reasonably priced northern Italian cuisine, including recipes brought back from the owners' annual trip home to Parma. *126 N. Main St., E. Hampton, NY 11937; tel. 516-324-8008. Open daily for dinner.*

◆ **Santa Fe Junction** (moderate). Casual southwestern decor, convincing southwestern dishes, and stellar margaritas have won this restaurant regulars. Starters include cornmeal-coated oysters, black bean ravioli, and seafood tamales; among the entrées are mesquite-grilled fajitas, seafood pasta, and grilled free-range chicken with a jalapeño, sweet pepper, and cactus peach glaze. *8 Fresno Pl., E. Hampton, NY 11937; tel. 516-324-8700. Open daily for dinner.*

NIGHTLIFE

Private parties make up much of East Hampton's nightlife, but the area's rich artistic climate also draws some top-rate entertainers in a few small venues.

◆ **Stephen Talkhouse.** This seafood restaurant is also the area's primo music club. *161 Main St., Amagansett, NY 11930; tel. 516-267-3117. Open daily. Admission.*

SHOPPING

East Hampton's Main Street is lined with tony boutiques, and on Main Street in Amagansett there are some charming little shops plus Amagansett Square. This collection of factory outlets on a village green includes Joan & David, Bass Outlet Clothing, and Geoffrey Beene.

BEST FOOD SHOPS

SANDWICHES: ◆ **Villa Italian Specialties.** 7 *Railroad Ave., E. Hampton, NY 11937; tel. 516-324-5110. Open daily. Closed Sun. in winter. From Main St., turn onto Newtown Lane and then turn left onto Railroad Ave.*

SEAFOOD: ◆ **Claws on Wheels.** 27 *Race Lane, E. Hampton, NY 11937; tel. 516-324-5090. Open daily. From Main St., turn north onto Newtown Lane and then left onto Railroad Ave. and left onto Race Lane.*

FRESH PRODUCE: ◆ **Amagansett Farmers Market.** This landmark has produce and much, much more. Lawn furniture under the trees for civilized picnics. *Box 746, Amagansett, NY 11930; tel. 516-267-3894; fax 516-267-1013. Closed Dec.-Mar. On the east end of Main St.*

BAKERY: ◆ **Georgica Bakers.** *Box 1856, Amagansett, NY 11930; tel. 516-267-6773. Closed Tue. and closed Tue.-Wed. in winter. Montauk Hwy. at Cross Hwy.*

BEVERAGES: ◆ **A&P.** *Newtown Lane, E. Hampton, NY 11937; tel. 516-324-6215. Open daily.*

WINE: ◆ **Amagansett Wine & Spirits.** *Main St., Amagansett, NY 11930; tel. 516-267-3939. Closed Sun.*

SPORTS
BOATING

Several marinas are located on Three Mile Harbor, mainly for boat owners. Rentals available in Montauk and Hampton Bays.

◆ **B&T Boat Co.** Sales and service; no rentals. *Montauk Hwy., E. Hampton, NY 11937; tel. 516-537-3662. Closed Sun.*

◆ **Aliento Charters.** Captain George Wilson runs a 50-foot teak sailboat on half-day, full-day, and sunset charters for groups of up to 12 people. *284 Old Stone Hwy., E. Hampton, NY 11937; tel. 516-267-6817. Open mid-May-mid-Nov. At E. Hampton Point Marina, Three Mile Harbor.*

SURFING

◆ **Main Beach Surf & Sport.** Surfboards, fashions, and surf reports (tel. 516-537-SURF). *Montauk Hwy., Wainscott, NY 11975; tel. 516-537-2716. Open daily.*

BICYCLING
◆ **Bermuda Bikes.** *36 Gingerbread Lane, E. Hampton, NY 11937; tel. 516-324-6688. Open daily Apr.-Dec. and Sat. 10-5 Jan.-Mar.*

GOLF
The closest public courses are Poxabogue Golf Course, Bridgehampton (tel. 516- 537-0025), Sag Harbor Golf Club (tel. 516-725-2503), and Montauk Downs (tel. 516-668-5000).

TENNIS
◆ **Racquet Club of East Hampton.** There are 19 Har-Tru courts. *Buckskill Rd., E. Hampton, NY 11937; tel. 516-324-5155. Open daily May-Sep. Admission. Take Montauk Hwy. west to Buckskill Rd.*

NATURE
◆ **Cedar Point County Park.** More than 600 acres; nature walks. *Alewive Brook Rd., E. Hampton, NY 11937; tel. 516-852-7620. Open daily. From Main St., follow Three Mile Harbor Rd. north to Springy Banks Rd., which becomes Hands Creek Rd. Turn left onto Alewive Brook Rd.*

SAFETY TIPS
Crimes against individuals are rare in East Hampton, but property crime occurs from time to time. According to one police officer, the most common complaint is cellular phone theft (from a parked car with its windows or top down).

TOURIST INFORMATION
◆ **East Hampton Chamber of Commerce.** *37A Main St., E. Hampton, NY 11937; tel. 516-324-0362. Open Mon.-Sat. 10-4. The office is in a commercial alley off the sidewalk.*
◆ **Streetwise East Hampton.** This company makes laminated fan-fold maps for destinations around the world. The East Hampton map is useful and particularly precise because this is the firm's home turf. *Box 2219, Amagansett, NY 11930; tel. 516-267-8617. Maps available in bookstores.*

CHAPTER 3

Southampton

Beauty	A
Swimming	A
Sand	B-
Hotels/Inns/B&Bs	B
House rentals	B-
Restaurants	B
Nightlife	C
Attractions	B
Shopping	A
Sports	B
Nature	B

If the resort towns of Long Island's South Fork are like a string of pearls, Southampton is the most lustrous on the strand. And small wonder, because to continue the metaphor, it has been cultivated long and expertly by sophisticated—and very wealthy—caretakers.

In 1640, Southampton became the first English settlement in New York State, the land bought from the Shinnecock Indians in exchange for corn. By the late 1800s, it was designated the Summer Colony by 200 wealthy New York families whose early beach cottages evolved into the hedge-obscured estates that today are one of the town's most distinguishing features.

They also founded such institutions as the Shinnecock Hills Golf Club, the Meadow Club for lawn tennis, the Beach Club, the Parrish Art Museum, and the Rogers Memorial Library. This imposing old money distinguishes Southampton from the other Hamptons and, because it also sends prices soaring, leads many vacationers to steer clear. Indeed, much of New York City's upper crust consider it more of a birthright than a resort.

It's unfortunate that some people are intimidated by the town and pass it up, because Southampton has an extraordinary beach and more than a dozen access points along a seven-mile stretch from Flying Point Road on the east to Shinnecock Inlet on the

HOW TO GET THERE

◆ Driving from New York City, take the Long Island Expwy. (Rte. 495) east to Exit 70 (Manorville), then south to Sunrise Hwy. (Rte. 27). Go west on Rte. 27 to Southampton. In smooth traffic the trip takes 2 hr.

◆ From Philadelphia and South Jersey, take the New Jersey Tpke. north to I-278 and go over the Verrazano Bridge. Take the Belt Pkwy. to the Southern State Pkwy. Continue east to Rte. 27 and on to Southampton. In smooth traffic the trip from Philadelphia takes 3 1/2 hr.

◆ Southampton is a stop on the Long Island Rail Road; call for schedule and fare information (tel. 718-217-5477).

◆ Regular bus service is provided from Manhattan to Southampton aboard the Hampton Jitney; call for information (tel. 516-283-4600, 800-936-0440).

west. In summer, traffic and parking can be problems. Many lots require permits that are costly unless you're a local resident, and those lots available to nonresidents are often small (the Wyandanch Lane parking area, for instance, has only about 20 spaces). Further, local ordinances prohibit most street parking near the beach.

Beating the system means either getting an early start to grab one of the few spaces, shuttling in from your motel by taxi or other vehicle, biking, or walking. Central Southampton is less than a mile from the closest beach. Parking is available for a daily fee at a few beaches, and some hotels provide permits for guests. Beaches are divided between Southampton Village and Southampton Town, each with its own permit procedures, which only adds to the confusion.

BEACHES
FLYING POINT BEACH

One of the most distant beaches from central Southampton, it has a rural character, with just a few beach houses nearby. Up the beach to the west, ocean-front estates rise in the distance. *From Montauk Hwy., follow Flying Point Rd. south.*

Beauty	A
Swimming	A
Sand	A
Amenities	C

Swimming: Clean surf rolls in, with waves a milky green. Lifeguard on duty.
Sand: Fine and light tan, uniformly textured, rolling slightly and backed by a fenced dune.
Amenities: Rest rooms, showers, and a bike rack.
Sports: None.
Parking: Town resident permit or seasonal nonresident permit required.

FOWLER'S BEACH

This beach, long attracting a gay crowd, was the focus of protests when new "No Parking" signs were installed along Fowler Street, greatly reducing spaces. Using donations, beachgoers hired a lawyer to fight the changes.

Beauty	A
Swimming	A
Sand	A
Amenities	D

The beach dips, and except for one large beach house, the dunes obscure much of the view east and west, providing a secluded atmosphere. *From Montauk Hwy., turn south onto Flying Point Rd., then right onto Wickapogue Rd. Jog left onto Fowler Rd., which goes through farmland to the beach.*

Swimming: Aquamarine waves caress the beach. No lifeguard.

Sand: Fine, uniform, light tan, rising to an eroding, fairly high dune.

Amenities: None.

Sports: None.

Parking: A few dozen diagonal and parallel parking spaces on the road just before it dead-ends at the beach. No permit needed.

OLD TOWN BEACH

This village beach is an access point for off-road vehicles, so there is some rutting where they come on and off. Two-story beach houses are more prominent here, perched just above the beach at dune's edge. *From Hampton Rd. in cen-*

Beauty	**B+**
Swimming	**A**
Sand	**A**
Amenities	**C**

tral Southampton, follow Old Town Rd. to the beach.

Swimming: Water clean and foamy as it spreads smoothly across the sand. Vigorous wave action. No lifeguard.

Sand: Fine and tan, sloping smoothly from water and rising to a dune. Some erosion may be present.

Amenities: None.

Sports: None.

Parking: Lot with about 40 spaces. No permit needed.

Wyandach Lane Beach

Just west of—and similar to—Old Town Beach, with about 20 parking spaces (no permit needed).

LITTLE PLAINS BEACH

This fine beach has one of the most elegant approaches anywhere—it's lined on both sides by very high, perfectly trimmed hedges that belong to private estates but create a lush, block-long

Beauty	**A**
Swimming	**A**
Sand	**A**
Amenities	**D**

avenue to the sand. These estates border the beach, but the beach is so wide that they fade into the background. *From Hampton Rd., go south on Little Plains Rd.*

Swimming: Good waves glide gently up the sloping beach. No lifeguard.

Sand: Fine and light tan, occasionally mixed with tiny pebbles. Very wide, rising to a medium-high grassy dune.

Amenities: None.

Sports: None.

Parking: Lot with about 50 spaces; village permit required.

SOUTH MAIN STREET

This village beach along the private Southampton Beach Club and St. Andrews Dune Church has a developed atmosphere, although there is plenty of sand to go around. Some wooden jetties and jetty remnants extend into the

Beauty	B
Swimming	B
Sand	B
Amenities	B

water. *From central Southampton, follow S. Main St. to where it jogs right and then left along Agawam Lake.*

Swimming: Robust waves break at shoreline but not too roughly. Sandbars offshore may affect waves. No lifeguard.

Sand: Uniformly fine and tan, sloping rather sharply to water's edge. Dunes at the back of beach, but presence of beach club and other development interrupts any sense of a natural dune.

Amenities: None.

Sports: None.

Parking: Large lot. Some spaces require a village permit, but over 150 do not.

COOPER BEACH

This is Southampton's main beach, spacious and well-equipped, extending hundreds of yards in either direction. It's also the most crowded, but with more than 300 parking spaces and a daily fee for those without permits,

Beauty	A
Swimming	A
Sand	A
Amenities	A

you're practically guaranteed a spot. *From Hill St. (Rte. 27A) turn south on either Halsey Neck Lane or First Neck Lane, both of which intersect Meadow Lane. Cooper Beach is off Meadow Lane, about halfway between the two.*

Swimming: Wave after wave rolls in gently to shore. Lifeguard on duty.

Sand: Clean, fine, and light tan, stretching wide between dune and water. West of the bathhouse, some dune grass continues off the dune onto the beach itself.

Amenities: Bathhouse with rest rooms, showers, and food.

Sports: None.

Parking: Lot with about 350 spaces, requiring either a village permit or a daily fee of at least $11 on weekdays, $16 on Saturday and Sunday.

BARRIER ISLAND BEACHES

West of Cooper Beach, Southampton's beach extends onto a barrier island for about three and a half miles from Halsey Neck Lane to the Shinnecock Inlet. Although parking is very limited, there is no lifeguard and there's scarce-

Beauty	A
Swimming	B
Sand	A
Amenities	D

ly a portable toilet. The beach is gorgeous and uncrowded. There is also limited access to the wetland along Shinnecock Bay. *A single two-lane road on the barrier island is known from east to west as Meadow Lane, Beach Rd., and Dune Rd.*

Halsey Neck Beach

This fine, big beach rolls and dips, and from the parking lot you can't see over it to the water's edge because it drops more steeply than others. The sand is almost powdery. There are about 22 parking spaces that do not require a permit.

Road D

From the parking lot, a deer-tracked, sandy road leads through the dune, opening onto a medium to wide beach of fine sand, sometimes mixed with tiny pebbles, and waves that break about 100 yards out and roll in gently. Some evidence of past erosion. Dunes to the east rise higher than average for this area. There are about 30 parking spaces that do not require a permit, plus about 25 more on the bayside, which has egrets and other water birds wading along the fringes.

Dune Beach

A six-foot-wide boardwalk leads across 250 yards of hillocklike dunes to a glorious beach reminiscent of a national seashore, with waves crashing white and foamy upon a wind-swept expanse of fine, light sand. Sunset is spectacular. From mid-June to mid-September, a village permit is required for the few parking spots. Cyclists should put this beach on their must-see list.

Road G/Shinnecock East County Park

This park occupies much of the last quarter mile of the barrier island, before it hits the Shinnecock Inlet. The park is virtually all sand, including high, rolling dunes. Only off-road vehicles with a permit can drive into the park and through the dunes, and they must stay on a winding, deep-sand road that is difficult to walk on. The wide beach has a wild feel. At the entrance to the park at Road G, there's a trailer office and a small lot requiring a village permit.

HOTELS/INNS/B&BS

◆ **The Village Latch Inn** (very expensive). Estate life meets artistic whimsy, and the result is seductively appealing. The five-acre property has a main building with 23 distinctive guest rooms, plus three mansions that can be rented in whole or part. Pool and tennis courts are just outside. Grandness aside, what makes the place is that every room is furnished with crafts, antiques, and other collectibles accumulated from owner Marta Byer's lifetime of travel. Duplexes here are just right for kids and pets. *101 Hill St., Southampton, NY 11968; tel. 516-283-2160, 800-545-2824.*

◆ **Southampton Inn** (expensive). With 90 units on two levels, this is Southampton's biggest motel. Rooms have a chain-motel sameness but are comfortable, with king-size or two full beds, pastel decor, blond furniture. Best views overlook the pool. Amenities include tennis, volleyball, and—importantly—a shuttle to the beach. *Hill St. at First Neck Lane, Southampton, NY*

11968; tel. 516-283-6500. In central Southampton.

◆ **The Old Post House Inn** (expensive). This seven-room B&B began as a farmhouse in 1684 and is on the National Register. Despite its age, all rooms have private baths and air-conditioning, as well as period furniture and country decor. The first floor has the spacious Albert Post Room; there are four rooms on the second floor, two on the third. The inn's restaurant, the Post House, is a local institution with a splendid bar. A mile from the beach. *136 Main St., Southampton, NY 11968; tel. 516-283-1717. Closed for a few weeks Dec.-Jan. Central Southampton.*

◆ **The Hill Guest House** (inexpensive). Staying here is like staying in a relative's farmhouse—simple, plain, unpretentious— except you're in lush, plush Southampton. Mauro Salerno and his family have been cultivating regular customers, many of them from Europe, for years. Rooms are individually furnished, family style. This is easily the least expensive lodging in the area. About a mile and a half from the beach. *53 Hill St., Southampton, NY 11968; tel. 516-283-9889, 718-461-0014. Closed Nov.-Apr. On Montauk Hwy. (locally called Hill St.), 1 mi. west of central Southampton.*

HOUSE RENTALS

Most summer rentals are for the season, though monthly—and occasionally weekly—rentals are also available. Memorial Day to Labor Day, they run from perhaps $15,000 for a basic house or condo far from the water to $325,000 or more for a big, ocean-front place with pool and tennis court. Try the North Sea area for something cheaper.

◆ **Coldwell Banker Cook/Pony Farm.** *30 Nugent St., Southampton, NY 11968; tel. 516-283-9600. Open daily.*

RESTAURANTS

◆ **Savanna's** (expensive). This restaurant opened in 1995 in the former village hall and immediately became a Southampton hot spot for its people-watching and coastal cuisine, flavored with southern and Caribbean influences. The menu includes a heavenly soft-shell-crab sandwich (actually, *sandwich* is too bland a word), lobster en brochette, grilled halibut, and garlic-encrusted lamb chops. Patio dining available. *268 Elm St., Southampton, NY 11968; tel. 516-283-0202. Open daily for dinner; Sat.-Sun. afternoon tea in the garden; Sun. brunch 10-2.*

◆ **Shippy's Pumpernickels Restaurant** (expensive). This longtime local fixture has an intimate Germanic atmosphere—dark wood, dark paneling, dark leather booths—and is known for its schnitzel and bratwurst. Other favorites are steak, scampi, and seafood. The bar is extensive. *36 Windmill Lane, Southampton, NY 11968; tel. 516-283-0007. Open daily for dinner and Mon.-Sat. for lunch.*

◆ **La Parmigiana** (moderate). Family-friendly restaurant with dozens of kinds of pasta, Neapolitan and Sicilian pizza, and hot sandwiches. House specialties include the penne with fresh sausage and mushrooms and the fettuccini Alfredo with broccoli. Large portions. The restaurant's deli sells great appetizers and sandwiches to go. *44-48 Hampton Rd., Southampton, NY 11968; tel. 516-283-8030. Open for lunch and dinner Tue.-Sun.*

◆ **Le Chef** (moderate). This comfortable, quiet, and friendly restaurant offers a Continental menu with a French accent, and many of the specials are available as part of an $18 prix fixe menu. Popular dishes include the rack of New Zealand spring lamb; lobster, shrimp and scallops with herbs, tomatoes, and snow peas over penne; grilled swordfish and other seafood steaks served with sauces that vary daily. In fall and winter, game is added. There's also a cozy, elevated bar up front. *75 Job's Lane, Southampton, NY 11968; tel. 516-283-8581. Open daily for lunch and dinner.*

NIGHTLIFE

◆ **75 Main** (expensive). Besides brick-oven pizzas and seafood, this modern Italian restaurant also offers live entertainment during the summer. *75 Main St., Southampton, NY 11968; tel. 516-283-7575. Open daily for breakfast, lunch, and dinner late May-early Sep.; shorter hours Sep.-May.*

◆ **Green Derby Saloon.** This neighborhood bar has DJs or sometimes a live band on Fridays and Saturdays. *813 North Hwy., Southampton, NY 11968; tel. 516-283-9750. Open daily.*

◆ **Take 5.** This casual supper club has ladies' night on

Wednesday, comedy on Friday, and piano music on Saturday. *720 N. Sea Rd., Southampton, NY 11968; tel. 516-283-7228. Open daily.*

ATTRACTIONS

◆ **Parrish Art Museum.** American art from the 19th and 20th centuries. *25 Job's Lane, Southampton, NY 11968; tel. 516-283-2118. Open Thu.-Tue. 11-5 Jun.-Aug., Thu.-Mon. 11-5 Sep.-May, and Sun. 1-5. In central Southampton.*

◆ **Southampton Historical Museum.** Located in the home of whaling captain Albert Rogers, it features a sea captain's living room and bedroom, a colonial bedroom, and Shinnecock Indian relics, toys, and other memorabilia. Also on the grounds are a one-room schoolhouse and other exhibits. *Box 303, Southampton, NY 11968; tel. 516-283-2494. Open daily 11-5 and by appointment. Closed Mon. Jun.-Sep. On Meeting House Lane near Main St.*

SHOPPING.

◆ **Deerfield Clothing & Supply Company.** Outdoor clothing and accessories. *62 Hampton Rd., Southampton, NY 11968; tel. 516-283-0700. Open daily.*

◆ **Hildreth's.** This engaging store, established in 1842, calls itself America's oldest department store, featuring everything from baby clothes and bed-and-bath goods to cookware and furnishings for home and garden. *Main St., Southampton, NY 11968; tel. 516-283-2300. Open daily.*

BEST FOOD SHOPS

SANDWICHES: ◆ **Sip-N-Soda.** Vintage luncheonette. Homemade ice cream, too. *40 Hampton Rd., Southampton, NY 11968; tel. 516-283-9752. Open daily for breakfast, lunch, and dinner.*

SEAFOOD: ◆ **Clam Man Seafood.** *50 Jagger Lane, Southampton, NY 11968; tel. 516-283-7705. Open daily.*

FRESH PRODUCE: ◆ **Schmidt Brothers Produce Co.** *120 N. Sea Rd., Southampton, NY 11968; tel. 516-283-5777. Open daily.*

BAKERY: ◆ **The Beach Bakery.** *30 Hampton Rd., Southampton, NY 11968; tel. 516-287-6741. Open daily.*

BEVERAGES: ◆ **Peconic Beverage.** *74 County Rd. 39, Southampton, NY 11968; tel. 516-283-0602. Open daily.*

WINE: ◆ **Herbert & Rist Inc.** *63 Job's Lane, Southampton, NY 11968; tel. 516-283-2030; fax 516-283-6331. Closed Sun.*

SPORTS
FISHING

◆ **Conscience Point Marina.** *1976 N. Sea Rd., Southampton, NY 11968; tel. 516-283-8295. Open daily Apr.-Nov. Follow N. Sea Rd. north to the harbor.*

SURFING

◆ **Espo's Surf & Sport.** Surfboard rentals and sales, plus clothes and Rollerblades. *28 Main St., Southampton, NY 11968; tel. 516-287-0075. Open daily Apr.-Dec. Closed Tue.-Thu. Jan.-Mar.*

BICYCLING

◆ **Rotations Bicycle Center.** Rentals, sales, and service. *32 Windmill Lane, Southampton, NY 11968; tel. 516-283-2890. Open Thu.-Tue. year-round.*

GOLF

Southampton is renowned for its golf, but most clubs, including Shinnecock Hills, site of several U.S. Opens, are private.

TENNIS

◆ **Nort'sea Racquet Club.** *665 Majors Path, Southampton, NY 11968; tel. 516-283-5444. Open daily May-Oct. Admission.*

◆ **Southampton High School.** *Narrow Lane, Southampton, NY 11968; tel. 516-283-6800.*

◆ **Southampton Village Tennis Courts.** *Rosko Dr., Southampton, NY 11968; tel. 516-283-0247. From downtown, go west on Hill St. and turn left onto Rosko Dr.*

TOURIST INFORMATION

◆ **Southampton Chamber of Commerce.** The office has useful brochures, but for beach questions expect to be referred to Town Hall (tel. 516-283-6011). *76 Main St., Southampton, NY 11968; tel. 516-283-0402; fax 516-283-8707. Open Mon.-Fri. 10-4 and Sat.-Sun. 11-4.*

CHAPTER 4

Hampton Bays

Beauty	B+
Swimming	A
Sand	A
Hotels/Inns/B&Bs	B-
House rentals	B
Restaurants	B
Nightlife	B
Attractions	B
Shopping	C
Sports	B
Nature	B

Hampton Bays, a middle-class community where the atmosphere and economy have long been tied to the surrounding waters of Shinnecock Bay and, to the north, Great Peconic Bay, sits just west of one of the narrowest pieces of land on Long Island's South Fork. Its reputation, unlike that of the other Hamptons, isn't linked to the rich and famous. It is, instead, a place where visitors can feel comfortable wearing cut-off shorts on Main Street.

That narrow neck—less than one mile across—is where the Shinnecock Indians once portaged their canoes between the two bays, thus it acquired the name Canoe Place. In 1892, a canal was completed, and with improvements over the years it has become a busy boating and fishing channel.

Shinnecock Bay is renowned for its abundant quantities of little neck, cherrystone, and chowder clams, as well as flounder, fluke, and eels. Ocean fishing is also popular, thanks to Shinnecock Inlet, another busy channel that owes its existence to the great hurricane of 1938, which knocked a hole in the bar-

HOW TO GET THERE

◆ Driving from New York City, take the Long Island Expwy.(Rte. 495) east to Exit 70-Manorville. Go south to Sunrise Hwy. (Rte. 27), then east to Exit 65 (Rampasture) and south to Rte. 27A (Montauk Hwy.). Turn left to Hampton Bays. In smooth traffic the trip takes 2 hr.

◆ From Philadelphia and S. Jersey, take the NJ Tpke. north to I-278. Go over the Verrazano Bridge to the Belt Pkwy. and then the Southern State Pkwy. Continue east to Rte. 27 and get off at Exit 65 (Rampasture). Go south to Rte. 27A, then make a left to Hampton Bays. In smooth traffic the trip from Philadelphia takes 3 1/2 hr.

◆ Hampton Bays is a stop on the Long Island Rail Road from New York's Penn Station. Call for LIRR schedule and fare information (tel. 718-217-5477).

◆ The Hampton Jitney offers regularly scheduled service from Manhattan to Hampton Bays. Call for information (tel. 516-283-4600, 800-936-0440).

rier island between the bay and the Atlantic Ocean. In the 1950s the inlet was bolstered with rock jetties, where jetty fishermen cast for striped bass and bluefish.

The inlet, which can be reached by car via the Ponquogue Bridge, is also a good place to wander on foot and experience the rushing water and raw beauty where ocean meets bay. A Coast Guard station, marina, and restaurant are nearby.

Until 1922, Hampton Bays was known as Good Ground, and it retains its friendly, down-to-earth atmosphere today. The city encourages tourism and tries to make things easy once you've arrived. Directional signs point the way to beaches, fish markets, and motels. Those seeking a quiet time should know that some motels cater to a weekend party crowd—one such place even requires guests to post a $100 deposit!

Visitors arriving on the Montauk Highway usually head either for the town center at Ponquogue Avenue, the Shinnecock Canal and marina just east of downtown, or south to the Ponquogue Bridge.

That new bridge leads to some of Hampton Bays' strongest recreational assets: dazzling beaches with plenty of daily-fee parking. Or, if you'll be around for awhile, you can buy a Southampton seasonal permit for $100 from the town's Parks & Recreation department (tel. 516-283-6011).

BEACHES
PONQUOGUE BEACH

Take Ponquogue Bridge south across Shinnecock Bay and the first beach you see, virtually dead-ahead, is Ponquogue Beach, part of Shinnecock County Park West. It's a sprawling stretch of sand that continues east to the inlet. Because

Beauty	A
Swimming	A
Sand	A-
Amenities	A

it's a park, there's no development—not even beach houses. And because it's a barrier island, with the big bay on one side and the ocean on the other, the feeling of escape is complete. *From Montauk Hwy. in central Hampton Bays, head south onto Ponquogue Ave. and turn left onto Shinnecock Ave. Make a right onto Foster and continue onto Light House Rd., heading for the Ponquogue Bridge.*

Swimming: On calm days, waves roll in gently, breaking against the shore more with a kiss than a smack—although rougher surf is not uncommon. Lifeguard on duty.

Sand: Fine, light tan, and spacious, backed by a medium-high, grassy dune. Some seaweed, gravel, and shells are scattered about, and there may be signs of erosion.

Amenities: Bathhouse, with rest rooms, showers, and concessions, plus picnic tables and a bike rack.

Sports: Fishing.

Parking: Lot with hundreds of spaces for a daily fee (at least $10) or with a Southampton town permit.

ROAD K AND ROAD L—TIANA BEACH

These locations west of Ponquogue Beach take you away from the bathhouse crowds and the Shinnecock Inlet boat traffic. It's all in all a more remote atmosphere. Looking east or west, you see only ocean, beach, and dunes.

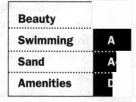

Beauty	
Swimming	A
Sand	A
Amenities	D

Coming off the Ponquogue Bridge, turn right.

Swimming: Waves vary from gentle to forceful. No lifeguard.

Sand: Fine, light tan, mixed in places with coarser ingredients. These beaches are less sweeping, with the dune line closer to the water. There may be evidence of an erosion scarp.

Amenities: None.

Sports: Surfing.

Parking: Each road has a small lot with room for a couple dozen cars. Southampton Parks & Recreation permit needed July 1 through Labor Day.

TIANA BEACH

To the west, the stilted beach houses of East Quogue come into view, extending almost to the waterline. *From Ponquogue Bridge, turn right. This beach, like the other Hampton Bays ocean beaches, can also be reached from the Westhampton/Quogue section of the barrier island.*

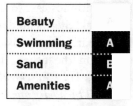

Beauty	
Swimming	A
Sand	B
Amenities	A

Swimming: Plenty of wave action, but generally swimmer-friendly. Lifeguard on duty.

Sand: Uniformly fine and tan, with clusters of stone washed ashore. There may be remnants of erosion scarp or other signs of erosion.

Amenities: Bathhouse, with rest rooms, showers, and concessions, plus picnic tables and a bike rack.

Sports: On the bay side, sailing and swimming instruction.

Parking: Lot with several hundred spaces. Daily parking fee or Southampton town permit.

MESCHUTT BEACH COUNTY PARK

This beach on Great Peconic Bay is a contrast to local ocean-front areas, abuzz with offshore activity near the northern entrance to busy Shinnecock Canal. It's bracketed by the canal and a residential area and attracts residents.

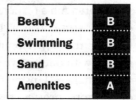

Beauty	B
Swimming	B
Sand	B
Amenities	A

The modest dune at the back of the beach isn't high enough to hide nearby homes. The view over the bay makes for great sunset gazing. *From Montauk Hwy., turn north (on the east side of the canal) onto North Shore Rd. Bear left onto Canal Rd. and continue to Old North Hwy.*

Swimming: Clear water, sometimes with scant seaweed, gently laps the shore. The first few yards offshore are rocky; then the bottom becomes a sandy shelf where barefooted waders sometimes step on—and get pinched by—the occasional crab. Lifeguard on duty.

Sand: Fine, light, almost powdery, mixed with shells and rocks.

Amenities: Bathhouse with rest rooms, concessions.

Sports: None.

Parking: Lot for more than 200 cars. Daily fee or Southampton town permit.

HOTELS/INNS/B&BS

Motels, co-op properties, and cottages line Tiana and Shinnecock bays. Some cater to the sporting crowd, others to families, still others to young partiers. Room rates, on average, are lower than elsewhere in the Hamptons, but some of the low-end motels are not well furnished or insulated from noise.

◆ **Drake Motor Inn** (expensive). This 15-unit waterside motel with rooms, efficiencies, and suites is carefully maintained, and the rooms have homey touches, such as wreaths, eucalyptus sprigs, and country curtains. Fishermen like it, but it's more than a bare-bones anglers' inn. Some units have slab front porches with picnic tables. Rooms 11 and 12 open onto a grassy yard at water's edge. Barbecue grills available. *16 Penny Lane, Hampton Bays, NY 11946; tel. 516-728-1592; fax 516-728-8770. From Montauk Hwy., go south on Ponquogue Ave. Turn left onto Shinnecock Ave. and right onto Penny Lane.*

◆ **Hampton Arms** (expensive). This 28-unit two-floor complex of co-op apartments is well maintained and has a stellar pool overlooking the bay. About 16 units are on the rental program. Each—with one or two bedrooms and modern furnishings—has a full kitchen. Upstairs units have skylights, and the balconies offer more privacy than the first-floor terraces. The resort caters to families and has a playground. *61 W. Tiana Rd., Hampton Bays, NY 11946; tel. 516-728-4161. From downtown, go west on Montauk Hwy. and then turn south onto W. Tiana Rd.*

◆ **Colonial Shores** (moderate). This 24-unit complex is built on a slope from road to bay, with motel rooms, suites, and eight cabins, some of which can be linked for family gatherings. Furnishings vary from traditional to modern and are simple and comfortable. The area is grassy, with picnic tables, a pool, and water access. Rowboats available. *83 W. Tiana Rd., Hampton Bays, NY 11946; tel. 516-728-0011; fax 516-728-0897. From Montauk Hwy. west of downtown, turn south onto W. Tiana Rd.*

◆ **The Caffrey House** (moderate). A bumpy dirt road leads to this spartan 18-room Victorian inn on the edge of Tiana Bay, a true find for those who favor funk over frills. Two turn-of-the-century houses connected by a wide porch are furnished with sturdy old furniture. Owner Bob Van Dyke has strong links to the music and film worlds—he produced documentaries for Dylan, The Beatles, and The Stones—and his collection of jukeboxes and broadcast equipment is world class. *2 Squires Ave., E. Quogue, NY 11942; tel. 516-728-9835. From Montauk Hwy., about 2 1/2 mi. west of Hampton Bays, turn south on Jones Rd. (aka*

Great Hwy.) and make a left onto Squires Ave. Bear left onto a dirt road marked by a "Caffrey House" sign.

HOUSE RENTALS

Rentals tend to be seasonal, although shorter periods are available if you plan far enough ahead.

◆ **Bob Johnson Realty.** *3 Ponquogue Ave., Hampton Bays, NY 11946; tel. 516-728-8500; fax 516-728-8508. Open daily.*

◆ **The Real Estate Store.** *6 W. Montauk Hwy., Hampton Bays, NY 11946; tel. 516-728-5600. Open daily.*

RESTAURANTS

◆ **Sunset Deck** (expensive). From the outside it looks like a large, weather-beaten bait-and-tackle shop, but the seafood served inside or on the deck makes this a hot spot in summer. Perched on Shinnecock Bay, it's the perfect place for watching the sun set over the water. Live music on deck weekend nights. *Dune Rd., Box 1020, Hampton Bays, NY 11946; tel. 516-728-1040. Open daily for lunch and dinner. Closed Sep.-May. Cross the Ponquogue Bridge and turn left.*

◆ **La Casserola** (moderate). This family-style Italian restaurant is a hit with groups and those who want bang for their buck (big servings). When busy, the spacious dining room—done in wood paneling, acoustic ceiling tiles, green plants, and white-over-red tablecloths—can have a feeding-frenzy atmosphere. Live music on Friday nights. *336 Montauk Hwy., Hampton Bays, NY 11946; tel. 516-728-7254; fax 516-728-7262. Open for lunch and dinner Mon.-Fri. and for meals mid-afternoon Sat.-Sun.*

◆ **Oakland's Restaurant and Marina** (moderate). Take in the sunset and the boats cruising Shinnecock Inlet at this shingle-style faux-lighthouse eatery with a big outdoor deck and plenty of window seating. Decorated in light woods and a nautical theme, the circular dining room with its central bar rises to a high peak. The wharfside location gives it an edge in the fresh-seafood department. *Dune Rd. and Rd. H, Hampton Bays, NY 11946; tel. 516-728-6900. Open daily for lunch and dinner. Closed Sep.-mid-Apr. Cross Ponquogue Bridge, turn left, and go to the end of Dune Rd.*

◆ **Rip Tide** (moderate). This restaurant is on the east bank of Shinnecock Canal, and from the outdoor deck you can hear the

41

canal's fast-moving current and the whooshing of nearby bridge traffic. The background noise and passing boats give the place a kinetic feel. The menu emphasizes seafood and pasta, with specials like grilled tuna with fresh basil, plum tomatoes, and black olives and wild mushroom ravioli with bell pepper cream sauce. *7 North Hwy., Hampton Bays, NY 11946; tel. 516-728-7373. Open Fri. dinner and Sat.-Sun. lunch and dinner mid-Apr.-mid-Jun.; daily mid Jun. early Sep., weekends only the rest of Sep. Closed Oct.-mid-Apr. From Montauk Hwy., turn north at the canal.*

◆ **Villa Paul** (moderate). For more than 35 years this family-run institution has been serving up Italian specialties in an elegant, dark-walled dining room. The menu includes a range of pastas, seafood, and steaks. Favorites are duck and veal. *162 Montauk Hwy., Hampton Bays, NY 11946; tel. 516-728-3261. Open daily for dinner.*

◆ **Tully's Harbor Restaurant** (inexpensive). Diners flock here because of the renown of the parent business, Tully's Lobster Co. seafood store and supplier (516-728-9043), housed in the same location. The restaurant's simply prepared seafood can be ordered in a no-frills dining room or at the outdoor snack bar. *78 Foster Ave., Hampton Bays, NY 11946; tel. 516-728-9111. Open daily for dinner mid-Mar.-mid-Oct. Just north of the Ponquogue Bridge.*

NIGHTLIFE

◆ **Beach Bar.** Raw bar, dancing, DJs, live music on weekends. *58 Foster Ave., Hampton Bays, NY 11946; tel. 516-723-3100. Open May-Sep. Just north of the Ponquogue Bridge.*

◆ **Canoe Place Inn.** It draws big crowds from all over the Hamptons for live rock music, DJs, dancing, and billiards. *Montauk Hwy., Hampton Bays, NY 11946; tel. 516-728-4121. Open nightly May-Sep. On Montauk Hwy. east of the Shinnecock Canal.*

SHOPPING

The shopping district (such as it is) is Montauk Highway and Ponquogue Avenue. For power-shopping, try Southampton, Westhampton, or East Hampton.

BEST FOOD SHOPS

SANDWICHES: ◆ **Katrinka's Delicery.** *150 Montauk Hwy.,*

Hampton Bays, NY 11946; tel. 516-728-1441. Open daily.

SEAFOOD: ◆ Cor-J Seafood. *36 Lighthouse Rd., Hampton Bays, NY 11946; tel. 516-728-5186, 516-728-5187; fax 516-728-0465. Open daily. Just north of the Ponquogue Bridge.*

FRESH PRODUCE: ◆ Nurel Produce. A blue roadside stand. *226 E. Montauk Hwy., Hampton Bays, NY 11946; tel. 516-878-9367. Open late May-late Oct. East of downtown.*

BAKERY: ◆ Krieg's Bake Shop. *39 W. Main St., Hampton Bays, NY 11946; tel. 516-728-6524. Closed Mon. Jan.-mid-Mar. In the Village Plaza.*

ICE CREAM: ◆ Big Dipper. *9 Montauk Hwy., Hampton Bays, NY 11946; tel. 516-728-0834. Open daily.*

BEVERAGES: ◆ Hampton Beverage. *156 E. Montauk Hwy., Hampton Bays, NY 11946; tel. 516-728-1353. Open daily.*

WINE: ◆ Hampton Bays Liquor. *7 Ponquogue Ave., Hampton Bays, NY 11946; tel. 516-728-0740. Closed Sun.*

SPORTS
FISHING

Charter fishing boats operate from Shinnecock marinas. Boats tend to specialize in canyon fishing—way out in the ocean—or offshore or bay fishing. Overnight ocean trips are also available. At the bay end of roads like Foster Avenue and Penny and Gardners lanes are small beaches that abound with clams, but you'll need a license. The nearby Shinnecock Bay Fishing Station and Marina rents 15-foot fiberglass skiffs by the full or half day (tel. 516-728-6116).

◆ Oakland's Marina. A handful of captains operate from here; call the marina for referrals. *Dune Rd. and Rd. H, Hampton Bays, NY 11946; tel. 516-728-6900. Open mid-Apr.-Sep. Cross the Ponquogue Bridge and go left on Dune Rd.*

BOATING

◆ Spellmans Marine. Full-service marina with rentals. *262 E. Montauk Hwy., Hampton Bays, NY 11946; tel. 516-728-9200. Open daily. On the Shinnecock Canal.*

SURFING

Surfable waves break just west of Ponquogue Beach.

◆ **Bedford's Surf Shop.** Surf reports, surfboards, Boogie boards, skateboards, wet suits. *38 W. Montauk Hwy., Hampton Bays, NY 11946; tel. 516-723-2363.*

BICYCLING
◆ **P&M Bicycles.** *38 E. Montauk Hwy., Hampton Bays, NY 11946; tel. 516-728-6686. Open daily. Closed Wed. Oct.-May.*

GOLF
Hampton Bays has no golf courses, but there are more than a dozen public courses within a 45-minute drive. One of the closest is Indian Island in Riverhead (tel. 516-727-7776).

TENNIS
◆ **Hampton Bays High School.** Two outdoor courts available, first-come, first-served, outside school hours. *88 Argonne Rd., Hampton Bays, NY 11946; tel. 516-723-2110. Open daily. From Montauk Hwy., go south on Ponquogue Ave. and left on Argonne Rd.*

NATURE
◆ **Sears Bellows County Park.** The park has 690 acres with a lake, rowboat rentals, camping, picnicking, hiking, nature trails, and horseback riding. *Bellows Pond Rd., Hampton Bays, NY 11946; tel. 516-852-8290. Open daily 8-4. From central Hampton Bays, take Montauk Hwy. west and turn right at Bellows Pond Rd.*

TOURIST INFORMATION
◆ **Hampton Bays Chamber of Commerce.** *Box 64, Hampton Bays, NY 11946; tel. 516-728-2211. Open daily 10:30-4:30 Memorial Day -Labor Day and Sat.-Sun. May and Sep.; phone inquiries answered year-round. The information office is on Montauk Hwy., east of downtown, across from St. Rosalie's Catholic Church.*

◆ **Southampton Town Parks & Recreation.** Hampton Bays is part of the town of Southampton, which has jurisdiction over parking at town beaches, such as Tiana and Ponquogue. *116 Hampton Rd., Southampton, NY 11968; tel. 516-283-6011. Open 8:30-4 Mon.-Fri.*

CHAPTER 5

Westhampton

Beauty	A
Swimming	A
Sand	B
Hotels/Inns/B&Bs	B+
House rentals	C
Restaurants	A
Nightlife	B+
Attractions	NA
Shopping	A
Sports	B
Nature	B

esthampton calls itself the gateway to the South Fork, but for many people it is also their final destination—and little wonder. Its beautiful bays and long strip of barrier island make it a prime vacation land, but equally significant is its proximity to New York City. Along with nearby hamlets, such as Quogue and East Quogue, this locale is less than two hours away and can be reached by expressway without having to cope with the slow and narrow Montauk Highway farther down the road.

The range of lodging in the area is good, and some of its restaurants are superb. Westhampton Village is less stodgy than well-manicured Southampton, which isn't to say it doesn't have its share of showpiece properties. But in Westhampton the trimmed hedges aren't quite so high, the atmosphere is more nouveau riche than old money, and many of the ocean-front mansions along Dune Road are modernistic pleasure palaces whose builders were not at all influenced by the understated elegance of the archetypal estates.

This setting has a price, which is paid on July and August

HOW TO GET THERE

◆ Driving from New York City, take the Long Island Expwy. (Rte. 495) east to Exit 70-Manorville and go south to Sunrise Hwy. (Rte. 27). Take Exit 63 south to Westhampton Beach. In smooth traffic the trip takes under 2 hr.

◆ From Philadelphia and S. Jersey take the NJ Tpke. north to I-278. Go over the Verrazano Bridge and onto the Belt Pkwy. Then take the Southern State Pkwy., continuing east to Rte. 27. Take Exit 63 south to Westhampton Beach. In smooth traffic the trip from Philadelphia takes about 3 1/4 hr.

◆ The Long Island Rail Road stops in both Westhampton and Quogue. Call the LIRR for schedule and fare information (tel. 718-217-5477).

◆ The Hampton Jitney offers regular bus service from Manhattan to Westhampton and Quogue. Call for information (tel. 516-283-4600, 800-936-0440).

weekends, when the traffic and competition for parking can be fierce. If Westhampton seems too cluttered with people and Mercedes, the nearby Quogues offer a more countrified setting.

Ironically, Quogue was a center of resort activity well before Westhampton Beach. It was first settled by Puritans in 1640, and then in the 1830s was a stopover on the stagecoach route from Brooklyn to Southampton. That exposure brought raves for Quogue's beaches, and when railway service began in 1844, the number of summer vacationers soared. In 1868, Westhampton Beach got its first hotel, Howell House, built with the support of circus impresario P. T. Barnum, and when a railway stop was initiated in 1870, its fate as a resort was sealed. The first beach shacks rose at the foot of Beach Lane—today the site of Rogers Beach, the city's biggest.

BEACHES
DOLPHIN LANE BEACH

This beach is an access point for off-road vehicles, and the sand near the entrance may be chewed up with tire tracks. Just east of the ingress are high, rolling dunes, with beach houses visible behind them. *From Montauk Hwy., turn*

Beauty	B
Swimming	A
Sand	B
Amenities	C

south onto Quogue St. (aka Main St.) and then south onto Post Lane. Turn left on Dune Rd. and drive 1 3/4 mi.

Swimming: Waves roll in softly, breaking first about 100 yards offshore and then again fairly close to shore.
Sand: Fine and light tan, rising to a moderately high dune.
Amenities: None.
Sports: Fishing.
Parking: About 50 spaces.

HAMPTON BEACH

This pretty, moderately wide seashore has beach homes behind it, each with its own boardwalk leading over the dune. Looking east along the waterline you can see for a mile or so, to a point where the coast curves out of sight. To the west the beach

Beauty	B
Swimming	A
Sand	B
Amenities	B

goes on and on. *From Montauk Hwy., turn south onto Quogue St. (aka Main St.) and then south onto Post Lane, which intersects Dune Rd.*
Swimming: Waves roll in softly, breaking fairly close to shore with a swoosh and an occasional soft crash. Lifeguard on duty.
Sand: Same as Dolphin Lane Beach.
Amenities: Shingle-style bathhouse with showers and rest rooms and a boardwalk leading over the dune. Bike racks.
Sports: Surfing, fishing.
Parking: About 150 spaces requiring a village permit.

ROGERS BEACH

This is Westhampton's primary beach, a sprawling expanse of sand that, when you enter it off the boardwalk, seems to stretch forever. The illusion is created partly by a rise in the beach that obstructs the view of where water and sand meet.

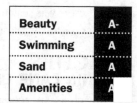

Beauty	A-
Swimming	A
Sand	A
Amenities	A

Walk to the edge of that rise on a good day and you can see the waves rolling in from a smooth sea. From the water's edge, one- and two-story beach houses rise behind the dune as far as you can see in both directions. The beach's wide sweep continues to the west and, to a lesser degree, the east. *From central Westhampton, follow Beach Lane across the recently reopened Quantuck Canal bridge.*
Swimming: Waves roll in gently. Lifeguard on duty.
Sand: Light tan and fine, almost powdery, with a little seaweed blowing around, rising to a low, very grassy dune.
Amenities: Bathhouse with showers, rest rooms, and a deck.
Sports: None.
Parking: Lot with about 180 spaces requiring village permit.

WESTHAMPTON BEACH
(ALSO KNOWN AS LASHLEY BEACH)

This medium-width beach is just west of the Dune Deck resort, also home of the popular Starr Boggs restaurant, so it doesn't exactly have a remote feel. A tight row of beach houses extends in each direction. If it's too crowded, walk

Beauty	B
Swimming	B
Sand	B
Amenities	B

west to a section known as Pikes Beach, where the only other access is from the big estates along Dune Road. *From either the Jessup Lane or Beach Lane bridges, turn right onto Dune Rd.*
Swimming: Steady but manageable wave action, with a boulder breakwater at the eastern edge. Lifeguard on duty.
Sand: Fine and light, rolling slightly from left to right and building back to a low dune. Some evidence of erosion may be present.
Amenities: Bathhouse with showers and rest rooms.
Sports: Surfing.
Parking: Lot with about 45 spaces requiring a village permit.

HOTELS/INNS/B&BS

◆ **1880 House** (very expensive). This well-appointed B&B has two guest suites in the main house and a third room above a small adjacent barn. Antiques, quilts, and heirlooms fill the house, and you can read by the fireplace in the library. The barn room, not as refined but quite appealing in a funky way, has its own kitchen and sunken tub. A pool and tennis court are just outside. *2 Seafield Lane, Box 648, Westhampton Beach, NY 11978; tel. 516-288-1559, 800-346-3290. Go east on Main St. and turn right on Seafield Lane.*

◆ **The Grassmere Inn** (expensive). This three-story B&B has 17 rooms, about half with private bathrooms, plus three cottages. The house dates to the late 1800s, but the family-run business makes no pretense of Victoriana. Furnishings include some antiques, but country simplicity prevails. The Jones Beach cottage has a spacious living room with a fireplace, white plank walls and ceiling, painted-green floors, and a sporting motif. Each of the two bedrooms has its own bath. The cottage porch, just off the parking area, has wicker furniture. *7 Beach Lane, Westhampton Beach, NY 11978; tel. 516-288-4021.*

◆ **The Inn on Main** (expensive). The Main Street location makes this inn Westhampton's most visible, with 15 individually furnished rooms, most with private bath. There is also a separate cottage. The two-story building is surrounded by a manicured lawn, hedges, and trees, making it an oasis amid the bustle. Decor is modern and comfortable but not plush. *191 Main St., Westhampton Beach, NY 11978; tel. 516-288-8900.*

HOUSE RENTALS

◆ **First Hampton Realty.** *50 Main St., Westhampton Beach, NY 11978; tel. 516-288-2122, 800-773-8267; fax 516-288-2270. Open daily.*

RESTAURANTS

◆ **The American Grill** (expensive). From the outside this restaurant doesn't look extraordinary, but inside it has a warm ambience in its several seating areas, including a fireplace and a lounge that sometimes has live music. One of the rooms has a library. The cuisine is billed as all-American (southwestern chicken and the popular barbeque baby back ribs), but there are other choices, such as pasta primavera and fettuccine Alfredo. *141 Montauk Hwy., Westhampton, NY; tel. 516-288-2255. Open daily for dinner Apr.-Dec.*

◆ **Starr's Hampton Square Restaurant** (expensive). This downtown sibling of the celebrated Starr Boggs restaurant on Dune Road also shines, but in a barnlike building with a fireplace, dark-wood bar, and bird prints precisely aligned on the paneled walls. The menu changes frequently, with items such as breast of Long Island duck, roast swordfish, and grilled organic free-range chicken with fresh applesauce, lemon, and herbs. *10 Beach Rd., Westhampton Beach, NY 11978; tel. 516-288-1877. Open daily for dinner; reduced hours during the off-season.*

◆ **Tierra Mar** (expensive). In a short time this restaurant has become one of the Hamptons' shining stars, with an elegant atmosphere and a creative menu of seafood, meats, and poultry. Popular dishes include the seared salmon with lemon-caper vinaigrette, grilled Black Angus sirloin with merlot wine sauce, and pan-roasted free-range chicken. The garden porch dining area in front is a bit less formal than the spacious main dining room. *62 Montauk Hwy., Westhampton, NY 11977; tel. 516-288-2700. Open daily for lunch and dinner.*

◆ **New Moon Cafe** (moderate). Texas sets the tone and the cuisine here, with, as the menu might say, a heap o' such Lone Star favorites as pit barbecue, fajitas, and *chimichangas*, plus seafood, soups, salads, and killer desserts made by Shana Campsey. Ribs and beef are prepared in a mesquite smoker. It's an informal place with a humorous edge. *Montauk Hwy., E. Quogue, NY 11942; tel. 516-653-4042. Open daily for dinner and Sat.-Sun. for brunch and lunch. Closed Tue. Sep.-Apr. On the main drag in E. Quogue.*

◆ **Eckart's** (inexpensive). This classic 1940s luncheonette is museum-worthy, but it's a working restaurant, too. Nothing gourmet here, just your basic tuna, cheeseburger, and BLT. Treat yourself to an ice-cream soda at the marble soda fountain. *162 Mill Rd., Westhampton, NY 11978; tel. 516-288-9491. Open daily for breakfast and lunch.*

NIGHTLIFE

◆ **Casey's.** Dance club with DJs. *Montauk Hwy., Westhampton Beach, NY 11978; tel. 516-288-5828. Open Wed. and Fri.-Sun.*

◆ **The Bay Club.** Nightclub with DJs, dancing, and occasional live music. *395 Montauk Hwy., E. Quogue, NY 11942; tel. 516-653-8165. Open Mon. and Thu.-Sat.*

BEST FOOD SHOPS

SANDWICHES: ◆ **Quogue Country Market.** *Box 1419, Quogue, NY 11959; tel. 516-653-4191, fax 516-653-6226. Open daily. On Jessup Ave. north of Main St.*

SEAFOOD: ◆ **Bennett Seafood.** *11 Parlato Pl., Westhampton Beach, NY 11978; tel. 516-288-2573. Open daily May-Sep. Off Library Ave.*

FRESH PRODUCE: ◆ **Fruit King.** Possibly the only fruit stand any-where with autographs from Bob Fosse, Howard Cosell, and Roy Scheider. *166 Montauk Hwy., Westhampton Beach, NY 11978; tel. 516-288-3852. Open Apr.-Dec.*

BAKERY: ◆ **The Beach Bakery.** *112 Main St., Westhampton Beach, NY 11978; tel. 516-288-6552. Open daily.*

ICE CREAM: ◆ **Main Street Sweets and Gifts.** *121 Main St., Westhampton Beach, NY 11978; tel. 516-288-5753. Open daily.*

BEVERAGES: ◆ **Circle M Beverage Barn.** *160 Montauk Hwy., Westhampton Beach, NY 11978; tel. 516-288-3040. Open daily.*

WINE: ◆ **Six Corners Liquors.** *166 Mill Rd., Westhampton Beach, NY 11978; tel. 516-288-1387. Open Mon.-Sat. Next to Eckart's.*

SPORTS
BOATING

◆ **Hampton Watercraft & Marine.** Boat rentals, sales, and dockage, as well as Jet Ski rentals and waterskiing lessons. *99B Old Riverhead Rd., Westhampton Beach, NY 19978; tel. 516-288-2900. Open daily Apr.-Sep. Closed Tue. Oct.-Mar.*

◆ **Remsenburg Marina.** Rentals, slips, and service. *Dock Rd., Speonk, NY 11960; tel. 516-325-1677. Open daily. West of Westhampton Beach on Montauk Hwy. in Speonk, turn south on Dock Rd.*

● **South Shore Boats.** Boat rentals, sales, and service. *Box 1706, Westhampton Beach, NY 11978; tel. 516-288-2400. Open daily. From Main St., go south on Library Ave.*

BICYCLING

◆ **Bike 'n' Kite.** Bike rentals, sales, service, and clothing. *112 Potunk Lane, Westhampton Beach, NY 11978; tel. 516-288-1210. Open daily.*

GOLF

Both the Westhampton Country Club and the Hampton Hills Golf and Country Club are private. The Indian Island Golf Club (tel. 516-727-7776), a public course, is located to the north, at Riverhead.

TENNIS

◆ **Westhampton Tennis & Sports Club.** *86 Depot Rd., Westhampton Beach, NY 11978; tel. 516-288-6060. Admission.*

NATURE

◆ **Quogue Bird Sanctuary.** *Quogue, NY 11942. Open daily. East of Suffolk County Airport along Old Quogue Riverhead Rd.*

SAFETY TIPS

Westhampton Beach Taxi & Limo has a van service that's proven popular among club-hoppers who want to avoid drinking and driving (tel. 516-288-3252, 800-649-4118).

TOURIST INFORMATION

◆ **East Quogue Chamber of Commerce.** *Box 877, E. Quogue, NY 11942; tel. 516-653-5143.*

◆ **Greater Westhampton Chamber of Commerce.** *173 Montauk Hwy., Box 1228, Westhampton Beach, NY 11978; tel. 516-288-3337. Open Mon.-Sat. 10-4 Jun.-Sep. and Mon.-Fri. 10-2 Oct.-May.*

CHAPTER 6

Fire Island

Beauty	A
Swimming	A
Sand	A
Hotels/Inns/B&Bs	C
House rentals	C
Restaurants	C
Nightlife	B
Attractions	C
Shopping	D
Sports	C+
Nature	A

ire Island stands alone among Middle Atlantic beach destinations, just a short ferry ride offshore but so far removed from daily routine that it casts a mesmerizing spell on those who visit. Life takes on a whimsical quality on this 32-mile barrier island. Roads and cars are supplanted by footpaths, hand-pulled wagons, bikes, and whitetail deer wandering freely, like cows in India.

HOW TO GET THERE

◆ From New York City, take Rte. 27 (Sunrise Hwy.) east. For the Bay Shore ferries (to Dunewood, Fair Harbor, Kismet, Ocean Bay Park, Ocean Beach, and Saltaire), take Exit 43 south (Fifth Ave.), and follow Fifth Ave. south past Main St. Turn left onto Gibson St. and right onto Maple Ave. to the Fire Island ferries (tel. 516-666-3600).

◆ For the Sayville ferries (to Cherry Grove, Fire Island Pines, Sailor's Haven, and the Sunken Forest), take Rte. 27 east. Turn right onto Lakeland Ave., left onto Montauk Hwy., and right onto Foster to the Sayville ferries (tel. 516-589-0810).

◆ For the Patchogue ferries (to Davis Park and Watch Hill), take Rte. 27 east. Turn south onto Patchogue Holbrooke Rd., left onto Montauk Hwy., and right onto West Ave. to the ferry (tel. 516-475-1665).

◆ From Philadelphia, take the NJ Tpke. north to Exit 13 (Staten Island). Cross Staten Island and the Verrazano Narrows Bridge. Pick up the Belt Pkwy. eastbound and take it to the Southern State Pkwy. eastbound. Take Exit 42 south (Bay Shore). Follow signs to the ferries.

◆ From New York City, the Long Island Rail Road stops at Bayside, Sayville, and Patchogue. Jitneys run between the train stations and the ferry docks in Bayside and Sayville. In Patchogue, the ferry is within walking distance. Call the LIRR for information (tel. 718-217-5477).

◆ **Village Transit Corp. provides van service between the Sayville train station and the ferry (tel. 516-563-4611). From the Bayshore railroad station, Tommy's Taxi (516-665-4800) and David's Taxi (516-665-1515) serve the Fire Island ferry terminals. These two taxi services also provide transportation between Manhattan and the ferry terminals.**

◆ **Ferry schedules can be found in the *Fire Island Tide*, a biweekly newspaper (49 Main St., Sayville, NY 11782; tel. 516-567-7470).**

◆ **South Bay Water Taxi serves Fire Island communities from Kismet to Watch Hill (tel. 516-665-8885).**

◆ **Aqualine Water Taxi serves Kismet, Saltaire, Fair Harbor, Dunewood, Atlantique, Ocean Beach, Point O'Woods, Sailors Haven, and Cherry Grove (tel. 516-665-5566).**

The island's eastern half is mainly uninhabited park land, but strung along the western end are 17 small, dense communities, each with its own personality. Interspersed are park and beach areas and, at one point, a rare natural phenomenon called the Sunken Forest. There, a boardwalk carries people away from the beach and down into a heavily wooded concavity complete with swamp and leafy canopy, an enchanted forest that gives no hint that it sits on a sandy island.

Nature throws its weight around on Fire Island. The ocean eats at the coastline, threatening beach homes that seemed safe only a decade ago. Some of the towns have little beach left, and storm surges bring with them a crisis atmosphere. Residents have a long history of avid environmentalism, but they also clamor for beach replenishment. Naysayers classify Fire Island as an overgrown sandbar and say it will eventually be reclaimed by the sea.

Sandy trails, wooden walks, and paved paths link the communities, but the prevailing transportation is the ferry. During the summer, the boats regularly cross Great South Bay from the Long Island towns of Bay Shore, Sayville, and Patchogue, and "lateral" ferries ply the island's shoreline between town docks.

At the west end of Fire Island is Robert Moses State Park, accessible by causeway from the mainland but lacking the secluded atmosphere of the rest of the island (*see* Chapter 7, Robert Moses State Park). At the island's east end, the Smith Point Visitors Center can also be reached by car.

Each town has a bay side and ocean side, but many have little to offer transient tourists beyond the spectacle of mazelike walkways that pass alluring homes and bungalows. Don't expect to find public rest rooms or changing facilities. Many communities are strictly residential, with no stores, shops, restaurants, or lodging. Rental houses are often passed among networks of acquaintances, although they are not impossible to find, especially among properties that for one reason or another haven't been reserved for the whole season. Hotels and guest houses are few, and many have a steady stream of repeat customers. Booking ahead means *way* ahead. The town of Ocean Beach has the most facilities, including restaurants and places to stay. Ocean Bay Park has a few hotels as well. The gay communities of Cherry Grove and Fire Island Pines have many more rooms.

Still, day-tripping to several communities is quite manageable. In half an hour or less, the boats carry passengers to beaches like Sailors Haven, Watch Hill, and Atlantique, all of which are geared to day-trippers and have food and bathing facilities. Parking at the ferry terminals is reasonably priced.

The National Park Service sites in particular—Sailors Haven, Watch Hill, and Fire Island Lighthouse—are hungry for visitors. In the politics of federal budgeting, the parks that draw the most people stand the best chance of surviving budget cuts. Fire Island gets a relatively small number of visitors and officials are happy to promote their prize territory.

Although there is a public school, and some people live here year-round, by early October, virtually all of Fire Island's occupants have departed until May, when the weather warms and the ferry service resumes a frequent schedule.

BEACHES
SAILORS HAVEN

This Fire Island National Seashore beach is huge and spectacular. The ferry from Sayville drops passengers at a pier near the visitors center, from which a boardwalk leads through the island's sandy midsection to the oceanside. The

Beauty	A
Swimming	A
Sand	B
Amenities	B

beach has a splendid, wild atmosphere with fortresslike dunes. Half a mile up the beach to the east, the beach homes of Cherry Grove are silhouetted in the distance; down the beach to the west, other beach houses are even more distant. A walkway from the visitors center leads to the Sunken Forest. *From Sayville, ferries for Sailors Haven depart regularly May-Sep.; tel. 516-589-8980. Visitors center tel. 516-597-6183. From Cherry Grove, the visitors center is about a 15-min. walk. From Ocean Bay Park, the visitors center is about a 30-min. walk, although a boardwalk to the beach is closer.*

Swimming: Waves break 30 to 50 yards out, then swoosh in gently on calm days. Beach angles gently into the water. Lifeguard on duty.

Sand: Light tan and mostly very fine, with occasional patches mixed with coarser granules and pebbles. Occasional signs of erosion.

Amenities: Visitors center on bayside with food, showers, rest rooms, picnic tables, volleyball, maritime forest exhibit; 42-slip marina (tel. 516-597-6171).

Sports: None.

Parking: No vehicles.

ATLANTIQUE BEACH

This beach park operated by Islip Village sprawls from bayside to ocean-side. The portion along the bay includes a marina and a big picnic and play area, with a boardwalk leading over the dune to the ocean. The beach is

Beauty	A-
Swimming	A
Sand	B
Amenities	A

humongous, although it loses something because it's geared to han-

dling large numbers of people. Beach houses are visible up and down the coastline, but none are located just behind the beach. *From Bay Shore, ferries depart for Atlantique Beach regularly May-Sep.*
Swimming: Waves wash in against a broad, gently sloping beachline. Lifeguard on duty.
Sand: Light tan and fine, rising to a dune.
Amenities: Marina, bathhouse with showers, rest rooms, food, playground, picnic areas.
Sports: Handball, volleyball.
Parking: No vehicles.

SALTAIRE

Perhaps Fire Island's most well-to-do community, Saltaire doesn't exactly cater to daytrippers, but it does have a beach with a lifeguard and an inviting network of boardwalk "streets" that are excellent for strolling. Steps lead from one of the boardwalks down

Beauty	B
Swimming	B
Sand	B
Amenities	B

to the medium-size beach, where the fence-protected dune rises to become the backyard of residences overlooking the ocean. *From Bay Shore, ferries run regularly to Saltaire May-Sep., dropping off passengers near a very nice boardwalk complex complete with benches and a gazebo.*
Swimming: Waves break 100 yards or more out, then break again just before the beach, providing sometimes choppy conditions. Lifeguard on duty.
Sand: Fine and tan, sloping fairly steeply from the waterline back to a moderately high dune.
Amenities: Foot showers. Grocery and other businesses near town pier.
Sports: None.
Parking: No vehicles.

WATCH HILL

Watch Hill has the Fire Island National Seashore's largest park complex and program of activities, including a big, mile-long beach and three miles of wooden walkway. A walkway about a third of a mile long leads west, to the

Beauty	A
Swimming	A
Sand	A
Amenities	A

edge of the Davis Park community, where the beach suffered storm damage in 1995 and early 1996. Watch Hill's broad beach was spared, and to the east is seven more miles of unspoiled beach in the Fire Island National Wilderness Area. *Ferries from Patchogue leave regularly May-Oct.; tel. 516-475-1665. Visitors center tel. 516-597-6455.*

Swimming: Waves tempered by a sandbar a few hundred yards out. Lifeguard on duty.

Sand: Fine and light tan, building to a healthy, grassy dune.

Amenities: Rest rooms, changing rooms, cold showers, picnic areas, camping, nature programs, visitors center, marina, concessions, restaurant.

Sports: None.

Parking: No vehicles.

NATIONAL SEASHORE— LIGHTHOUSE VISITORS CENTER

This section of Fire Island National Seashore is distinguished for two reasons: You can get near it by car, and it's the only *officially* clothing-optional stretch around. A boardwalk leads from below the lighthouse over a dune to the medium-size

Beauty	A
Swimming	B
Sand	B
Amenities	D

beach, which lost some girth to Hurricane Hugo and which during high tide shrinks to a fairly narrow size.

The beach has an isolated atmosphere, with the grassy dune blocking the view of the low-lying park land to the north. The towering lighthouse is occasionally visible, but it is a few hundred yards from the beach and does not create much of a presence.

To the west are the crowded beaches of the state park; going east just over a mile, the federal seashore runs into that of Kismet, a funky, sixties kind of place. This westernmost of Fire Island's communities is known (along with Ocean Beach) for attracting singles. *From New York, take Rte. 27 east. Go south on Sagtikos State Pkwy. and across the Robert Moses Causeway to its end at Robert Moses State Park. Turn east and go to the end of the park road. You must walk from Parking Field 5. In summer there is ferry service for tour groups from Bay Shore to the lighthouse dock. Lighthouse vis-*

itors center tel. 516-661-4876.

Swimming: Medium-size waves swell in from the open ocean. No lifeguard.

Sand: Fine, tan, uniformly spread, and rising to a medium dune.

Amenities: Rest rooms at lighthouse. Robert Moses State Park facilities within walking distance.

Sports: None.

Parking: Field 5 at Robert Moses State Park is about a quarter of a mile from the lighthouse. On foot, the beach is closer (daily fee charged).

HOTELS/INNS/B&BS

Because of the small number of hotels, booking early is often the only way to get a room. Several hotels take reservations even before they've opened for the season (but cancellations can mean last-minute openings.) Small lodgings tend to change hands or close, then reopen under new management. The Fire Island Tourism Bureau should know the latest (tel. 516-563-8448).

◆ **Fire Island Hotel & Resort** (expensive). This 46-unit hotel, one of Fire Island's biggest, occupies a former Coast Guard station that's about 90 years old but has recently been renovated. All of the rooms are simply furnished and have TVs but no phones. Some have balconies or decks. Many rooms are small, and hallways retain a barracks character. Pool and playground. Less than a block from the ocean. *Ocean Bay Park, NY 11770; tel. 516-583-8000; fax 516-583-7413. Closed Nov.-Apr. From the ferry dock, go east on Bay View Ave., then right onto Cayuga.*

◆ **Houser's Hotel** (expensive). New England-style B&B has 12 guestrooms, some with shared bath, most with bay views. Charming touches, such as fresh flowers and potpourri. A new deck overlooks the bay and Houser's restaurant and bar. *Bay Walk, East Side, Ocean Beach, NY 11770; tel. 516-583-7799. Open May-Sep.*

◆ **Clegg's Hotel** (expensive). A shingle-style structure offering single and double rooms, plus an apartment with a kitchen and bath. It's next to the tennis courts, just off the bay. *Ocean Beach, NY 11770; tel. 516-583-5399. Closed Oct.-mid-Apr. Next to the ferry basin.*

◆ **Four Seasons Bed & Breakfast** (moderate). All ten rooms have air-conditioning, some a fireplace and Jacuzzi. *468 Denhoff Walk,*

Ocean Beach, NY 11770; tel. 516-583-8295. Open May-Oct.
◆ **Land's End Motel & Marina** (moderate). The only lodging within walking distance of the Sayville ferry docks, this motel has 15 efficiency units with stove, refrigerator, sofa bed, double bed, and remote-control TV. A high wardrobe/drawer unit separates the bedroom from the living room area. New construction, plain furnishings. Just off the bay. *70 Brown's River Rd., Sayville, NY 11782; tel. 516-589-2040. Just beyond the ferry piers.*
◆ **Sea-Shore Motel** (moderate). This 22-unit motel has modest rooms, small but tidy and not worn, with pine walls and two twin beds. Most units have a refrigerator or efficiency kitchen. Across the street from the bay. *78 E. Bay Walk, Ocean Bay Park, NY 11770; tel. 516-583-5860. Closed early Sep.-late May.*

HOUSE RENTALS

House rentals are usually by the season or month but occasionally by the week for properties that aren't filled. A small and/or no-frills house rental for the Memorial Day-Labor Day season could cost $7,500 to $15,000, a large and luxurious one $14,000 to $30,000. A weekly rental could run from $1,300 to $2,000, depending on size, timing, and location. Most rentals are arranged between January and March. The *Fire Island News* and the *Fire Island Tide* may have listings.
◆ **Fire Island Summer Space.** Rentals and sales in several Fire Island communities. *Bay Walk E., Ocean Beach, NY 11770; tel. 516-583-7790, 212-674-6256. Open daily.*
◆ **Larson Realty.** Rentals and sales in Saltaire, Kismet, and Fair Harbor. *206 Broadway, Saltaire, NY 11706; tel. 516-583-9100. Open daily.*
◆ **Ocean Beach Real Estate Co.** Rentals and sales in several Fire Island communities. *310 Bay Walk, Ocean Beach, NY 11770; tel. 516-583-9393. Open daily.*
◆ **Pines Harbor Realty.** Rentals and sales in Fire Island Pines, Water Island, Cherry Grove, Davis Park. *Box 219, Sayville, NY 11782; tel. 516-597-7575. At the Boatel in Fire Island Pines. Open daily.*

RESTAURANTS

◆ **Sunset Grill Le Dock** (expensive). This informal restaurant with a view of the Fair Harbor bay-front offers entrées such as seared tuna with garlic, soy, ginger sauce and coconut rice; farfalle with grilled vegetables, sun-dried tomatoes, caramelized onions, and cream; and linguini à la vodka. Chicken and steak specials round out the menu. *60 Bay Walk, Fair Harbor, NY 11770; tel. 516-583-5200. Open daily for lunch and dinner May-mid-Oct. Near the dock in Fair Harbor.*

◆ **Top of the Bay** (expensive). This cozy second-floor restaurant looks out over the bay and the Cherry Grove ferry dock, where paddling swans offer a welcoming touch. Seafood with a southwestern accent; the menu includes steak and chicken dishes as well. *Dock Walk, Cherry Grove, NY 11782; tel. 516-597-6699. Open for lunch and dinner Wed.-Mon. early May-early Oct.*

◆ **CJ's Restaurant & Bar** (moderate). Ocean Beach's only year-round restaurant, CJ's offers dining at the bar or in the adjacent dining room—both informal and relaxed. Besides sandwiches and other light choices, specials such as chicken marsala, chicken parmesan, steak au poivre, cornish game hen, and the ubiquitous lobster are available. *Bayview Walk, Ocean Beach, NY 11770; tel. 516-583-9890. Open daily for lunch and dinner.*

◆ **Flynn's** (moderate). This celebrated restaurant has a big square bar plopped onto a cream linoleum floor and a big deck overlooking the bay and marina. *Bayview Ave., Ocean Bay Park, NY 11770; tel. 516-583-5850, 516-665-2751. Open daily for lunch and dinner May-Sep.*

◆ **Kismet Inn** (moderate). A prime gathering place for socializing and dining on steaks, chops, and seafood. *Kismet, NY 11770; tel. 516-583-5592. Open daily for lunch and dinner May-Sep.*

◆ **Seashore Inn** (inexpensive). This dockside restaurant offers standard entrées (stuffed flounder, shrimp scampi, and filet mignon), pastas (cappellini with smoked salmon and roasted peppers in a sun-dried tomato sauce), and appetizers (fried calamari, steamed mussels, and baked clams). *Box 128, Blue Point, NY 11715; tel. 516-597-6655. Open Tue.-Fri. for dinner and Sat.-Sun. for lunch and dinner mid-Jun.-early Sep.; bar open through mid-Oct. At the Watch Hill Marina.*

NIGHTLIFE

◆ **Maguire's Restaurant & Bar.** This restaurant with a dark, nautical decor, fireplace, and outdoor deck has dancing to a DJ on Friday and Saturday nights. Music varies widely. *Bungalow Walk,*

Ocean Beach, NY 11770; tel. 516-583-8800. Near the marina.

◆ **The Out.** This barnlike restaurant and bar, half of Kismet's "the Inn and the Out," is a lively après-beach scene, especially on weekends, offering packed late-night dancing to recorded music and sometimes live entertainment. The Out has been in business since 1974, and its happy hour has achieved cult status. *Kismet, NY 11770; tel. 516-583-7400.*

◆ **The Ice Palace.** Fire Island's best-known club caters to a gay audience but also attracts nongays, especially for the Miss Fire Island Contest, a competition for female impersonators that has been held each September for three decades. The club offers music, dancing, cabaret, and a piano bar. *At the Cherry Grove Beach Motel, Main Walk, Cherry Grove, NY 11770; tel. 516-597-6600. Open daily mid-May-mid-Sep.*

ATTRACTIONS

Fire Island doesn't have amusement parks, but it does have the Fire Island Lighthouse and a host of nature trails, including the Sunken Forest (*see* "Nature").

◆ **Fire Island Lighthouse.** The lighthouse visitors center has a maritime museum and regular 45-minute tours to the top. There's also a nature trail that starts at the lighthouse. *120 Laurel St., Patchogue, NY 11772; tel. 516-661-4876. Tours conducted at 10, 11, 12:45, 2 and 3. From Kismet, the lighthouse is a 1-mi. walk, or it can be reached by lateral ferry. The lighthouse is also accessible from Robert Moses State Park—it's a 1/4-mi. walk from Parking Field 5.*

BEST FOOD SHOPS

Most of the island communities have their own small food, liquor, and ice cream stores. Vacationers renting property can save money by ordering from businesses across the bay that will deliver groceries and other goods to the ferry terminals.

SANDWICHES: ◆ **Ocean Beach Trader.** *Ocean Beach, NY 11770; tel. 516-583-8440. Open daily May-Sep.*

SEAFOOD: ◆ **The Market Place at Matthew's Seafood House.** *E. Bay Walk, Ocean Beach, NY 11770; tel. 516-583-8016. Open daily May-Sep.*

FRESH PRODUCE: Some markets on Long Island offer ferry delivery to Fire Island, including Blue Point Farm &

Country Store (tel. 516-363-2244).

◆ **Ocean Beach Trader.** Near the ferry basin. *Bayview Walk, Ocean Beach, NY 11770; tel. 516-583-8440.*

BAKERY: Mermaid Market has a full-service bakery. *Ocean Beach, NY 11770; tel. 516-583-0303. Open daily May-Oct.*

BEVERAGES: Beverage Barn in Bay Shore (tel. 516-665-0320) offers ferry delivery to Fire Island.

◆ **Ocean Bay Park Market.** Beer and soda, seafood, dairy products, fruit, vegetables, sandwiches. *Ocean Bay Park, NY; tel. 516-583-8431. Open daily May-Sep.*

WINE: ◆ **Seaview Liquors.** *Seaview, NY 11770; tel. 516-583-5287. Open Mon.-Sat.*

◆ **The Pines Liquor Shop.** *Fire Island Pines, NY 11770; tel. 516-597-6442. Open Mon.-Sat. At the ferry pier.*

SPORTS
FISHING

◆ **Capt. T's.** Bait and tackle for surf, inshore, offshore, and freshwater fishing. *650-3 Montauk Hwy., Bayport, NY 11705; tel. 516-472-0302. Open daily Apr.-Dec. Closed Tue.-Sun. Jan.-Mar.*

BOATING

◆ **Schooner Inn Beach.** Jet Ski, Waverunner, sunfish, day sailer, fishing dory, and Hobie Cat rentals. Instruction. *Ocean Bay Park, NY; tel. 516-583-9561. Open daily May-Sep.*

SURFING

◆ **Phoenix Surfboards.** Rentals, sales, accessories. *60 W. Main St., Bay Shore, NY; tel. 516-665-5595. Open daily.*

◆ **Rick's Action Sports & Surf Shop.** Surfboards, body boards, wet suits, surf wear, accessories. Surf report (tel. 516-581-2299). *155 E. Carelton Ave., E. Islip, NY; tel. 516-581-9424. Open daily.*

BICYCLING

◆ **Ocean Beach Hardware.** Bicycle rentals, sales, and service. *482 Bayberry Walk, Ocean Beach, NY 11770; tel. 516-583-5826.*

◆ **Schooner Inn.** Bike rentals, sales, and repairs. *Ocean Bay Park, NY 11770; tel. 516-583-9561. Open daily in May-Sep.*

TENNIS

Kismet, Ocean Beach, Ocean Bay Park, and Seaview are among the communities with public courts. Their recreation departments have regulations for their use.

◆ **Ocean Beach.** These two courts are tucked in the thick of things, between the marina and the ferry basin. Hourly time can be secured at the Recreation Department office in the boat house on the north side of the ferry pier. *Recreation Dept., Ocean Beach, NY 11770; tel. 516-583-5153. Open mid-May-mid-Oct.*

NATURE

◆ **Sunken Forest Trail.** This amazing self-guided trail carries visitors into a rare maritime forest complete with thicket, marsh, bog, and a full range of trees and plant life that thrives below dune level. Within the forest, it's easy to forget you're on a barrier island. Pick up the Sunken Forest guide booklet at the visitors center. *Sailors Haven Visitors Center, tel. 516-597-6183.*

SAFETY TIPS

Ticks that carry Lyme disease are common on Fire Island. They aren't a problem on the beach, but health experts recommend avoiding deer and the grassy, wooded, or shrubby areas where ticks reside. Inspect yourself and children regularly. Poison ivy and mosquitoes are also present.

TOURIST INFORMATION

◆ **Fire Island National Seashore.** This office administers all the federal seashore sites, including Sailors Haven (tel. 516-597-6183), Watch Hill (tel. 516-597-6455), Fire Island Lighthouse (tel. 516-661-4876), and Smith Point (tel. 516-281-3010). *120 Laurel St., Patchogue, NY 11772; tel. 516-289-4810. Open Mon.-Fri. 8-4:30. South of Montauk Hwy., off West Ave.*

◆ **Fire Island Tourism Bureau.** Responds to mail and phone inquiries. *Box 248, Sayville, NY 11782; tel. 516-563-8448. Open Mon.-Fri. 10-3.*

◆ *The Fire Island Guide.* This authoritative guide to Fire Island is compiled by Trigar Publishing, which also publishes the weekly *Fire Island News.* A new edition was scheduled for summer 1996 ($8). *Box 486, Ocean Beach, NY 11770; tel. 516-583-5345.*

CHAPTER 7

Robert Moses State Park

Beauty	B
Swimming	A
Sand	A
Hotels/Inns/B&Bs	NA
House rentals	NA
Restaurants	NA
Nightlife	NA
Attractions	B-
Shopping	NA
Sports	B
Nature	B

he westernmost six miles of Fire Island are the domain of Robert Moses State Park, named for New York's visionary city and parks planner who, ironically, wanted to run a road the length of the island as a way to deter its erosion and open it to the masses. His road plan was expensive and unpopular with preservationists, and it was rejected in the 1930s and again in the early sixties. But his influence on the state's park system was pervasive, and today the park bearing his name attracts about three million people each year.

Besides its broad beaches, it has the advantage of accessibility—the Robert Moses Causeway carries thousands of people on hot summer days from West Islip, across South Oyster Bay, past Captree State Park, and over the Fire Island Inlet.

For nearly half a century after it became, in 1908, the first state park in New York, visitors had to ferry over from Babylon. In 1954 the causeway to Captree was completed, with a water shuttle providing the final connection. In 1964 the last bridge link was finished, the park was named in Moses's honor, and attendance soared astronomically.

The park's most prominent landmark as visitors approach on the causeway is a slender 202-foot-high water tower that looks more like a monument than a storage tank, sitting in the middle of a landscaped circle that is roughly in the middle of the park.

The park has four paved parking fields that can hold a total of about 8,300 cars, although not all are open all of the time. Fields 3 and 4 are closed mid-September to mid-May. At other times a field may be open just on weekends. Each field has a bathhouse and refreshment facilities near the entrance to its section of beach.

The beach itself is one long strand, and it's good to take note of

HOW TO GET THERE

◆ From New York City, go east on Rte. 27 (Sunrise Hwy.) or the Southern State Pkwy. and turn south onto the Sagtikos State Pkwy. Cross the Robert Moses Causeway to the park. (The park is about 50 mi. from Manhattan; from the turn off Rte. 27, it's about 7 mi.) From the Fire Island community of Kismet, the park is about a 1 1/4 mi. walk on a sandy road off-limits to traffic. It can also be reached by water taxi.

◆ The beach areas at Robert Moses State Park are designated by their parking lots: Fields 2, 3, 4, and 5.

any closed fields because the sand there will probably be less crowded—if you don't mind walking there from wherever you've parked.

Near the park's eastern end, a quarter-mile walk beyond Parking Field 5, is the black-and-white Fire Island Lighthouse and its red-roofed visitors center (*see* Chapter 6, Fire Island).

BEACHES
FIELD 2

This section of beach along the westernmost parking lot is backed by a high dune bluff for a few hundred yards to the east. To the west there's a lower dune, and the beach extends as far as you can see. At the beach entrance, a wide concrete plaza stands between the bath-

Beauty	B
Swimming	A
Sand	B
Amenities	A

house and the sand. Farther west, the beach is open to off-road vehicles and curls around to form the tip of Fire Island and one edge of the Fire Island Inlet. Because of the nearby inlet, there's a lot of fishing and other boating activity just offshore. *Enter the park at the circle and go right.*

Swimming: Waves break about 100 yards out then roll in fairly gently on calm days. Lifeguard on duty.

Sand: Fine and mostly light tan, though in some areas tinged with reddish sand of the same consistency.

Amenities: Bathhouse with showers and rest rooms. Refreshments, picnic area.

Sports: Surfing just west of beach. Pitch-and-putt golf course within walking distance.

Parking: Huge lot ($3 fee).

FIELD 3

This beach area, closest to the park's entrance, tends to be more family-oriented and has the largest picnic area. The beach setting has a more natural feel than at Field 2, partly because the higher dune bluff is closer and masks

Beauty	B+
Swimming	A
Sand	B
Amenities	A

the parking lot, although the park water tower looms nearby. *Enter the park at the circle and go right.*

Swimming: Waves roll in unthreateningly on calm days.

Lifeguard on duty.
Sand: Fine and mostly light tan.
Amenities: Bathhouse with showers and rest rooms. Refreshments, picnic area.
Sports: Body boards.
Parking: Huge lot ($3 fee).

FIELD 4

Aesthetically, this is the best of the park's beach areas, backed totally by a moderately high dune, except for the gap leading to the bathhouse. It's a huge beach, and its few visual imperfections—erosion traces, splotches of garnet sand, a tidal line of grav-

Beauty	A
Swimming	A
Sand	B
Amenities	A

el and shell—seem negligible against the beach's scale. Peeking over the dune to the west is the water tower, and a couple miles east rises the Fire Island Lighthouse. *Enter the park and follow the circle to the left.*
Swimming: Waves wash in rhythmically, breaking three or four times before reaching shore. Lifeguard on duty.
Sand: Fine and mostly light tan, with some small stones, rising to a moderately high dune.
Amenities: Bathhouse with showers and rest rooms. Refreshments, picnic area.
Sports: Body boards.
Parking: Huge lot ($3 fee).

FIELD 5

This easternmost beach area is wide and backed by a medium-size dune, although in spots the parking lot is visible. The beach maintains its width and dune line to the west, whereas to the east it narrows as it crosses into Fire Island

Beauty	B+
Swimming	A
Sand	B
Amenities	A

National Seashore territory, a swimsuit-optional area (*see* Chapter 6, Fire Island). West of the bathhouse, a wide boardwalk runs along the dune, arcing around to the parking lot. It has a couple of ramps that empty onto the beach, and at the west end of the boardwalk is a dune-protected picnic area with grills and tables. *Enter the park and follow the circle to the left.*

Swimming: Waves begin breaking about 100 yards out, with several other breaking points before the shore. Lifeguard on duty.

Sand: Fine and mostly light tan, with some goldish and purplish grains mixed in. At times, there may be an erosion cliff, with a lower, undulating beach level and a higher flat level rising to a moderately high dune with sparse dune grass.

Amenities: Bathhouse with showers and rest rooms. Refreshments, picnic area. Boardwalk.

Sports: Body boards.

Parking: Huge lot ($3 fee).

RESTAURANTS

Each parking field has a concession just outside the dune line, with such basic fare as hamburgers. They're usually open daily 9 to 6 from May through September.

◆ **Captree Cove** (moderate). This second-floor restaurant looks out over the charter fishing fleet and the State Boat Channel and serves, of course, seafood. Downstairs there's a cafeteria-style restaurant with lighter fare. *Captree State Park, Ocean Pkwy., Babylon, NY 11702; tel. 516-587-3495. Open daily for lunch and dinner Apr.-Oct. At the Captree Boat Basin off the Robert Moses Causeway.*

SPORTS
FISHING

Surf fishing is permitted in designated areas outside the swimming and surfing zones, which are marked by signs on the east side of each parking field. Fishing is also allowed from piers at the park boat basin. Across the inlet, there's a fishing pier at Captree State Park.

◆ **Captree Boat Basin.** Activity at the 298-acre Captree State Park centers on a boat basin where many charter fishing boats are based. Information on the boats can be obtained from the Captree Boatman's Association (tel. 516-669-6464). The park also has two fishing piers, a bait-and-tackle shop, a picnic area, and a playground. *Captree State Park, Box 247, Babylon, NY 11702; tel. 516-669-0449. Many of the boats operate daily most of the year; some operate Fri.-Mon. in the colder months, with departures at 5 or 6 a.m. Off the Robert Moses Causeway, at the end of Ocean Pkwy.*

on Captree Island, extending from Jones Beach State Park.

BOATING

A day-use boat basin located near the park entrance can handle 40 boats, with free pump-out station. No overnight use.

SURFING

Surfing is allowed in four designated areas to the east of each parking field. The areas near Fields 2 and 5 are particularly popular. Surfing is prohibited in areas designated for fishing and swimming. The surfing boundaries expand outside of the May through September swimming season.

BICYCLING

The park has no designated bike paths and discourages bike use, but some cycling occurs. It is possible to bike on a road that runs past the lighthouse and continues to Kismet, westernmost of the Fire Island communities.

GOLF

An 18-hole pitch-and-putt course is located at the west end of Parking Field 2. It operates from April through November, with hours varying from 8 to 4 at the beginning of the season to 7 a.m. to 6:30 p.m. as the days grow longer. The popular course sometimes has waits of two or more hours, although a reservation system was being considered. The course can be reached through the park's main number (516-669-0449, ext. 60).

TOURIST INFORMATION

◆ **Captree State Park.** Information can be obtained through Robert Moses State Park, which has the same phone number. *Box 247, Babylon, NY 11702; tel. 516-669-0449. Open daily sunrise to sunset. Off the Robert Moses Causeway, at the end of Ocean Pkwy. on Captree Island, extending from Jones Beach State Park.*

◆ **Robert Moses State Park.** The park office is to the right as you come onto the island. *Box 247, Babylon, NY 11702; tel. 516-669-0449. The park is open daily sunrise to sunset.*

CHAPTER 8

Jones Beach State Park

Beauty	A
Swimming	B
Sand	B-
Hotels/Inns/B&Bs	B
House rentals	B+
Restaurants	B
Nightlife	C
Attractions	B
Shopping	C
Sports	B
Nature	A

ones Beach is the colossus of American sandboxes, a place whose scale is matched only by the astounding crowds of summer sunbathers who swarm here—more than 200,000 on the Fourth of July, a mere 100,000 or more on slower days. In a year, six million people visit Jones Beach, more than you'll find at any other beach in the United States.

The six-mile-long strand is not a genteel escape

to quiet sun-splashed shores. This is the quintessential urban watering hole, a cooling ground for New York's teeming masses less than an hour from the Big Apple by rail and connecting shuttle bus ($11 or so round-trip).

For most visitors, Jones is not a beach to build a whole vacation around. But it is a spectacle, and whether sampled on a daytrip from New York City or as part of a swing toward the Hamptons or Montauk, it will be memorable. The Long Island traffic may back up, but there's no need to worry about parking; the big lots can accommodate more than 23,000 vehicles. (On occasion, pilots in trouble have safely landed their private planes here.)

On summer evenings, lifeguards stay on duty until 7 or 8, and the park is open until midnight. The one-and-a-half-mile-long boardwalk is lined with diversions, including restaurants, ball fields, shuffleboard and tennis courts, a band shell with free nightly entertainment, and an old-fashioned ice cream parlor. Some visitors like the night best, when the crush has abated and dreams hang in the cool evening air. Young Jack Kerouac and his friends whiled away the hours at Jones Beach after dark. Night

HOW TO GET THERE

◆ Jones Beach is about 40 mi. from Columbus Circle in Manhattan. By car, go east on the Long Island Expwy. or the Grand Central Pkwy. to the Northern State Pkwy. Then drive east to the Meadowbrook Pkwy. or the Wantagh Pkwy. and south to the park. You can also take the Southern State Pkwy. east to the Meadowbrook Pkwy. or the Wantagh Pkwy. and go south from there.

◆ By train from Pennsylvania Station, take the Long Island Rail Road to Freeport station. In the summer, a round-trip fare package includes the bus ride from Freeport station to the beach parking lot. Call for LIRR information (tel. 718-217-5477).

time is also prime time at the park's 11,200-seat open-air theater, which offers world-class rock and pop performers.

By day the beach is like a miniature city percolating with sun worshippers who prostrate themselves beneath the sun, marking their territory with beach blankets, inches apart, creating a huge and colorful patchwork. The air is thick with the sounds of seashore frolic and the scent of tanning lotion, and there are plenty of the usual diversions and, sometimes, the unusual. At least one baby has been born on the beach when its mother unexpectedly went into labor.

The density of activity would no doubt delight Robert Moses, the New York State parks commissioner under whose aegis the park opened in 1929. Then-governor Franklin D. Roosevelt spoke at the opening ceremonies. The park was named for Maj. Thomas Jones, who arrived on Long Island in 1692 and established a whaling station near the site.

Today, the park covers 2,431 acres at the western tip of the barrier island at Wantagh and includes both bayside and oceanside frontage. Besides the main ocean-front beach, there's a family-friendly bay beach near the theater.

BEACHES
JONES BEACH—OCEANSIDE

When you step onto the beach from the boardwalk or parking fields, it can seem impossibly wide, and in places you can't even see the distant surf because of rises and dips in the sand. But a two-minute walk will usually carry you to the water's edge.

Beauty	A
Swimming	A
Sand	B
Amenities	A-

During peak periods, the whole beach is packed, but the section just in front of the Central Mall is ground zero for crowd activity.

Many regulars have their favorite parking field. Families, of course, favor the ones between Ocean Drive and the beach because it's a shorter walk to the sand. The crowd thins at the west end, where the beach is appreciably wider, the walk from the parking areas longer, and the amenities far fewer.

Low dunes rise at the back of the beach, some more prominent than others, and miles of dune fence cast shadows. The boardwalk scene behind the beach is helter-skelter; the view out over the ocean

is long, wide, and impressive, a soothing antidote to the zany throngs.
Swimming: Good swimming in rolling waves. Lifeguard on duty.
Sand: Fine and light tan, sometimes showing signs of erosion that comes and goes with the stormy seas.
Amenities: Rest rooms, east and west bathhouses, snack stands along boardwalk.
Sports: Surfing at west end; fishing, softball diamonds, basketball, fitness course, roller skating, golfing.
Parking: Eight huge lots along Ocean and Bay drives, which circle the park (per-car fee).

JONES BEACH—ZACH'S BAY

Zach's Bay, located next to Parking Field 5 and the theater, offers a calm alternative to the ocean surf, especially for families with small children. It's a quarter-mile bay beach whose water rises and falls with the tide, but there are no waves. It lacks the fresh

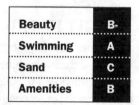

Beauty	B-
Swimming	A
Sand	C
Amenities	B

urgency of crashing surf, but its reeds and wetland grasses are soothing despite the traffic on Ocean Drive, a few hundred yards away.
Swimming: Wading and swimming in still waters. Lifeguard on duty.
Sand: Moderately fine and tan, mixed with shells and tidal debris; not impressive compared with ocean sand.
Amenities: Bathhouse, snack bar, rest rooms.
Sports: Playground.
Parking: Field 5 (per-car fee).

HOTELS/INNS/B&BS

There is no lodging in the park, but there are motels and hotels within ten miles.

◆ **Long Island Marriott Hotel** (expensive). This 617-room hotel has pools, racquetball, a health club, and restaurants. *101 James Doolittle Blvd., Uniondale, NY 11553; tel. 516-794-3800, 800-228-9290. Take the Meadowbrook State Pkwy. west from the park past Hempstead Tpke.*

RESTAURANTS

Besides the Boardwalk Restaurant and Terrace, the park has a number of refreshment stands.

◆ **Boardwalk Restaurant and Terrace** (moderate). The restaurant's high glass walls give it an open-air feel and make it a prime vantage point for watching the boardwalk pedestrian traffic and the ocean rolling in. The menu ranges from sandwiches to seafood and pasta, with daily specials. *Jones Beach State Park, Wantagh, NY 11793; tel. 516-785-2840, 516-785-2420. Open daily for lunch and dinner Mon.-Fri. (last seating 9 p.m.) and Sat.-Sun. (last seating 10 p.m.) and for Sun. brunch early May-early Sep.; open for lunch Mon.-Fri. and Sun. brunch mid-Mar.-mid-May and mid-Sep.-early Dec. At the boardwalk's Central Mall. The restaurant has its own parking lot, which costs $20, with the full amount applied to the cost of dining (to discourage beachgoers from using the lot).*

NIGHTLIFE

From June to early September, the park remains open until midnight, and the lively scene along the boardwalk consists of sideshows, from shuffleboard to roller skating. At the Central Mall Band Shell, free concerts or dancing are scheduled most evenings (schedules available from the park office). Near the band shell there's miniature golf, which on busy nights may require a wait of up to an hour.

◆ **Jones Beach Theatre.** The open-air theater attracts world-class performers, and in recent years more than 400,000 people have attended each summer concert series, which leans toward rock and pop. The theater looks out over the smooth water of Zach's Bay and was renovated in the early '90s. It seats 11,200. *Jones Beach State Park, Wantagh, NY 11793; tel. 516-221-1000, 516-785-1600. Most concerts are Jun.-Sep.; call for a schedule. Admission. The theater and its parking lot are at the east end of Bay Dr.*

ATTRACTIONS

The 200-foot Jones Beach Water Tower, the most prominent feature on Ocean Drive, was patterned after the campanile of St. Mark's Cathedral in Venice. It holds 315,000 gallons of water, drawn from four wells more than 1,000 feet deep.

SHOPPING

At the Central Mall there's a Beach Shop that sells basics, such as sunscreen, T-shirts, beach towels, lots of souvenirs, and Boogie boards (tel. 516-785-1600).

BEST FOOD SHOPS

ICE CREAM: The Ice Cream Parlor near the West Bathhouse is faux-fifties and has booth seating. Ice cream also available from boardwalk concessionaires. *Tel. 516-785-2420. Open daily 3-10 mid-Jun.-early Sep.*

SPORTS

In addition to ocean swimming, the park offers two large outdoor pools—one at the East Bathhouse and one at the West Bathhouse—plus a wading pool. The pools open in mid-June, and one closes in mid-August, the other in early September. Some people pay the bathhouse-use fee for the convenience of the lockers and showers but swim in the ocean rather than the pools (tel. 516-785-1600).

FISHING

The park has a bait-and-tackle shop and fishing piers near Parking Field 10. The shop also sells sweatshirts, souvenirs, and the like. Surf casting is popular near the West End 2 lot and Parking Field 6, although fishing is not permitted near swimming areas (tel. 516-785-1600).

BOATING

The park's western end has a 78-slip boat basin that opens into the state boat channel and Jones Inlet. No overnight docking (tel. 516-785-1600).

SURFING

The beach's designated surfing area is at the park's west end, closest to the West End 2 parking field.
◆ **Sea Mass Surf Shop.** *5368A Merrick Rd., Massapequa, NY 11758; tel. 516-797-5670.*

BICYCLING

Bicycling is allowed on the boardwalk from October to March only, but there's a four-and-a-half-mile bike path along the Wantagh State Parkway from Jones Beach to Cedar Creek Park.

GOLF

The park has an 18-hole pitch-and-putt golf course, located near the Central Mall and the park water tower (Parking Fields 4 and 5). No reservations. An 18-hole miniature golf course is also open just west of the band shell. *Tel. 516-785-1600. Open Sat.-Sun. 10-4 early Apr.-Memorial Day; open daily 10-4 Memorial Day-late Jun. and 10 a.m.-11 p.m. late Jun.-Labor Day, open Sat.-Sun. 10-4 Labor Day-late Oct.*

TENNIS

Fifteen paddle-tennis courts are located in the West Games Area between the band shell and the Ice Cream Parlor. Paddles and shuffleboard equipment are available for rent by the half-hour from a booth. *Tel. 516-785-1600. Open Sat.-Sun. 10-5 mid-Apr.-mid-May; open daily 10-5 mid-May-late Jun. and 10 a.m.-11 p.m. late Jun.-early Sep.; open Sat.-Sun. 10-5 early Sep.-late Oct.*

NATURE

At the west end of the park is the Interpretive Nature Program Center (tel. 516-785-1600), from which guided walks on topics such as shorebird identification and dune ecology sometimes depart. This is an undeveloped area that is home to many birds. A checklist called "Birds of Jones Beach State Park," with hundreds of species and a guide to which seasons they are present, is available.

SAFETY TIPS

Beware of poison ivy and ticks. Swim only when lifeguards are on duty. If the water's rough, stay out of reach of the wave break. Be careful in the massive parking lots: More accidents occur there than in the big traffic circle. Always lock cars and keep valuables out of sight.

TOURIST INFORMATION

◆ **Jones Beach State Park.** The Central Mall park office (tel. 516-669-1000, ext. 223) serves as an information center. Each of the parking fields along the beach has an umbrella rental site that also has information about the park. Group permits available. *Box 1000, Wantagh, NY 11793; tel. 516-785-1600. Open daily 8 a.m.-midnight late Jun.-Labor Day and 8-5 Sep.-mid-Jun. The Central Mall is on the boardwalk, just south of the water tower.*

CHAPTER 9

Lake George

Beauty	A
Swimming	B
Sand	C
Hotels/Inns/B&Bs	A
House rentals	B
Restaurants	B+
Nightlife	B
Attractions	A
Shopping	A-
Sports	A
Nature	A

*L*ake George spreads between the folds of the Adirondack Mountains, its water serene, clear, clean, and speckled with hundreds of islands. It is 32 miles long and 4 miles at its widest, running north and south, and since the end of the Civil War its shoreline has been a magnet for vacationers and others escaping the grind. Thomas Jefferson discovered the area even earlier, writing in a letter to his daughter, "Lake George is, without comparison, the most beautiful water I ever saw." Near its south end Georgia O'Keeffe owned a farm, now a condo development. Adolph Ochs, an early publisher of the *New York Times*, had a big place, the only remaining piece of which is now the waterside Boathouse restaurant. Across the way is St. Mary's on the Lake, where the Paulist Brothers of Boston have been sending their seminarians on retreat for more than a century. The grand Sagamore hotel and resort rises on its own island, lording over the lake.

As elegant as the retreats of the rich are, the mood of Lake George is set more by the hundreds of smaller properties to which generations of families have come for vacation. Some are privately owned, others are rented by the week or month. They're called by many names: housekeeping cabins, lodges, bungalows, cottages, resorts, estates, motels, hotels, guest rooms. As you drive along the roads that skirt the lake, especially Route 9N, these properties stream by, each with its own narrow access road that often winds down to the lake's edge and, perhaps, its own spit of sand, dutifully identified as a private beach.

The glacial lake's natural appeal notwithstanding, the area has also cultivated its fun-spot reputation. At the southern tip, the state built the "Million Dollar Beach" in 1957, hauling in sand by the truckload to Lake George Village, the biggest of the resort communities. The quintessential lake experience is a ride aboard one of several big tour boats that ply the waters in grand tradition. One, the *Lac du Saint Sacrement*, holds more than 1,000 passengers. Another, the *Minne-Ha-Ha*, is a steam-driven paddle wheeler built

HOW TO GET THERE

◆ Lake George Village is just off I-87, about 1 hr. north of Albany, NY, and about 4 hr. from New York City.

◆ From Philadelphia and points south, take I-95 north to the NJ Tpke. north, exiting onto I-287 and following it north to I-87 north.

expressly for service on Lake George. When it plays its calliope at the Steel Pier, tourists swarm alongside, snapping pictures as if they can capture the high-pitched strains of "God Bless America" for later consumption.

The lake was known as Lac du Sacrement until the British defeated the French in the French and Indian War and renamed it after King George III. Early American history provides an educational backdrop to the region, with abundant landmarks from Colonial times. Ticonderoga sits at the lake's northern end; overlooking the south is the restored Fort William Henry, which provided the setting for James Fenimore Cooper's *Last of the Mohicans.*

But history only goes so far with the vacation crowd. Theme parks and arcades are part of the region's scene, too, with places like Great Escape Fun Park and Water Slide World. Factory-outlet shopping looms large year-round. In winter, local ski areas take the baton from the lake's water-sports scene.

BEACHES

Lake George's beaches don't have the girth or wave action of an ocean beach. It is, after all, a lake. But the water is remarkably clear and fresh, and you'll never find yourself awash in seaweed or jellyfish.

Most of the lake's islands are public, and some have their own small beaches. You can either boat to them or arrange to be dropped off for your own private beach picnic.

MILLION DOLLAR BEACH

Formally known as Lake George Beach State Park, this beach in Lake George Village is the lake's biggest, made of sand originally hauled in to the tune of one million dollars. Plans were to name the beach after someone, but residents

Beauty	A
Swimming	B
Sand	C
Amenities	B

dubbed it the Million Dollar Beach, and it stuck.

The sand runs for about a quarter mile along the lake's edge, overwhelmed somewhat by the green hillsides rising along the water, the big lake boats nearby, and the village strung along the shore to the left.

In proportion to beach size, the bathhouse must be one of the largest anywhere. It actually dominates the center section of shoreline. The sand spans perhaps 50 yards from water's edge to a surrounding fence. There's an admission charge in summer. *From Rte. 9 (Canada St.) in Lake George Village, turn onto Beach Rd. The beach is just north of the Steel Pier.*

Swimming: Water is clear, cool, and inviting on hot days. No real waves, except for the residual wake of the big tour boats. Lifeguard on duty.

Sand: Moderately fine, tan. The beach is artificial, so the sand quality faltered a bit over time; it's been replenished in recent years.

Amenities: Bathhouse with showers, rest rooms, concessions.

Sports: None in the swimming area. Volleyball (including tournaments).

Parking: Large parking lot off Beach Drive, next to the beach.

SHEPARD PARK BEACH

Beauty	B
Swimming	B
Sand	C
Amenities	B

This beach is a narrow 100-yard strip at the lower edge of Shepard Park, a grassy, bench-filled retreat in Lake George Village. It's in the heart of the action at the south end of the lake, with marinas on either side and a wooden pier leading out over the water. The tour boats chug past as their trips begin and end. It's also one of the only beaches you'll ever see that has an occupancy limit posted (670). It's just on the busiest holiday weekends that the beach reaches its maximum.

The park is on Route 9 near the Beach Road intersection. The beach is obscured by the park's rise and not clearly visible from Route 9.

Swimming: Water clear and clean. Swimming area is marked, though proximity to motor boats may bother some. Lifeguard on duty.

Sand: Medium-fine, tan. Narrow stretch rising to park.

Amenities: Bathhouse with rest rooms, dining.

Sports: No water sports. Jet Ski rentals nearby.

Parking: There's metered parking on nearby street, but finding a space can be hard. Metered lot across from the Steel Pier is within walking distance.

HOTELS/INNS/B&BS

Lake George teems with lodging choices, from modest cabins to luxurious resorts and condos. Many regulars rent by the month or for the whole summer, so for the best selection, reserve early. Motels are concentrated in Lake George Village, but accommodations can also be found in nearby Warrensburg, Lake Luzerne, Glens Falls, and Bolton Landing. Many properties have narrow beach fronts available to guests, but the amount of sand is often small. If having a beach is a priority, ask for a description before you book. Among the best hotel beaches are the Golden Sands Resort at Diamond Point, Scotty's Resort Motel, the Blue Lagoon Resort, and the Marine Village Resort.

◆ **The Sagamore** (very expensive). Lake George's showpiece resort sits on its own island, with 100 rooms and suites in the historic and elegant main hotel and 240 rooms in contemporary lakeside lodges. The hotel rooms have period furnishings. Many of the 120 suites, such as Room 209, have memorable lake views. On the premises are a spa, several restaurants, a golf course, boat landing, and the Morgan, a working replica of a 19th-century touring vessel. *110 Sagamore Rd., Bolton Landing, NY 12814; tel. 518-644-9400, 800-358-3585. Open year-round. From Lake George Village follow Rte. 9N north to Bolton Landing, and turn right over the marked bridge.*

◆ **Best Western of Lake George** (expensive). One of Lake George Village's biggest year-round motels, it has 87 units and a few suites. Most standard rooms have two double beds. Room 187 is a spacious, well-equipped two-floor suite (not luxurious). Room 188 is a sprawling, houselike suite with two full bedrooms upstairs, a large stone fireplace, full kitchen, and washer/dryer. It's close to the interstate, but it's not on the lake and does not have views. *50 Canada St., Lake George, NY 12845; tel. 518-668-5701, 800-234-0265; fax 518-668-4926. Along the Exit 21 ramp of I-87.*

◆ **Fort William Henry Motor Inn** (expensive). Sitting on an 18-acre bluff overlooking the lake, this motel has the most spacious setting in Lake George Village and is next to the fort and the Steel

Pier lake boats. It has "hotel" and "motel" wings—the hotel rooms are closer to the restaurants and have larger bathrooms—otherwise, room furnishings are about equivalent (plain but more than adequate). In the motel section, second-floor lakeside views are best, though a few rooms have obstructed views. *50 Canada St., Lake George, NY 12845; tel. 518-668-3081, 800-234-0267; fax 518-668-1926. 1 mi. north of I-87 Exit 21.*

◆ **The Georgian** (expensive). The Georgian bills itself as "the affordable luxury resort," but while above average, with neat furnishings, it is not plush. Most of its 164 rooms face the parking lot, although a minority look out over the lake, as do the large pool and the dining room. The penthouse suites have the best views, particularly the third-level suites numbered 222 through 229. *384 Canada St., Lake George, NY 12845; tel. 518-668-5401, 800-525-3436.*

◆ **The Lamplight Inn B&B** (expensive). This very attractive B&B has ten Victorian antique-filled rooms, five with gas fireplaces, and many nice touches, such as decorative pine cones, tasteful stuffed toys, and period wall decorations. Innkeepers Gene and Linda Merlino say they redo one room every six months. The Skylight Room indeed has a skylight, plus exposed beams and a high-back oak bed. The Evergreen Room has windows on two sides. An inside sun porch, where breakfast is served, stretches across the front of the inn, as does the chair-lined outside porch. *2129 Lake Ave., Box 70, Lake Luzerne, NY 12846; tel. 518-696-5294. Bear left off I-87 Exit 21 down ramp, and make a left onto Rte. 9N south. Go 10 mi.; the inn is on the right.*

◆ **The Merrill Magee House** (expensive). This splendid inn has ten rooms, all with fireplaces, antiques, and many authentic touches, including patchwork quilts handmade by local women. Rooms are named for herbs. The Lavender has a queen-size canopy bed and Victorian settee. The Parsley has a low four-poster bed and white wicker furniture. The Coriander, a larger room, has a king-size brass bed and framed bird sketches. Well-regarded restaurant. Two-bedroom family suite. *2 Hudson St., Warrensburg, NY 12885; tel. 518-623-2449. On Rte. 9, 6 mi. north of Lake George Village. Or take I-87 to Exit 23, follow signs to Warrensburg, and go left at the third traffic light.*

◆ **Lake George Travelodge** (moderate). This 102-unit motel sits on a hill just south of Lake George Village, and it's well worth requesting a room on the lake-view side of the long, narrow building. Decor is basic motor-lodge—wood-veneer furniture and one window per room. Fifteen rooms have king-size beds, the rest have doubles. About a mile from the main beach. *50 Canada St., Lake George, NY 12845; tel. 518-668-5421, 800-234-0586; fax 518-668-4926. Closed Nov.-Apr. Take I-87 to Exit 21 and turn right onto Rte. 9N.*

HOUSE RENTALS

◆ **Camps, Condos & Castles Real Estate.** *Box 751, Lake George, NY 12845; tel. 518-668-3240, 518-668-5190. Open daily.*

◆ **Properties by Tuttle.** Vacation rentals—condos, houses, cabins, chalets—with docks on Lake George. *16 Tuttle Lane, Lake George, NY 12845; tel. 518-668-5367. Open daily.*

◆ **Warren County Association of Realtors.** *296 Bay Rd., Queensbury, NY 12804; tel. 518-798-3425.*

RESTAURANTS

◆ **Algonquin** (expensive). The Algonquin offers perfect lakeside atmosphere, as if you've stepped into a painting with a pristine lake, little islands ahead, majestic pines reaching up from the water's edge, and boats docked just outside. The shrimp is popular, and specials include the nut-encrusted mahimahi with rum and pineapple sauce and the scallop and broccoli au gratin en casserole. Best seats are upstairs by the broad window—unless you prefer the outdoor deck. The gray clapboard building is inconspicuously tucked among the pines. Casual. *Box 728, Lakeshore Dr., Bolton Landing, NY 12814; tel. 518-644-9442. Open daily for lunch and dinner late Apr.-mid-Oct.; open for dinner Fri. and lunch and dinner Sat.-Sun. mid-Oct.-Apr. Go 10 mi. north of Lake George Village on Rte. 9N (Lake Shore Dr.) to Bolton Landing.*

◆ **Grist Mill** (expensive). One of those rare places where setting, cuisine, ambience, and attitude combine to delectable effect. Located in an 1824 mill on the Schroon River, the restaurant offers "American heritage" cooking: thyme-roasted loin of lamb, Louisiana panfried catfish, and a chef's sampler in six courses. Best seats are the bay window tables, which jut over the river, and the Mill Stone Table, a circular table built around the original mill stone. An air of elegant simplicity prevails. What's more, it's a museum of American mill history. *River St., Warrensburg, NY 12885; tel. 518-623-3949; fax 518-623-4011. Open daily for dinner Memorial Day-Labor Day; Wed.-Sun. for dinner Sep.-May. From Rte. 9 in Warrensburg turn onto Rte. 418. Go over the bridge and then follow the curve to the right.*

◆ **The Log Jam** (moderate). This friendly landmark restaurant amid factory-outlet stores is built of thick timbers and has a real lumberjack flavor, with heavy furniture and well-worn wooden floors. Just being there works up your appetite. Besides a renowned salad bar with dozens of fresh ingredients, it has hefty entreés, such as scallops *fromage*, swordfish Portuguese, and charbroiled steaks. For more daylight, ask for the greenhouse room, a combination of cabin chic and fern bar. *1484 State Rte., Lake George, NY 12845; tel. 518-798-1155. Open daily for lunch and dinner. From Lake George Village, go south a couple mi. on Rte. 9, just past Rte. 149.*

◆ **Sutton's Market Place** (inexpensive). The café is part of a multibusiness dynasty including clothing, furniture, gifts, and gourmet food. Local residents rave over the breakfasts and lunches. Grilled smoked turkey and salads are popular, especially the Pacific Rim salad (grilled chicken, mixed greens, Oriental vegetables, and crispy noodles). At peak weekend times, you may wait for a table, but you can roam the stores until you're paged. Country-kitchen ambience. *1066 Rte. 9, Queensbury, NY 12804; tel. 518-798-1188; fax 518-793-5963. Open daily for breakfast and lunch; dinner on Fri. only. From Lake George Village, go south on Rte. 9 past the outlet stores and the Great Escape Fun Park. It's on the left.*

NIGHTLIFE

Many of the area's motels and resorts have lounges with nightly entertainment during the summer and on weekends in spring and fall.

◆ **Brass Ring.** Live entertainment in the Ramada Inn. *7034 Lake Shore Dr., Bolton Landing, NY 12814; tel. 518-644-9955. Open Wed.-Sun. at 8. At the House of Scotts Restaurant.*

◆ **Brier Patch Lounge.** Live entertainment. *Box 351, Lake George, NY 12845; tel. 518-668-3131. I-87 to Exit 21.*

◆ **DJ's Outdoor Cafe & Nite Club.** Live entertainment, DJs, dancing, billiards, pinball. *89 Canada St., Lake George, NY 12845; tel. 518-668-9803. Open nightly May-Sep. and Thu.-Sun. Oct.-May.*

◆ **Lake George Dinner Theatre.** Actors Equity performances. *Rte. 9, Lake George, NY 12845; tel. 518-668-5781. Open nightly Tue.-Sun. with matinees Wed. and Sun. late Jun.-mid-Oct. Admission. In the Holiday Inn Turf at Lake George, north of Exit 21.*

ATTRACTIONS

◆ **Fort William Henry.** Re-created British fort that was overrun and destroyed in 1757 by French and Indians, who massacred its occupants, a story recounted in *The Last of the Mohicans*. The restored fort includes a museum, living history guided tours, movie screenings. *Canada St., Lake George, NY 12845; tel. 518-668-5471. Open daily 9 a.m.-10 p.m. mid-Jun.-early Sep. and 10-5 May-mid-Jun. and early Sep.-mid-Oct. Admission. From Rte. 9 in Lake George Village turn onto Beach Rd. The fort is on the right, across from the Steel Pier.*

◆ **Fort Ticonderoga.** Reconstructed fort dating to 1750s, with fife and drum corps, reenactments, costumed guides. *Box 390, Ticonderoga, NY 12883; tel. 518-585-2821. Open daily 9-5 early May-late Oct. and 9-6 Jul.-Aug. Admission. At north end of Lake George, on Rte. 74; take I-87 Exit 28 and go 8 mi.*

◆ **Great Escape Fun Park and Splashwater Kingdom.** Theme parks with about 100 rides, including giant roller coaster, kiddie rides, raging-river raft ride, high-dive show and wildlife, street shootouts. *Rte. 9, Lake George, NY 12845; tel. 518-792-3500. Open daily late May-early Sep. Admission. South of Lake George; take I-87 Exit 20.*

◆ **Historical Association Museum.** In the National Register of Historic Places. History exhibits, 19th-century jail cell, bookstore with maps and prints. *Box 472, Lake George, NY 12845; tel. 518-668-5044. Open Mon.-Fri. 10-5 and Sat.-Sun. 1-5 Jun.-early Oct.; Mon.-Fri. 10-4 mid-Oct.-late May. At Rte. 1 and Amherst St. in the old Warren County Courthouse.*

◆ **Lake George Steamboat Co.** Largest cruise operation on the lake, including the biggest boat, the *Lac du Saint Sacrement*, plus the paddel wheeler *Minne-Ha-Ha* and the *Mohican*. A variety of cruises are offered, most one to two and a half hours, some with a meal or themes. *Steel Pier, Beach Rd., Lake George, NY 12845;*

tel. 518-668-5777, 800-553-2628. Multiple cruises daily May-early Sep.; reduced schedule in Oct. Admission.

◆ **Shoreline Cruises.** One- to two-and-a-half-hour cruises on one of five boats. Dinner, shoreline, and entertainment cruises. *2 Kurosaka Lane, Lake George Village, NY 12845; tel. 518-668-4644. Daily cruises late Jun.-early Sep.; reduced schedule late Apr.-late Jun. and Sep.-late Oct. Admission. At Rte. 9 and Beach Rd.*

◆ **Water Slide World.** Water theme park with more than 35 slides, attractions, and services. *Rtes. 9 and 9L, Lake George, NY 12845; tel. 518-668-4407. Open daily mid-Jun.-Labor Day. Admission. 1/2 mi. south of Lake George Village on Rte. 9.*

SHOPPING

Canada Street in Lake George Village is lined with shops selling souvenirs and gifts, but the heavy-duty shopping takes place to the south, at the factory-outlet complexes.

◆ **Factory Stores of America.** A dozen stores, including L'Eggs/Hanes/Bali, Levi's Outlet by Design, Carter's Childrenswear, Famous Footwear, Leather Loft, Colours by Alexander Julian, Maidenform, Perfumania. *Rte. 9, Lake George, NY 12845; tel. 518-792-5316. Open daily. At Rte. 149 intersection, next to the Log Jam Restaurant.*

◆ **Lake George Plaza Factory Stores.** More than a dozen stores, including Anne Klein, Bass Shoes, Dansk International, Jones New York, Jones New York Woman, Nautica, Polo/Ralph Lauren, Timberland, and Van Heusen. *Rte. 9, Lake George, NY 12845; tel. 518-798-7234. Open daily. Near the I-87 Exit 20 ramp.*

◆ **Sutton's Market Place.** A gourmet-food shop brimming with jellies, jams, marmalades, spreads, dipping sauces, hot sauces, relishes, seasonings, spices, candles, potpourri, and sweet-smelling things ad infinitum. *1066 Rte. 9, Queensbury, NY 12804; tel. 518-798-1188; fax 518-793-5963. Open daily. Just south of Great Escape Fun Park.*

◆ **Syd & Dusty's Outfitters.** Large outdoor store with full range of clothing and equipment for hiking, backpacking, climbing, fishing, biking, paddle sports, and more. Also arranges a wide variety of outdoor trips and rentals. *Rtes. 9 and 149, Lake George, NY 12845; tel. 518-792-0260; fax 518-792-3429. Open daily.*

BEST FOOD SHOPS

SEAFOOD: ◆ **Art's Seafood Market Down Under.** *62 1/2 Main St., Warrensburg, NY; tel. 518-623-3477. Open Mon.-Sat. May-Oct.; Open Tue. - Sat. Oct.-May. From Lake George Village, take Rte. 9 north about 5 mi. into Warrensburg.*

BAKERY: ◆ **Bluebird Bakery.** *10 Hudson St., Warrensburg, NY 12885; tel. 518-623-3301. Open. 7:30-4 Tue.-Sat. and 8-2 Sun. Closed Mon. Next to the Merrill Magee House.*

ICE CREAM: ◆ **Martha's Dandee Creme.** *1133 Rte. 9, Queensbury, NY 12804; tel. 518-793-0372. Open daily. Closed Oct.-May. On Rte. 9 across from the Great Escape Fun Park.*

WINE: ◆ **Duffy's Wines & Liquors.** *46 Amherst St., Lake George Village, NY 12845; tel. 518-668-2103. Closed Sun.*

SPORTS

In addition to water sports, cycling, golf, and tennis, Lake George offers some fine horseback riding.

FISHING

Fishing requires a state license, available at town clerk offices in all communities. Other purchase sites include the Warren County Municipal Center in Lake George, the Ellsworth Sport Shop in Lake George (tel. 518-668-4624), and the Outdoorsman Sport Shop in Diamond Point (tel. 518-668-3910). Species in Lake George include trout, salmon, yellow perch, small- and largemouth bass, and northern pike.

◆ **E&R Sport Fishing Charters.** Salmon, trout, and bass fishing on Lake George. *21 Underwood Rd., Hudson Falls, NY 12839; tel. 518-747-6987, 800-336-6987. Open daily. On Rte. 9N at the Sand N' Surf Motel, 3 mi. north of Lake George Village.*

◆ **Lockhart Charter Fishing & Guide Services.** Fishing packages on Lake George and other Adirondack lakes and ponds. *70 Library Ave., Warrensburg, NY 12885; tel. 518-623-2236. Open daily.*

◆ **Ted's Charter Fishing Service.** Three-, four-, and five-hour charter-fishing trips available. *Lake Shore Dr., Lake George, NY 12824; tel. 518-668-5334. Open daily Apr.-Oct. Treasure Cove Resort Motel at Diamond Point, 3 mi. north of Lake George Village on Rte. 9N.*

BOATING

Dozens of marinas around the lake offer boating rentals and services.

◆ **U-Drive Boat Rentals.** Speedboats, pontoon boats, and bowriders available for hourly, half-day, and full-day rentals. *2 Kurosaka Lane, Lake George Village, NY 12845; tel. 518-668-4644. Open daily May-Oct. At the Shoreline Cruise docks.*

◆ **Waters Edge Marina Inc.** Outboard rentals for fishing, sightseeing, waterskiing. *Sagamore Rd., Bolton Landing, NY 12814; tel. 518-644-2511. Open daily mid-Apr.-mid-Oct. Just off Rte. 9N, at bridge to Sagamore Island.*

DIVING

Lake George has some of the cleanest inland freshwater diving in the country. The lake has no massive hulls for divers to explore, but it has three interesting wreck sites: the 52-foot *Land Tortoise*, a seven-sided war ship scuttled in 1788 (in 110 feet of water); the historic Waiwaka Bateaux Cluster north of the Camp Waiwaka boathouse, and a 1920s-era launch. *Land Tortoise* dives require a permit from the state Department of Environmental Conservation ranger on Long Island. The Historical Association Museum has information on the wrecks. Diving operators come and go here, so ask the Chamber of Commerce for recommendations.

◆ **Submerged Heritage Preserve.** *Dept. of Environmental Conservation, Rte. 86, Box 296, Ray Brook, NY 12977; tel. 518-897-1277.*

◆ **Bateaux Below Inc.** This nonprofit group has helped chart the area's wrecks. *Box 2134, Wilton, NY 12866.*

BICYCLING

The 10-mile-long Warren County Bikeway starts in Lake George Battleground Park and goes south to Queensbury over flat terrain and gentle hills. The Warren County Mountain Bike Trail System has 180 miles of trail with 11 loops from 8 to 21 miles. Some sections require trail permits, available from Warren County Parks and Recreation. *261 Main St., Warrensburg, NY 12885; tel. 518-623-5576, 518-623-2877.*

◆ **Flipflop Cycleshop.** Bike rentals by the hour, half day, full day, or longer. *285 Canada St., Lake George Village, NY 12845; tel. 518-668-*

2233. Open daily. Closed Mon. Nov.-Jan. Across from Shepard Park.

GOLF

Five 18-hole golf courses are in the area and even more 9-hole courses.

◆ **Cronin's Golf Resort.** It has 18 holes overlooking the Hudson River. Lodging available. *Golf Course Rd., Warrensburg, NY 12885; tel. 518-623-9336. Closed Nov.-Mar. Admission. From Lake George, take Rte. 9 north to Warrensburg. Bear left at the third light and follow Hudson St. for 2 mi.*

◆ **Queensbury Country Club.** An 18-hole course and driving range. *Rte. 149, Queensbury, NY 12804; tel. 518-793-3711. Open daily Apr.-Nov. Admission. From Lake George Village, go south on Rte. 9, then left onto Rte. 149.*

◆ **Sagamore Golf Course.** Donald Ross-designed course built under his supervision in 1928 and restored in 1985 according to his original blueprints. Guests of the resort have priority. *Lake Shore Dr., Bolton Landing, NY 12814; tel. 518-644-9400, 800-358-3585. Open daily Apr.-Nov. Admission. From Lake George Village, go 10 mi. north on Rte. 9N.*

TENNIS

Public courts are available in several area communities, including Bolton Landing, Chestertown, Glens Falls, Lake Luzerne, Queensbury, and Warrensburg. Most of them are at schools or parks and are first come, first served. In Lake George, such courts are at Lake George High School and Ushers Park.

◆ **Queensbury Racquet Club.** Indoor and outdoor courts open to the public at hourly rates when not being used by club members. *91 Glenwood Ave., Queensbury, NY 12804; tel. 518-793-5353. Open daily. Admission.*

HORSEBACK RIDING

◆ **Bennett's Riding Stables.** Horseback and pony rides ranging from one hour to all day. *RR 2, Box 208, Gage Hill Rd., Lake Luzerne, NY 12846; tel. 518-696-2174. Open daily 9-5 in summer; open weekends and by appointment only on weekdays in spring and fall. Admission. 5 mi. south of Lake George on Rte. 9N in Lake Luzerne.*

NATURE

◆ **Adirondacks Mountain Club.** Maps and information on the trails of the lake region. *814 Goggins Rd., Lake George, NY 12845; tel. 518-668-4447. Open Mon.-Sat. May-mid-Oct.; Mon.-Fri. mid-Oct.-Apr.*

◆ **Natural Stone Bridge and Caves.** Self-guided tours of stone arch, caves, gorge, waterfalls, mill sight. *Rte. 87, Exit 26, Pottersville, NY; tel. 518-494-2283. Open daily 9-7 late May-early Sep.; 10-6 early Sep.-early Oct. Admission. 23 mi. north of Lake George Village.*

SAFETY TIPS

Crime keeps a low profile, but traffic can snarl the area during peak summer months. The 50-cent Village Trolley (tel. 518-792-1085) operates daily at 25-minute intervals along Canada Street and Lake Shore Drive.

TOURIST INFORMATION

◆ **Lake George Regional Chamber of Commerce.** *Box 272, Rte. 9, Lake George, NY 12845; tel. 518-668-5755. Open Mon.-Fri. 9-5 and Sat.-Sun. 10-2 late May-early-Sep.; Mon.-Fri. 9-5 Sep.-May.*

◆ **Bolton Landing Chamber of Commerce.** *Box 368, Rte. 9N, Bolton Landing, NY 12814; tel. 518-644-3831. Open daily 9-5 Jul.-Aug.; Mon.-Fri. 10-2 Sep.-Jun.*

CHAPTER 10

Spring Lake

Beauty	B
Swimming	B
Sand	B
Hotels/Inns/B&Bs	A
House rentals	C
Restaurants	B
Nightlife	C
Attractions	C
Shopping	B
Sports	B
Nature	C

$\mathcal{S}$pring Lake is a community whose Victorian persona demurely waves off modern intrusion, while at the same time beckoning visitors with some of the most come-hither architecture and accommodations in the Mid-Atlantic. Two big beach pavilions house saltwater swimming pools and second-story observation floors, throwbacks to an era long gone but not hard to imagine alongside the many stately structures from the turn of the century.

The median value of a single-family home here is more than $400,000, and a short stroll along the wide, tree-lined streets underscores the luxury. Over and over you see sprawling three-story properties that appear to be elegant country inns, only to realize that they are simply someone's home. Three lakes punctuate the flat topography, including Spring Lake, surrounded by a city park whose huge American flag suggests that traditional values matter here. They do.

The main business district is on Third Avenue, about four blocks lined with awninged shops and restaurants that, while attractive, possess little of the contrived cutesiness that marks the shopping districts of many upscale resorts. Clearly, most of the stores are there for the year-round population of about 4,000, rather than for the tourists.

Three blocks east of downtown, Ocean Avenue and the boardwalk run north-south for nearly two miles. To the south is Sea Girt, with its own lighthouse and noncommercial boardwalk. To the north is Belmar, the flip side of the coin, with a lively club scene and a McDonald's on the boardwalk, overlooking the ocean.

A handful of these neighboring towns haven't always seemed day-tripper friendly. In 1989, Spring Lake, Belmar, Sea Girt, Avon, and Bay Head were brought to court by the state Public Advocate's Office after they attempted to charge higher-than-

HOW TO GET THERE

◆ From New York and points north, take the Garden State Pkwy. south to Exit 98. Then take Rte. 34 south to the first traffic circle and Rte. 524 to the ocean.

◆ From Philadelphia and points south, take the NJ Tpke. north to I-195 east. Exit at Rte. 34 south and take Rte. 524 to the ocean.

◆ Spring Lake is a stop on the New Jersey Coast Line commuter train from Manhattan (tel. 201-762-5100).

average beach fees and apply the proceeds to municipal expenses other than beach projects. After a wrist-slapping, they cut back on the charges. In any case, guesthouses and hotels usually provide beach tags for guests.

BEACHES
BELMAR

The beach along the one-and-a-half-mile boardwalk is moderately wide. At the north end, around Fifth Avenue, is the Belmar Fishing Club Pier, and north of that is a stone jetty marking the entrance to the Shark River Inlet.

Beauty	B-
Swimming	B
Sand	B-
Amenities	B

Ocean Avenue along the beach is lined on one side with mainly undistinguished two-story businesses. Looking north from the middle of the beach you see the fishing pier; look south and the coastline goes on for miles, with shops, lodgings, and residences following its curve. There are no businesses on the boardwalk, except for a McDonald's at 13th Avenue. *From Rte. 35, take 16th St. to the Belmar water front.*

Swimming: Good swimming in surf that can be quite calm. Beach tags required. Lifeguard on duty.

Sand: Light tan, ranging from fine to coarse with shells and pebbles mixed in, rising to a low dune in front of the boardwalk.

Amenities: Pavilion with facilities at Fifth and Tenth avenues, plenty of snack shops along Ocean Avenue.

Sports: Volleyball, surfing from 16th to 18th avenues.

Parking: Meters along Ocean Avenue.

SPRING LAKE

The moderately wide beach is lined by a two-mile boardwalk. Look north and the view is mostly beach, with a few jetties protruding into the water and the low-rise buildings of Belmar extending up the coast. From the middle of the

Beauty	B
Swimming	B
Sand	B
Amenities	B

beach, you can see the north and south pavilions at sand's edge, and on Ocean Avenue the Breakers Hotel is prominent, as is the old, columned Essex & Sussex Hotel. At the south end of the boardwalk, the beach narrows and the southern view is cluttered with breakwaters that begin in Sea Girt. Between the south end of the Spring Lake boardwalk and the north end of the Sea Girt boardwalk are a few blocks of beach with no road or construction behind, big dunes, and a more remote feel. *From Third Ave. in Spring Lake follow any street east to the water front.*

Swimming: Good. Waves are controlled by jetties; some sections have more wave action than others. Beach tags required. Lifeguard on duty.

Sand: Light tan, moderately fine, mixed in places with pebbles and shell fragments, sloping up to a grassy dune that is higher than the boardwalk in places. The beach has a roll to it in spots.

Amenities: Rest rooms at the pavilions.

Sports: Surfing. Saltwater pools available to residents only.

Parking: Metered spaces on Ocean Avenue.

SEA GIRT

The beach along the Sea Girt boardwalk is divided by jetties. To the north is the Spring Lake beach front, running straight up the coast. The beach is generally less spacious than in Spring Lake. Behind the beach are two- and three-

Beauty	B-
Swimming	B
Sand	B
Amenities	B

story residences that rise on grassy terraces. The view of the ocean is extremely wide and unimpeded. *From Spring Lake, follow First Ave. south into Sea Girt.*

Swimming: Waves roll in between the jetties, varying in force. Beach tags required. Lifeguard on duty.

Sand: Light tan, moderately fine, rising slightly to the boardwalk.

Amenities: Snack bar at the north end of the boardwalk has rest rooms.

Parking: Large parking area along the boardwalk.

HOTELS/INNS/B&BS

The area has more than two dozen charming B&Bs and historic inns; a map showing their names and locations is available from the Greater Spring Lake Chamber of Commerce (tel. 908-449-0577). A brochure, "Classic Inns of the Garden Coast," is also available (tel. 800-523-2587). Some chain-type motels are on routes 71 and 35, including a fairly new Quality Inn (tel. 908-449-6146) and a basic, refurbished Travelodge (tel. 908-974-8400).

◆ **Spring Lake Inn** (expensive). The nine guest rooms in this gabled B&B have distinctive shapes and furnishings, including rugs on wooden floors, antiques, and private sitting areas. Room 12 has a pineapple canopy bed, Room 18 a cannonball four-poster. A number of rooms have angel-theme wall decor. Fruit and home-baked muffins and breads are served in a huge dining room with a 12-foot ceiling and sunny eastern exposure. One block from the beach. *104 Salem Ave., Spring Lake, NJ 07762; tel. 908-449-2010.*

◆ **The Breakers** (expensive). A most-visible hotel, it rises five stories just across Ocean Avenue from the beach, a focal point for guests and residents, who pack the elegant restaurant or loll on the wraparound porch. Room decor is seashore modern. Room 600, on the fourth floor, has a round bed and a swath of bay windows. *1507 Ocean Ave., Spring Lake, NJ 07762; tel. 908-449-7700.*

◆ **The Chateau** (expensive). This delicious Victorian sits perfectly at the western tip of the town's namesake lake, columned and balconied on the outside, seductively decorated on the inside. Most rooms have tin ceilings and Waverly or Laura Ashley wallpaper. Each room is different, but all are well-appointed with period prints and floral designs. Room 44, like the much-requested Honeymoon Suite, has a wet bar, fireplace, and private balcony. Five blocks from the beach. *500 Warren Ave., Spring Lake, NJ 07762; tel. 908-974-2000.*

◆ **Hollycroft** (expensive to moderate). In appearance and ambience, this B&B marches to a different drummer. Built in 1908, it's a refined log cabin, with ironstone fireplaces and individually decorated rooms. Antique beds, lace curtains, and beamed ceilings provide an aura of rustic romanticism. The new second-floor Anniversary Suite is stunning, with private screened porch, soaking tub looking out on Lake Como, queen-size canopy bed, and fireplace. Several blocks from the beach. *506 North Blvd., Box 448, Spring Lake, NJ 07762; tel. 908-681-2254, 800-679-2254. From Spring Lake, follow Third Ave. north to Lake Como. Turn right onto North Blvd. and then left up a narrow road marked by a Hollycroft sign.*

HOUSE RENTALS

House rentals are usually by the season, and there aren't a large number of them. From Memorial Day through Labor Day, the rental range is anywhere from $15,000 for a place within a few blocks of the beach to $40,000 for one of the few ocean-front properties. Occasionally, monthly rentals become available.

◆ **Edmonds Realty Co.** *305 Washington Ave., Spring Lake, NJ 07762; tel. 908-449-4600. Open daily.*

◆ **The Mary Holder Agency.** *Jersey and Third Aves., Spring Lake, NJ 07762; tel. 908-449-3113. Open daily.*

RESTAURANTS

Several of Spring Lake's best year-round restaurants are in hotels and inns. The area also has quite a few social dining spots, often with an Irish bent, that offer tasty if not fancy selections.

◆ **The Breakers** (expensive). This tasteful dining room off the hotel lobby overlooks the sea across Ocean Drive. It serves seafood and classic Italian cuisine, with such menu choices as veal *rollatini* (veal rolled with prosciutto and mozzarella and sautéed in wine and mushrooms) and country-style chicken (sautéed with sausage, mushrooms, and hot or sweet peppers). *1507 Ocean Ave., Spring Lake, NJ 07762; tel. 908-449-7700. Open daily for breakfast, lunch, and dinner Apr.-Dec.*

◆ **Whispers Restaurant** (expensive). This understated and elegant dining room at the Hewitt-Wellington Hotel operates under executive chef Mark Mikolajczyk, who prepares simple dishes without heavy sauces. The menu changes regularly, and there's a weekly prix-fixe tasting menu; one week it offered warm baked mozzarella, mescalun salad with fontina cheese, fresh lemon sorbet, and a choice of coriander-encrusted salmon, pork tenderloin with parsnip, or filet mignon with saffron risotto, followed by *crème brûlée* or homemade ice cream. *200 Monmouth Ave., Spring Lake, NJ 07762; tel. 908-449-3330. Open daily for dinner.*

◆ **The Sandpiper Restaurant** (moderate). This inviting spot below the Sandpiper Inn has an air of refined informality, with china set beneath painted rafters. Windows line two sides of the pink-washed dining room; at night, candles and strings of tiny white lights set the mood. The menu changes seasonally. Sample selections include fillet of sole stuffed with crabmeat and topped with lobster sauce; penne with broccoli florets and sweet sausage tossed in garlic oil; and marinated beef *jardinière* served with duchess potatoes. *7 Atlantic Ave., Spring Lake, NJ 07762; tel. 908-449-6060, 800-824-2779. Open daily for breakfast, lunch, dinner. On Atlantic Ave., just off Ocean Ave.*

ATTRACTIONS

◆ **Ocean Grove Great Auditorium.** This historic 6,500-seat wooden auditorium has hosted many well-known speakers, including Billy Graham and Richard Nixon. Call for the entertainment schedule. *Auditorium Sq., Ocean Grove, NJ 07756; tel. 908-988-0645. In Ocean Grove, about 15 min. north of Spring Lake.*

SHOPPING

◆ **Irish Centre.** With the area's concentration of Irish-Americans, this shop is well-stocked with crystal, china, clothing, books, records, and food items. *1120 Third Ave., Spring Lake, NJ 07762; tel. 908-449-6650. Open daily.*

BEST FOOD SHOPS

SANDWICHES: ◆ **Who's on Third.** Full-service deli makes sandwiches and serves breakfast and lunch. *1300 Third Ave., Spring Lake, NJ 07762; tel. 908-449-4233. Open daily.*

SEAFOOD: ◆ **Klein's Fish Market & Waterside Cafe.** *708 River Rd., Belmar, NJ 07719; tel. 908-681-1177. Open daily.*

FRESH PRODUCE: ◆ **Matt's Farm Market.** *Rte. 71 and 18th Ave., Belmar, NJ 07719; tel. 908-449-1557. Open May-Oct.*

BAKERY: ◆ **Freedman's Bakery.** *1203 Third Ave., Spring Lake, NJ 07762; tel. 908-974-9227. Open daily.*

ICE CREAM: ◆ **Hoffmans Ice Cream.** *569 Church St., Spring Lake Heights, NJ; tel. 908-974-2253. Open daily.*
WINE: ◆ **Spring Lake Bottle Shop.** *1400 Third Ave., Spring Lake, NJ 07762; tel. 908-449-5525. Open daily.*

SPORTS

FISHING

The area's fishing hub is the Belmar Marina, home to a dozen party boats and more than a dozen charters, including some that take diving parties.

◆ **Belmar Marina.** *900 Marina Ave., Belmar, NJ 07719; tel. 908-681-2266. Open daily. On Rte. 35, south of the Shark River bridge.*
◆ **Captain Bill's Bait & Tackle.** Rents 16-foot skiffs—some wood, some fiberglass—for river fishing. Summer rates are about $35 a day. *900 Marina Ave., Belmar, NJ 07719; tel. 908-681-6677. Open daily 5 a.m.-7 p.m. At the Belmar Marina.*

BOATING

◆ **Shark River Jet Ski Rentals.** Rents Jet Skis, ocean kayaks, wet suits. *618 Fifth Ave., Belmar, NJ 07719; tel. 908-280-0419. Open daily. On the Shark River Inlet near the Rte. 71 bridge.*

SURFING

Surfing is permitted in designated areas: in Spring Lake, at the north and south ends of the beach; in Belmar, between 16th and 18th avenues.

◆ **Eastern Lines Surf Shop.** Surfing equipment rentals, accessories, and clothing. Wave report (tel. 908-681-6401). *1603 Ocean Ave., Belmar, NJ 07719; tel. 908-681-6405. Open daily in season.*

BICYCLING

◆ **D.J.'s Cycles.** Rentals, sales, and service. *At 15th Ave. and Main St., Belmar, NJ 07719; tel. 908-681-8228. Open daily.*

GOLF

The area is rich with public golf courses beyond the Spring Lake borders: nine in Monmouth County and seven in Ocean County, to the south.

◆ **Bel-Aire Golf Club.** An 18-hole, executive par-60 and a 9-hole, par-3 course. Pro shop. *Rte. 34 and Allaire Rd., Allenwood, NJ 08720; tel. 908-449-6024. Open daily. Admission. Go west 3 mi. on Allaire Rd.*

◆ **Spring Meadow Golf Course.** *4181 Atlantic Ave., Farmingdale, NJ 07727; tel. 908-449-0806. Open daily. Admission. Go west on Allaire Rd., which becomes Atlantic Ave.*

TENNIS

Spring Lake's public courts require a nominal fee for a permit, available from the police department (tel. 908-449-1234). Courts are in the park along Spring Lake and in Marucci Memorial Park at Third Avenue and South Boulevard.

NATURE

◆ **Allaire State Park.** This park has a nature center, horse trails, picnic areas, playgrounds, a restored 19th-century bog-iron-mining community, and a steam railway. *Box 222, Farmingdale, NJ 07727; tel. 908-938-2371. Open daily. From Spring Lake, take Rte. 524 west past the Garden State Pkwy.*

TOURIST INFORMATION

◆ **Belmar Chamber of Commerce.** *702 Sixth Ave., Belmar, NJ 07719; tel. 908-681-2900. Open Mon.-Fri. 9-noon.*

◆ **Greater Spring Lake Chamber of Commerce.** Responds to phone and mail inquiries. *Box 694, Spring Lake, NJ 07762; tel. 908-449-0577.*

◆ **Monmouth County Promotion/Tourism.** *25 E. Main St., Freehold, NJ 07728; tel. 908-431-7310, 800-523-2587. Open Mon.-Fri. 9-5.*

CHAPTER 11

Point Pleasant Beach/ Island Beach State Park

Beauty	B+
Swimming	A
Sand	B
Hotels/Inns/B&Bs	B
House rentals	B
Restaurants	B
Nightlife	C
Attractions	C
Shopping	B
Sports	B
Nature	A

The 22 miles from Point Pleasant Beach to Barnegat Inlet, mostly barrier island, embrace a mulligatawny of shoreline personalities—seafood-rich Point Pleasant, the handsomely shingled town of Bay Head, the boardwalk nirvana of Seaside Heights, and the stunning Island Beach State Park.

Route 35 connects all these points and runs past other communities as well, including some with row after row of tiny beach homes packed like sardines into narrow side streets. The star of this stretch is the last stop on the road: Island Beach State Park, whose 3,000 acres of dunes and coast are a lush natural treasure.

The park offers swimming and surfing, biking and bird-watching, boating and fishing, all in a spectacular setting. It's no secret getaway, though. On hot summer weekends, the 2,300 parking spaces are filled by 10 a.m. and the gatekeepers block the entrance, usually reopening it in the afternoon as the early-birds trickle out.

The park and the governor's summer house there had star-ring roles—with Jodie Foster and Mark Harmon—in the 1988 film *Stealing Home.*

North of the park, Seaside Heights is the quintessential boardwalk town, rich in amusement piers and water slides. It also boasts an aerial tram that provides a gull's-eye view, ski-lift-style, from above the boardwalk. And there's a working gem of

HOW TO GET THERE

◆ From New York and points north, take the NJ Tpke. south to Exit 11 and the Garden State Pkwy. south to Exit 98. Take Rte. 34 to the second circle, then take Rte. 35 to Point Pleasant and all towns south.

◆ From the Philadelphia area, the fastest route to Point Pleasant Beach is I-276 or the NJ Tpke. north to I-195 east. Follow Rtes. 34 and 35 south as directed above. For Seaside Heights and Island Beach State Park, a more direct route from the Ben Franklin Bridge is Rte. 70 east to Rte. 37 at Lakehurst. Continue on Rte. 37 east across Barnegat Bay to Seaside Heights.

◆ Point Pleasant Beach and Bay Head are the last stops on the NJ Coast Line commuter train from Manhattan (tel. 201-762-5100).

a carousel—a 1910 hand-carved Dentzel Loof. April through October the town has a constant lineup of activities centering on the boardwalk and its environs, including regular volleyball tournaments and fireworks.

To the north, Bay Head calls itself a "country village by the sea," and its historic homes and shops are attractive, as is its mile-long beach, although it offers no public facilities and lodging is limited.

Point Pleasant Beach is a boardwalk town, too, its walkway distinguished by Jenkinson's Aquarium, with reefs, sharks, and touch tanks. It also has plenty of rides, games, and dining spots. Seafood is big in Point Pleasant, because it's home to a commercial fishing fleet, with many restaurants at the north end of town, near the Manasquan Inlet.

BEACHES
ISLAND BEACH STATE PARK

The atmosphere here is glorious, a real surf-and-sand playground without commercial development. Substantial dunes abound, both behind the beach and across the park, many of them heavily vegetated. The long, narrow park is

Beauty	A
Swimming	A
Sand	A
Amenities	B+

divided into three zones: a northern natural area near the entrance, a central recreational zone with swimming, and the southern natural area.

The scene on the nearly mile-long swimming beach is clean and refreshing, full of that away-from-it-all feel—if you don't count the few thousand other people lounging nearby in the summer. The atmosphere is a reminder of what barrier island beaches were like before development. *Follow Rte. 35 south (and continue on Central Ave. in Seaside Park) to the entrance.*
Swimming: Excellent, with clear waves breaking sweetly against the beach. Lifeguard on duty.
Sand: Fine, powdery white, rising to a fine natural dune with thick dune grass.
Amenities: Bathhouses, rest rooms, and some concessions near swimming beach.

Sports: Fishing, biking, canoe and kayak launch, mobile sport fishing.

Parking: Two huge lots and other designated spaces within the park (per-car entrance fee).

SEASIDE HEIGHTS

The sand shares the spotlight with the boardwalk, amusement piers, and other diversions. From the wide beach between the two amusement piers there's an unusual feeling of being in the outdoors while being boxed in by the

Beauty	B
Swimming	B
Sand	B
Amenities	A

two hulking piers and the boardwalk behind, with no view at all up or down the coast. South of the piers, the beach broadens and takes on a different tone. From a distance, the towering Ferris wheel and other pier rides have a postcard quality, and the coast to the south is quite pleasing, with the beach rising to a stable dune and low residences lining Ocean Avenue into the distance. The boardwalk extends to the south beyond Seaside Heights into adjacent communities, totaling two and a half miles. *From Rte. 35, the beach is just east.*

Swimming: Good, with waves breaking 50 to 100 yards out, then breaking again a few times before reaching shore. Beach tags required; some free days. Lifeguard on duty.

Sand: Fine, uniformly light tan, almost powdery, running up to the boardwalk or, farther south, rising to a grassy dune.

Amenities: Boardwalk has all amenities; south of the boardwalk, none.

Sports: Volleyball, fishing, surfing.

Parking: Metered street parking and lots.

BAY HEAD

The moderately wide beach has an almost private feel, partly because it's backed by a well-maintained dune and an orderly line of expensive beach homes that would fit right into any New England coastal community. It's a pub-lic beach, but it's privately owned and maintained by the Bay

Beauty	A-
Swimming	B
Sand	A
Amenities	D

Head Improvement Authority. Jetties keep the sand under control. Overall, it's a very appealing stretch of sand, with no boardwalk or arcade chaos. And the lack of amenities keeps the crowds down. *From Rte. 35, the beach is just east.*

Swimming: Vigorous waves tamed in places by jetties. Beach tag required. Lifeguard on duty.

Sand: Fine, fluffy, light tan, rising steeply in places from the water, extending to a grassy dune.

Amenities: No rest rooms; businesses blocks away.

Sports: Surfing, fishing.

Parking: Limited street parking.

POINT PLEASANT BEACH

The wide beach stretches refreshingly long, straight, and uninterrupted, in contrast to some jetty-laden beach fronts elsewhere in the area. Just south of Manasquan Inlet, the boardwalk begins, geared to a lot of activity, with

Beauty	B
Swimming	B
Sand	B
Amenities	A

businesses lining the west side of the boardwalk and others extending over the sand on the oceanside. Farther south, the arcade atmosphere gives way to an unrailed pedestrian boardwalk, a hefty dune appears, and the beach atmosphere is calm and soothing, backed only by two-story condos and other low-key housing. *From Rte. 35, take Broadway, Arnold Ave., or other streets east to Ocean Ave.*

Swimming: Active waves, with surf often breaking close to shore, forcefully at times. Beach tag required. Lifeguard on duty.

Sand: Fine to moderately fine, tan, rising to a healthy dune past the boardwalk businesses.

Amenities: Rest rooms, food on boardwalk, aquarium. Private bathhouses.

Parking: Street parking and plenty of lots.

HOTELS/INNS/B&BS

Point Pleasant Beach has quite a few motels and hotels, which tend to be on the basic side and fill up during peak season. Bay Head has several charming B&Bs and inns. Seaside Heights and

Seaside Park, just outside Island Beach State Park, have a number of basic motels and motor inns.

◆ **White Sands** (expensive). This beach-front motel offers standard rooms and efficiencies, plus two ocean-front pools and its own private beach. *1100 Ocean Ave., Pt. Pleasant Beach, NJ 08742; tel. 908-899-3370.*

◆ **Grenville Hotel** (expensive to moderate). This Victorian hotel, the best-known in the area, is tastefully filled with antiques and tradition. The four-story inn has 31 individually furnished rooms, and some have interesting shapes, including the water-view bridal suite, one of two rooms in turrets. In a neighborhood of shingled homes a block from the beach. *345 Main Ave., Bay Head, NJ 08742; tel. 908-892-3100, 800-756-4667. On Rte. 35, just south of Pt. Pleasant Beach.*

HOUSE RENTALS

Point Pleasant Beach has many houses available, often rented by the season or half-season, although weekly rentals also arise. Expect weekly rates to begin in the $650 to $1,000 range, depending on size and location. The city has acted to cut down on rowdy group homes; would-be renters can expect to be grilled about who will be occupying their summer residence.

◆ **Ralph S. Hayes.** *106 Ocean Ave., Pt. Pleasant Beach, NJ 08742; tel. 908-899-2222. Open daily.*

◆ **Ward Realty.** *705 Ocean Ave., Pt. Pleasant Beach, NJ 08742; tel. 908-892-2700. Open daily.*

RESTAURANTS

◆ **Grenville Restaurant** (expensive). This columned dining room in the Grenville Hotel has a rich carpet, a fireplace, tables set with maroon tablecloths, elegant flowers, and stained glass, which nicely sets the stage for such entrées as braised Norwegian salmon, Caribbean-spice-and-tortilla-encrusted swordfish, and pistachio-rosemary New Zealand rack of lamb. The menu changes regularly. *345 Main Ave., Bay Head, NJ 08742; tel. 908-892-3100. Open Tue.-Sun. for lunch and dinner Sept.-Jun.; open daily for breakfast, lunch, and dinner Jul.-Aug.*

◆ **Clarks Bar & Grill at Clarks Landing** (moderate). The big picture windows in this polished place, opened in mid-1995, look out onto the Manasquan River and Treasure Island, and the decor includes a 759-pound great white shark. The food is creative, including the best-selling "The Landing": chitwood-grilled swordfish steak, scallops, and garlic shrimp with seared plum tomato sauce over pasta. Crab cakes, grilled shrimp, and burgers are other favorites. There's often live music. *847 Arnold Ave., Pt. Pleasant, NJ 08742; tel. 908-899-1111. Open daily for lunch and dinner Mar.-Nov. and Wed.-Sun. Dec.-Feb.; Sun. brunch Dec.-Mar.*

◆ **Redingtons Seafood** (moderate). Local residents practically line up to testify on behalf of this 15-table, simply appointed seafood restaurant. The Salmon Jacqueline draws raves. The menu includes blackened mako, salmon, and snapper; grilled mahi mahi Florentine topped with spinach, crabmeat, and hollandaise; and a pasta/seafood combo. *816 Arnold Ave., Pt. Pleasant, NJ 08742; tel. 908-892-4343. Open daily for lunch and dinner Jul.-Sep.; closed Mon. Oct.-Jun.*

NIGHTLIFE

Much of Point Pleasant Beach's nightlife unfolds on the boardwalk at Jenkinson's and at nearby Martell's Sea Breeze, both restaurant/clubs that cater to families by day and adults by night. To the south, in Seaside Heights, the Aztec Motel has a lounge with live music on summer weekends, and Tunney Boulevard, two blocks west of the beach, has a strip of clubs offering a mix of DJs, live music, and karaoke.

ATTRACTIONS

◆ **Jenkinson's Aquarium.** Sharks, penguins, alligators, seals, live coral, touch tanks, and tropical birds are all part of this local landmark. *Parkway and Ocean Aves., Pt. Pleasant Beach, NJ 08742; tel. 908-899-1212. Open daily 10-10 mid-Jun.-Labor Day and Mon.-Fri. 9:30-5 and Sat.-Sun. 10-5 Oct.-Apr.; longer hours May-early Jun. Feeding schedule available for seals, sharks, penguins, alligators. Admission.*

◆ **Jenkinson's South & Jenkinson's Pavilion.** Jenkinson's dominates the water front, with dining, entertainment, concerts, rides, arcades, ice cream, and other attractions on the boardwalk. A "beach train" provides transportation. *3 Broadway, Pt. Pleasant*

Beach, NJ 08742; tel. 908-899-0569. Open daily. On the boardwalk at Parkway and Ocean Aves.

◆ **North American Lighter Museum.** Tours of this 7,000-lighter collection are by escort only in Gold Fever, a store that sells jewelry and watches. *700 Arnold Ave., Pt. Pleasant 08742; tel. 800-540-3534. Open daily. At Arnold and Bay Aves.*

◆ *River Belle and River Queen.* These riverboat replicas offer sightseeing and specialty tours on the Manasquan River, Point Pleasant Canal, and Barnegat Bay. *Box 307, Brielle, NJ 08730; tel. 908-528-6620, 908-892-3377. Open late Jun.-early Sep. Admission. The* River Belle *sails from the Broadway Basin, 47 Broadway, Pt. Pleasant Beach. The* River Queen *sails from Bogan's Brielle Basin, 800 Ashley Ave., Brielle, across the bridge from Pt. Pleasant Beach.*

SHOPPING

Point Pleasant Beach is an antiquing center, and Bay Head has more than 40 specialty stores and boutiques. Just north in Manasquan, Circle Factory Outlets has about 20 stores.

◆ **Point Pleasant Antique Emporium.** More than 100 dealers under one roof. Other antiques dealers are also in the neighborhood. *Box 1651, Pt. Pleasant Beach, NJ 08742; tel. 908-892-2222. Open daily 11-5. At Bay and Trenton Aves.*

BEST FOOD SHOPS

SANDWICHES: ◆ **Ebby's Deli, Cafe & Market.** Specialty sandwiches and submarines. *Central Ave., S. Seaside Park, NJ 08752; tel. 908-830-4775. Open daily. Just outside the entrance to Island Beach State Park.*

SEAFOOD: ◆ **Point Lobster Company.** Live lobsters, shellfish, scallops, shrimp, clams. *1 St. Louis Ave., Pt. Pleasant Beach, NJ 08742; tel. 908-892-1729. Open daily Apr.-Nov. Closed Mon. Dec.-Mar. Just off Channel Dr., on the water.*

ICE CREAM: ◆ **Hoffman's Ice Cream and Yogurt.** *800 Richmond Ave., Pt. Pleasant Beach, NJ 08742; tel. 908-892-0270. Open daily.*

SPORTS
FISHING

Surf fishing is allowed in Island Beach State Park 24 hours a day but is prohibited in the bathing zone May through September.

◆ **Bogan's Deep Sea Fishing Center.** Head boats and charters offering half-day and longer fishing trips. *800 Ashley Ave., Brielle, NJ 08730; tel. 908-458-3188, 908-528-5720. Daily trips spring through fall and Wed. and Sat.-Sun. Nov.-mid-Apr. Brielle is across the inlet from Pt. Pleasant Beach.*

◆ **Mobile sportfishing permits.** The southern end of the park is designated for four wheel-drive mobile sportfishing. Annual permits cost $125. *Island Beach State Park, Box 37, Seaside Park, NJ 08752; 908-793-0506.*

◆ **Wheelhouse Marina.** Crab and pontoon boat rentals, bait and tackle, clamming licenses. *267 24th Ave., S. Seaside Park, NJ; tel. 908-793-3296. Open daily 7-5 May-Sep. and 9-5 Oct.-Apr. On the bay.*

BOATING

◆ **Bay Cruiser Excursions.** Sightseeing and sunset cruises aboard a 35-foot pontoon boat. *Wheelhouse Marina, 267 24th Ave., S. Seaside Park, NJ; tel. 908-793-3296. Morning and afternoon cruises Wed., Fri.-Sun. On the bay.*

◆ **Canoe tours.** Canoe tours of the Sedge Islands of Barnegat Bay, guided by a park naturalist. These trips are very popular, and the whole summer quickly books up. Reservations are taken beginning in early June. *Island Beach State Park; tel. 908-793-0506. Late Jun.-Aug. Tours meet at parking area A-21, 7 1/2 miles south of park entrance.*

SURFING

Surfing sites include the beach at Bay Head and the southern end of the designated swimming zone at Island Beach State Park.

DIVING

Scuba diving is permitted along two and a half miles of Island Beach State Park north of Barnegat Inlet, but divers must register at the park office before their first dive each year and provide proof of certification.

BICYCLING

The area is flat and good for bicycling. While the boardwalks are sometimes off-limits, Island Beach State Park has a bike trail along both sides of the road between the toll gate and the recreational zone.

◆ **Tyre's Bicycles.** Rentals, sales, and service. *1900 Boulevard,*

Seaside Park, NJ 08752; tel. 908-830-2050. Open daily. In Seaside Park, outside Island Beach State Park. If the park is closed to cars because it's full, you can still bike in at no charge.

GOLF

The closest courses are on the mainland: Cedar Creek at the Berkeley Municipal Golf Course in Bayville (tel. 908-269-4460) and the Bey Lea Municipal Golf Course in Toms River (tel. 908-349-0566).

NATURE

◆ **Island Beach State Park.** The park's northern natural area is covered with maritime vegetation and is available for nature tours, fishing, and strolling. The southern natural area includes the inlet and a wildlife sanctuary. Nature tours are conducted by park naturalists, and programs are offered at the Aeolium Nature Center. *Box 37, Seaside Park, NJ 08752; tel. 908-793-0506. Open daily. Parking fee; no charge for additional tours.*

◆ **Whale watching cruises aboard the *Atlantis*.** This 110-foot boat ventures out in search of humpbacks, finbacks, minkes, and dolphins. *Bogan's Brielle Basin, 800 Ashley Ave., Brielle, NJ 08730; tel. 908-528-6620, 908-528-5014. Departures Sat.-Sun. 9-2 late Dec.-Mar. Admission. Brielle is across the inlet from Point Pleasant Beach.*

SAFETY TIPS

Poison ivy is present in the state park.

TOURIST INFORMATION

◆ **Bay Head Business Association.** The association offers a brochure of summer events. *Box 135, Bay Head, NJ 08742; tel. 800-422-9433.*

◆ **Greater Point Pleasant Area Chamber of Commerce.** *517-A Arnold Ave., Pt. Pleasant Beach, NJ 08742; tel. 908-899-2424. Open Mon.-Fri. 9-3.*

◆ **Island Beach State Park.** *Box 37, Seaside Park, NJ 08752; tel. 908-793-0506. Open daily 8-sunset.*

◆ **Seaside Business Association.** Brochures and information on Seaside Heights, including summer activity schedules. *Box 98, Seaside Heights, NJ 08751; tel. 800-732-7467.*

CHAPTER 12

Long Beach Island

Beauty	A
Swimming	A
Sand	B
Hotels/Inns/B&Bs	B
House rentals	A
Restaurants	B
Nightlife	B
Attractions	B
Shopping	B-
Sports	B
Nature	B

Ending its beeline through the Pine Barrens of South Jersey, Route 72 crosses Manahawkin Bay onto Long Beach Island, a barrier island whose low-key temperament disguises its recreational abundance. It has 18 miles of dune-guarded beaches on one side and a long bay front of marinas, salt-marsh grass, and weathered bulkheads on the other. In many ways it is the Jerseyite's Jersey shore. Less known than its fellow beaches to the south and north—some mapmakers don't even show it—the island's 20 or so communities offer everything from modest motels to megabucks neighborhoods that literally rise above the rest of the island.

Richard Nixon spent two weeks here in 1986, staying in a luxurious private home with a rooftop hot tub looking out across the dunes to the ocean. While the occasional star lands in the island's tonier quarters, celebrity-watching isn't why people come to Long Beach Island; rather, it's the classic mix of shore attractions that quench the seasonal appetite for sun, sand, and recreation.

Partly because it has about 10,000 year-round residents, the island also possesses a sense of community that remains in place even when summer vacationers astronomically inflate the population.

The island's northern end is crowned by historic Barnegat Lighthouse (affectionately known as Old Barney), a landmark open to visitors and set in a small gem of a state park. Below the tower, fleets of fishing party boats and working fishermen bring in their haul around the clock through the turbulent inlet to Barnegat Bay. At the island's south end is a wildlife refuge and bustling Beach Haven, a center for shopping, recreation, and nightlife, including an amusement park and water slides.

In between are miles of such hamlets as Beach Haven Terrace, Surf City, North Beach, and the more posh and picturesque Harvey Cedars and Loveladies—all sharing Long Beach Boule-

HOW TO GET THERE

◆ Long Beach Island is nearly 60 mi. from the Ben Franklin Bridge in Philadelphia. From the bridge, take Rte. 70 east to Rte. 72 east, which ends in Ship Bottom.

◆ From New York City or S. Jersey, take the Garden State Pkwy. to Rte. 72 east.

◆ In summer, New Jersey Transit may provide bus service from Philadelphia, New York, and other shore towns (tel. 215-569-3752).

vard, which runs like a spinal cord down the island's middle and is lined, especially on the south, with movie theaters, seafood markets, restaurants, shops, and venues for miniature golf, ice cream, and salt water taffy. (Long Beach Boulevard is also known in places as Ocean Avenue, Bay Avenue, or, almost universally, The Boulevard.)

Vacationers who favor the north half of the island tend to stock up on supplies so they don't need to regularly drive south, where more businesses are located. The north, though, does have some choice restaurants and shopping in Barnegat Light.

Unless you arrive by boat or parachute, there's only one way onto the island—the Route 72 Manahawkin Bridge. This highway bottleneck can cause moderate traffic jams on summer weekends but may also contribute to the island's rather slow development.

In the late 1700s, the island attracted whalers, fishermen, and hunters. Then Quaker farmers began ferrying across the bay in the summer. By the late 1800s a train tressel carried visitors to the island, and in 1914 a bridge for vehicular traffic was completed. Almost all those early visitors headed for the southern portion of the island. By the late 19th century, hotels and summer homes were cropping up, particularly in Beach Haven.

In the 1920s, Scandinavian fishermen established a community near the lighthouse. To this day a commercial fleet is based there, in Viking Village, as are whale-watching cruises.

As with most shore regions, the sea has provided a colorful heritage, with stories of pirates, shipwrecks, rumrunners, and storms.

One of the island's seminal events was a ferocious winter storm in 1962 that decimated the area around Loveladies, sweeping away whole houses. In the aftermath, the building code was revised, giving rise to the Loveladies of today, which is practically a fantasy world of elaborately designed beach homes standing high on pilings to guard against future storm tides.

BEACHES

Long Beach Island has more than a dozen towns that fall under the umbrella of Long Beach Township (including Loveladies, Brant Beach, and Holgate), as well as the independent towns of

Barnegat Light, Harvey Cedars, Surf City, Ship Bottom, and Beach Haven. Each has its own beach rules and sets its own prices on beach tags, which are required on bay- and oceanside beaches from mid-June through Labor Day.

BARNEGAT LIGHT

Barnegat Light's ocean front is about 28 blocks long, with the beach reaching gigantic proportions between 8th and 18th streets. This is the widest beach front on the island, and getting to it from the lighthouse parking lot means a calf-torturing trek through low, wide dunes.

Beauty	A
Swimming	B
Sand	B
Amenities	C

The reward is an extremely spacious beach where the ocean is so far from the shoreline houses that it has a wild, away-from-it-all atmosphere.

Down the beach to the south are the large homes of Loveladies; to the north are the swirling waters of Barnegat Inlet and a lot of boating traffic moving slowly in and out. *Upon reaching Long Beach Island, turn left onto Long Beach Blvd. and follow it to its end in Barnegat Light, where you can park in the lighthouse parking lot (tel. 609-494-9196). All numbered streets also end at the beach.*

Barnegat Light also has a bayside beach park at 25th Street and Bayview Avenue that includes a playground. *Follow Long Beach Blvd. to 25th St. and turn west to Bayview Ave.*

Swimming: The waves are clear and strong, with water roughest near the inlet. (In general, the northern end of the island has a reputation for rougher water.) Lifeguards on duty at about eight locations.

Sand: Fine and light tan, sprawling on a flat plain from the waterline back to low, rolling dunes.

Amenities: Most facilities are in the state park near the lighthouse, including rest rooms. Restaurant and gift shop also near the lighthouse.

Sports: None.

Parking: Free at the lighthouse lot. Barnegat Light also has a bayside beach park with playground equipment at 25th Street and Bayview Avenue.

SHIP BOTTOM

In beaches as in real estate, location is everything, and Ship Bottom's mile of sand tends to get crowded because the sole route onto the island empties right into town, making this beach very convenient for day-trippers. (It

Beauty	A
Swimming	A
Sand	B
Amenities	A

has good amenities too.) Buildings behind the beach are low-rise and unimposing, and the atmosphere is basic low-key beach fun. Besides location, the beach also is distinguished by the presence of a snack bar—something you won't find on the other island beaches. *From Long Beach Blvd., turn east to reach the beach. Ship Bottom also has a bathing beach on the bay side between 14th and 16th Sts.*

Swimming: Waves break several times on the way in, often lapping the shore calmly. Lifeguard on duty.

Sand: Medium fine, light tan, building to a protected dune.

Sports: Surfing at times.

Parking: Street parking and commercial lots nearby.

BEACH HAVEN

This is ground zero for beach activity on the island, and in August the sand is hopping with swarms of people drawn by the restaurants, ice cream shops, and amusements in town. At Centre Street, the beach is moderately wide, and the

Beauty	B
Swimming	B
Sand	B
Amenities	A

atmosphere is a classic blend of whooshing surf, romping kids, lifeguard whistles, and the smell of suntan oil. The beach is lined with motels and beach homes, and a lot of leisure boats cruise just offshore, as does another seashore tradition—small boats and airplanes towing advertising banners and billboards. If Beach Haven's two miles of sand get too crowded for you, stroll north or south; the sand may grow narrower, but there will be fewer people. *From Beach Ave., turn east to reach the beach.*

Swimming: Waves roll in steadily but not roughly when the weather's good. Lifeguards on duty.

Sand: Medium fine and light tan, sloping up to a low, fenced dune.

Amenities: Rest rooms at Centre Street and the beach; the main street is a block away, with a full range of restaurants and stores.
Sports: None.
Parking: Street parking and commercial lots nearby.

HOLGATE

This beach near the wildlife refuge is often ignored because of its size and distance from the action. But as a charming "pocket beach," it offers a nice respite from the busier spots. Boxed in by dunes, with the refuge nearby and

Beauty	B
Swimming	B
Sand	B
Amenities	C

most of Holgate's residential neighborhood out of view, it feels cozy and remote. It has a family atmosphere—parents and children walk over from the nearby summer homes. *The beach is at the southern end of Long Beach Blvd.*
Swimming: Ocean waves lap the shore. No lifeguard.
Sand: Medium fine and light tan, building to high, grassy dunes.
Amenities: Across the street is a beach store for snacks. Rest room near the boulevard.
Sports: None.
Parking: The wildlife refuge has a midsize lot that charges a fee.

HOTELS/INNS/B&BS

The island has more than two dozen motels, most of them in Ship Bottom, Beach Haven, and Beach Haven Inlet. A brochure called "Places to Stay" is available from the Southern Ocean County Chamber of Commerce. Beach Haven also has a historic district with eight bed & breakfasts.

◆ **Sea Shell Motel** (very expensive). This two-story ocean-front motel, renovated in 1987, has standard and ocean-front rooms and two suites with kitchenettes. The units are neat and simply furnished, most with two double beds. Ocean-front accommodations overlook a large pool and deck. There's also a restaurant/beach club on the property. *10 S. Atlantic Ave., Beach Haven, NJ 08008; tel. 609-492-4611. Closed Nov.-Mar. From the causeway, go right 7 mi. and turn left onto Engleside Ave.*

◆ **Drifting Sands Motel** (expensive). Driving off the causeway into Ship Bottom, you'll see this two-story, 53-unit motel rising straight ahead. It's basic and ideally located for quick arrival and departure without a traffic tangle. Room types include standard, family (three double beds), efficiency, and suite. Some have kitchenettes. Prime rooms are the 24 ocean-front units with balconies overlooking the beach. *119 E. 9th St., Ship Bottom, NJ 08008, tel. 609-494-1123. Continue straight off the causeway on 9th St. to the beach.*

◆ **Pierrot by the Sea** (expensive). This three-story Victorian has nine guest rooms, four with air-conditioning. Rooms 1, 2, and 3 share a bathroom. Room 6, on the top floor, has a queen-size bed, a big mirror, and an ocean view. Antiques, Victorian-pattern wallpaper, and lacy curtains abound. Breakfast is served in the dining room or on the porch. *101 Centre St., Beach Haven, NJ 08008; tel. 609-492-4424. After crossing the causeway, turn right onto Long Beach Blvd. Go 7 mi. to Beach Haven and turn left on Centre St.*

◆ **The Bayberry Barque** (moderate). This Victorian B&B's eight rooms have been renovated and are furnished with antiques, period touches, and floral arrangements. Five have private bath, all have ceiling fans. Room 3, done in dark green, has its own bathroom and a queen-size brass bed. Room 1 is the largest. The beach is a short walk away. A wraparound porch is furnished with rockers. *117 Centre St., Beach Haven, NJ 08008; tel. 609-492-5216, 908-369-7461 (off-season). Open daily late May-early Sep. and weekends early May-mid-May and mid-Sep.-Oct. From the causeway, turn right and go 7 mi. to Beach Haven. Turn left onto Centre St.*

HOUSE RENTALS

A wide range of weekly, monthly, and seasonal rental properties is available, varying in price depending on size and location. "Ocean-front" property is costlier than "oceanside." The island is narrow enough that all housing is within walking distance of both the ocean and the bay. An oceanside three-bedroom in Ship Bottom might cost $8,000 for the season, or $600 to $900 per week. An oceanside four-bedroom in Loveladies might run $1,500 to $2,700 per week.

◆ **Oceanside Realty.** *212 N. Long Beach Blvd., Surf City, NJ 08008; tel. 609-494-3800; fax 609-361-1759. Open daily.*

◆ **Weichert Realtors.** Sales and rentals. *326 W. 9th St., Ship Bottom, NJ 08008; tel. 609-494-6000. Open daily. Just over the causeway.*

RESTAURANTS

◆ **La Spiaggia** (expensive). This well-regarded Italian restaurant's attentive staff and reliable cuisine have built a loyal clientele. Appetizers such as fire-roasted peppers in a warm bath of slow-cooked garlic, anchovy, and olive oil with grilled polenta set the stage for an excellent range of meat, chicken, and seafood entrées. BYOB. *357 W. 8th St., Ship Bottom, NJ 08008; tel. 609-494-4343. Open daily for dinner Jun.-Sep. and Thu.-Sun. Oct.-Dec. and Mar.-May. On the left, just as you arrive on the island.*

◆ **The Owl Tree** (expensive). A longtime favorite at the north end, it features such creative dishes as seared sea scallops with sweet oven-dried tomatoes and cider-vinegar butter sauce, nut-encrusted pork shops with a multinut coating served with stewed Granny Smith apples and garlic mashed potatoes. *80th St. and Long Beach Blvd., Harvey Cedars, NJ 08008; tel. 609-494-8191. Open daily for lunch and dinner.*

◆ **Morrison's Restaurant** (moderate). Situated on Little Egg Harbor Bay, this restaurant has fine views, good food, and half a century of tradition to live up to. Seafood stews and combinations are the specialty, with a wide range of fresh seafood platters, both fried and broiled. The atmosphere is unpretentious and cozy. *2nd St. at the Bay, Beach Haven, NJ 08008; tel. 609-492-5111. Open daily for breakfast, lunch, and dinner Memorial Day-Labor Day and for lunch and dinner Fri.-Sun. Feb.-Apr. and Oct.*

◆ **The Terrace Tavern** (moderate). This place looks, feels, and sounds like a bar—but at mealtime it's packed with locals and visitors lured by good food and a surprisingly varied selection. Where else can you find conch fritters, smoked Norwegian salmon, and dim sum on the same appetizer menu? Entrées range from twin filet mignon with bearnaise sauce to barbecued St. Louis ribs and ravioli with roasted red pepper cream sauce. *13201 Long Beach Blvd., Beach Haven Terrace, NJ 08008; tel. 609-492-9751. Open daily for lunch and dinner.*

◆ **Mustache Bill's Diner** (inexpensive). A classic diner serving classic diner food, all freshly prepared, including salads, platters, clam chowder, and sandwiches off the griddle. In business since 1959. *8th St. and Broadway, Barnegat Light, NJ 08008; tel. 609-494-0155. Open Sun.-Thu. for breakfast and lunch and Fri.-Sat. for breakfast, lunch, and dinner.*

NIGHTLIFE

Live music in restaurants and bars makes up much of the island's nightlife, although the municipalities offer various early-evening entertainment options in the summer. Movie theaters are in Beach Haven, Beach Haven Park, and Brant Beach.

◆ *Black Whale III.* This 100-foot cruiser makes runs to Atlantic City, docking at the Trump's Castle marina. Reservations required. *Centre St. at the Bay, Beach Haven, NJ 08008; tel. 609-492-0333, 609-492-0202; fax 609-492-7575. Departures daily from Beach Haven at 10 and 2 May-Oct., returning from Atlantic City at 6:30 p.m. and 10:30 p.m. Admission. The Beach Haven Fishing Centre is 7 mi. south of the causeway on Long Beach Blvd. Turn right at the Colonial Movie Theatre.*

◆ **Quarter Deck.** Night club and restaurant features live entertainment and dancing. *351 W. 9th St., Ship Bottom, NJ 08008; tel. 609-494-3334. Open nightly. On the causeway.*

◆ **Surflight Theater.** Summer stock theater for adults and children. *Box 1155, Beach Haven, NJ 08008; tel. 609-492-9477. Shows nightly in summer. Admission. Engleside and Beach Aves.*

ATTRACTIONS

◆ **Barnegat Lighthouse State Park.** Climb the 217 steps to the top of the lighthouse for a sweeping view of the island, Barnegat Inlet, and Island Beach State Park to the north. *Barnegat Light, NJ 08008; tel. 609-494-2016. Lighthouse open daily 9-4:30 Memorial Day-Labor Day and weekends the rest of May. Park open 8 a.m.-10 p.m. Jul.-Aug. and 8-4 Oct.-May, with longer hours Jun. and Sep. Follow Long Beach Blvd. to its northern end, then swing left for a few blocks to the park.*

◆ **Fantasy Island Amusement Park.** Family amusement park with arcade, rides, games, refreshments, and a Ferris wheel. *7th St. and*

Long Beach Blvd., Beach Haven, NJ 08008; tel. 609-492-4000. In season, arcade opens daily at noon; rides open Mon.-Thu. at 5 and Fri.-Sun. at 2.

◆ **Historic Trolley Tours.** Weekly three-hour tours vary, providing a behind-the-scenes look at a different destination or theme each week. Past trips have included "Beach Haven: A Look Inside the Little Egg Harbor Yacht Club," "Barnegat Light: Behind the Scenes at the Coast Guard Station," and "Ship Bottom: Original Life-Saving Station and Houseboats." *Ship Bottom, NJ 08008; tel. 609-494-6828. Usually on Thu. Jul.-Aug.; call for a schedule. Admission. Trolley departs from the Chamber of Commerce parking lot (265 W. 9th St. in Ship Bottom).*

◆ **Long Beach Island Historical Association Museum.** *Engleside and Beach Aves., Beach Haven, NJ 08008; tel. 609-492-0700. Open Mon., Wed.-Thu., and Sat.-Sun. 2-4 and 7-9 and Tue. and Fri. 10-12, 2-4, and 7-9 Jul.-Aug.; open Sat.-Sun. 2-4 Jun. and Sep.*

SHOPPING

◆ **Bay Village/Schooner's Wharf.** These adjacent shopping malls have a fishing village motif and dozens of stores with clothing, jewelry, gifts, crafts, and restaurants. *9th St. and Bay Ave., Beach Haven, NJ 08008; tel. 609-492-2800 (Bay Village), 609-492-4400 (Schooner's Wharf). Both open daily Memorial Day-Labor Day; Bay Village open weekends the rest of the year and Schooner's Wharf open weekends in spring and fall. Take Long Beach Blvd. to 9th St. in Beach Haven (where the boulevard is known as Bay Ave.).*

◆ **Pier 18 Mall.** More than 20 shops and eateries under one roof, including jewelry, CDs, books, sunglasses, crafts, and boutique gift stores. *3rd St. and Bay Ave., Beach Haven, NJ 08008; tel. 609-492-0107. Open daily Memorial Day-Labor Day and weekends in spring and fall.*

BEST FOOD SHOPS

SANDWICHES: ◆ **Subs & Such Sandwich Shoppe.** *1211 Long Beach Blvd., N. Beach Haven, NJ 08008; tel. 609-492-7114. Open daily for lunch and dinner May-Sep.*

SEAFOOD: ◆ **Surf City Fishery.** *10th St. and Long Beach Blvd., Ship Bottom, NJ 08008; tel. 609-494-8171. Open daily late Feb.-Dec.*

FRESH PRODUCE: ◆ **Foster's Farm Market.** *400 N. Bay Ave.,*

Beach Haven, NJ 08008; tel. 609-492-1360; fax 609-492-5049. Open daily May-Oct.

BAKERY: ◆ Jack's Bakery. Breads, cakes, pastries, buns, pies, and bagels. *14 S. Bay Ave., Beach Haven, NJ 08008; tel. 609-492-1129. Open daily.*

ICE CREAM:◆ Show Place. This popular parlor is noteworthy for its singing waiters and waitresses. *200 Centre St., Beach Haven, NJ 08008; tel. 609-492-0018. Open daily Memorial Day-Labor Day. On Centre St. at Beach Ave.*

BEVERAGES: ◆ IGA Supermarket. *24th St. and Long Beach Blvd., Ship Bottom, NJ 08008; tel. 609-494-8400. Open daily.*

WINE: ◆ Rommel's Liquor Store. *201 S. Bay Ave., Beach Haven, NJ 08008; tel. 609-492-6101. Open daily.*

SPORTS

Long Beach Island is a hotbed of sporting activity—ocean and bay fishing, surfing, windsurfing, waterskiing, sailing, tennis, biking, and diving are all popular. The Chamber of Commerce publishes an annual regional directory that has an activities section with scores of listings.

FISHING

The island has a wealth of marinas and tackle shops. Charter fishing and party boats are centered at Barnegat Light and Beach Haven. The Southern Ocean County Chamber of Commerce offers a brochure, "Fishing & Boating," that lists tackle shops, boat ramps, charter companies, and seasonal fishing guides.

◆ *Black Whale II.* This 80-foot party boat runs six-hour trips from 8 a.m. to 2 p.m., providing rods, bait, and tackle. Evening sightseeing trips. *Centre St. at the Bay, Beach Haven, NJ 08008; tel. 609-492-0333, 609-492-0202; fax 609-492-7575. Sails mid-Jun.-mid-Sep. from the Beach Haven Fishing Centre, 2 blocks south of Morrison's.*

◆ **Fishermen's Headquarters.** Clamming licenses. *280 W. 9th St., Ship Bottom, NJ 08008; tel. 609-494-5739. Open daily.*

◆ *Miss Barnegat Light.* Deep-sea fishing on a 91-foot catamaran party boat. *18th St. Dock, Barnegat Light, NJ 08008; tel. 609-494-2094. Departs daily at 8 a.m. and 7:30 p.m. from the Barnegat Light Yacht Basin*

BOATING

Besides fishing and recreational boating, the island is a hot spot for windsurfing, particularly at Brant Beach and its popular launch site in Bayview Park at 68th Street.

◆ **George's Boat Rental.** Fishing, crabbing, and clamming boats for rent, plus pleasure boats, waterskiing and speed boats, and Jet Skis and Waverunners. *20th St. at the Bay, N. Beach Haven, NJ 08008; tel. 609-492-7931. Open daily mid-Apr.-mid-Oct. and Mon.-Fri. the rest of the year. Turn west off Long Beach Blvd. onto 20th St.*

◆ **Horizon Sailing.** Rentals of 18- and 21-foot Precision sailboats, plus instruction and captained sailings. *Beach Haven, NJ 08008; tel. 609-492-5900. Open daily in summer. On Engleside at the bay, across from Tucker's.*

◆ **Island Surf & Sail.** This windsurfing store offers rentals, sales, lessons, service, and apparel. *3304 Long Beach Blvd., Brant Beach, NJ 08008; tel. 609-494-5553. Open daily.*

◆ **Kelly's Boat Rental.** Rental of fiberglass Bayrunners. Bait and tackle. *8th St. and Bayview Ave., Barnegat Light, NJ 08008; tel. 609-494-1520. Open daily.*

SURFING

Surfing thrives on Long Beach Island, with most of the communities designating surfing zones and having the usual restrictions on sites where lifeguards and swimmers are present. Among good locations are Holyoke Avenue in Beach Haven, 7-Eleven Beach in Ship Bottom, Harvey Cedars, and Surf City.

◆ **Ron Jon Surf Shop.** Full range of surf equipment and fashions. *9th St. and Central, Ship Bottom, NJ 08008; tel. 609-494-8844; fax 609-494-6811. Open daily. On the right after crossing the causeway onto Long Beach Island.*

DIVING

◆ **Long Beach Island Scuba.** Diving equipment and instruction. *819 Barnegat Ave., Ship Bottom, NJ 08008; tel. 609-494-5599. Open daily Apr.-Dec. and Thu.-Mon. Jan.-Mar.*

◆ **Neptune Dive Center.** Full-service dive center offers New Jersey wreck dives, dive vacations, and instruction. *291 Rte. 72*

E., Manahawkin, NJ; tel. 609-978-0666; fax 609-978-0007. Open daily. On Rte. 72, just west of Long Beach Island.

BICYCLING

◆ **Walters Bicycles.** A wide range of bicycle rentals, including tandems, adult trikes, and specialty bikes. Accessory, clothing, and Rollerblade sales. *5th St. and Long Beach Blvd., Ship Bottom, NJ 08008; tel. 609-494-1991, 609-597-7450 (off-season). Open daily in season. North of the causeway at Long Beach Blvd. and 5th St.*

GOLF

Long Beach Island has a swarm of miniature golf courses, but for real golf the closest links are the Ocean County Golf Course at Atlantis in Little Egg Harbor (tel. 609-296-2444) and the Ocean Acres Country Club in Manahawkin (tel. 609-597-9393).

TENNIS

Dozens of courts are available to the public, some free on a first-come, first-served basis; others require reservations and fees.

◆ **Harvey Cedars.** Two outdoor public courts. *Harvey Cedars, NJ 08008; tel. 609-361-9733. Open daily 7-7 May-Sep.; reservation booth open 10-4. In the Harvey Cedars Recreation Area on Burlington Ave. at Long Beach Blvd.*

◆ **LBI Foundation of the Arts & Sciences.** Eight outdoor courts. Members have priority when courts are full. Instruction, children's clinics, and round robins. *120 Long Beach Blvd., Loveladies, NJ 08008; tel. 609-494-1241. Open year-round to members and Memorial-Labor Day to nonmembers. Admission. On the west side of Long Beach Blvd.*

NATURE

◆ **Ecology of Long Beach Island.** Three-hour guided tours of the shore ecosystem aboard the Long Beach Island Trolley, including beach, dunes, wetlands, and bay. Sponsored by the Alliance for a Living Ocean (204 Centre St., Beach Haven, NJ 08008; tel. 609-492-0222). *For ticket information, call the Chamber of Commerce (tel. 609-494-7211). Tours depart at 9 on Wed. and Fri. from the Chamber of Commerce parking lot (265 W. 9th St. in Ship Bottom). Admission.*

◆ **EcoTour Inc.** Environmental kayaking trips through the salt marshes and waterways around the bay, observing birds and marine life. *Box 304, Ship Bottom, NJ 08008; tel. 609-492-6235. By appointment. Admission.*

◆ **Forsythe National Wildlife Refuge.** This would be a good place to escape the summer crowds—except it's closed during the height of the season because of nesting shorebirds. *Box 544, Barnegat, NJ 08005; tel. 609-698-1387, 609-652-1665. Open daily dawn-sunset early Sep.-Mar. Follow Long Beach Blvd. to its southern end.*

SAFETY TIPS

August brings jellyfish and green flies that can be a real nuisance on hot, calm days. As for crime, take the usual precautions and don't leave valuables exposed. Even with the island's sense of community, the summer's transient population means that some petty property crime occurs.

TOURIST INFORMATION

◆ **Municipal governments.** Most of the island's municipalities are part of Long Beach Township, and information on beach tags and other township fees can be obtained by calling 609-361-1200 (open Mon.-Fri. 9-4 and Sat.-Sun. 9-3 Apr.-early Sep.). *Towns that have separate governments and fees are Beach Haven (tel. 609-492-0111; open Mon.-Fri. 9-3), Ship Bottom (tel. 609-494-2171; open Mon.-Fri. 9-4:30), Surf City (tel. 609-494-3064; open Mon.-Fri. 9-4:30), Harvey Cedars (tel. 609-494-2843; open Tue.-Fri. 8:30-3:30 and Sat. 8:30-1), and Barnegat Light (tel. 609-494-9196; open Mon.-Fri. 8:30-3:30).*

◆ **Southern Ocean County Chamber of Commerce.** The chamber has a brochure-packed information office to greet arriving visitors and provides information on mainland destinations elsewhere in the county. *265 W. 9th St., Ship Bottom, NJ 08008; tel. 609-494-7211. Open Mon.-Sat. 10-4. The chamber office is on the left just after you cross the causeway.*

Atlantic City

Beauty	B-
Swimming	B-
Sand	B-
Hotels/Inns/B&Bs	B
House rentals	C
Restaurants	A
Nightlife	A
Attractions	A
Shopping	B+
Sports	B
Nature	B

*A*tlantic City holds a unique place in the annals of American leisure destinations, a pioneering city that won global renown as a seaside resort, only to falter and then, with a roll of the dice, reinvent itself as a gambling mecca.

Today, its dozen casino resorts are often packed, as are the famous boardwalk and the beach alongside, one of the few free beaches in New Jersey. And while the prime tourist zone is confined to a relatively narrow strip of the city, nearby beach areas like Ventnor and Margate, to the west, provide ample room to stretch out and sightsee.

Atlantic City's boardwalk, built around 1870 and said to be the first ever, laid the foundation for the town's glory days. Besides boardwalk hotels, huge entertainment piers eventually led from the walkway far out over the surf. One even supported a luxury hotel where guests could look out and easily imagine that they were at sea. (The best-known, the 2,000-foot Steel Pier, now has a new life under the ownership of Donald Trump.)

During the first half of the century, the boardwalk sizzled with excitement and style, and the city itself joined the realm of Americana. The Miss America Pageant thrived here, and the city's thorough-farcs—Park Place, Baltic Avenue, New York Avenue—became part of the Monopoly game board, perhaps the marketing coup of all time.

But in the 1950s the city lost much of its cachet and began a

HOW TO GET THERE

◆ From Philadelphia, Atlantic City is about 1 hr. away on the Atlantic City Expwy. From the Ben Franklin Bridge, stay on Rte. 42 east until it becomes the Atlantic City Expwy. Follow this into town.

◆ From New York, the drive takes about 2 hr. in smooth traffic. Take the Garden State Pkwy. south to the Atlantic City Expwy. and follow this into town.

◆ Regular train service operates between Philadelphia and Atlantic City on Amtrak (tel. 800-872-7245) and New Jersey Transit (tel. 215-569-3752).

◆ Greyhound Bus Lines serve Atlantic City (tel. 800-231-2222).

◆ Atlantic City International Airport has recently been improved but handles mainly charter and general aviation aircraft.

period of decline that left it a shadow of its former self. In 1976, New Jersey legalized gambling on behalf of Atlantic City, inadvertently setting the stage for America's current rush to the gaming tables. With salvation now resting in a gambling-based economy, the first casino opened in 1978.

A couple of years later, Susan Sarandon played a struggling casino worker in Louis Malle's movie *Atlantic City*. And Burt Lancaster portrayed an aging hoodlum longing for the past. "You should've seen the Atlantic Ocean in those days," he wistfully says from the boardwalk. Today, most slot-pumping visitors pine not at all for the past. They come by the busload, often just for the day, numbering more than 30 million a year.

Some traditions remain. The six-and-a-half-mile boardwalk is still a lively promenade, with its rolling chairs available for hire. Jitneys still make frequent runs down Pacific Avenue, although often at a pace that can hardly be called relaxing. Saltwater taffy shops abound. A rich blend of society is on parade, from international high-rollers to day-tripping grandmas and pawn-shop regulars.

The gambling houses, with about 12,000 hotel rooms available and more under construction, have been criticized for not doing more to help the city beyond the casino zone. Their big-name stage shows and in-house restaurants aim to keep customers off the streets. But, increasingly, there are signs that the city is on the upswing.

A huge new convention center is expected to draw groups that will stay longer, and a 500-room hotel currently in the works will be the city's first major hotel not tied to a casino. Meanwhile, a $1 billion complex with two new casinos is planned by Circus Circus and Mirage Resorts, offering the kinds of theme parks and rides that helped turn Vegas into one of the hottest family destinations in the country.

BEACHES
MAIN BEACH

The main beach along the boardwalk and the casino strip is segmented every several blocks by the massive piers— Ocean One, Central Pier, Steel Pier— under which beach goers can stroll. This is the spot where Miss America

Beauty	C
Swimming	B-
Sand	C
Amenities	A

sticks her toe in the water each September.

It's a long stretch of sand with plenty of room for strolling, swimming, and sunbathing, but the casinos overshadow the beach. Even the boardwalk has a thriving life of its own, so it's as if the beach has to compete for visitors' attention.

More than most resort beaches, this one gets a lot of fully clothed foot traffic. People wander down from the casinos, ankle-splashing jubilantly if they're winners or strolling wistfully if they're not. For kids, of course, none of this matters. It's plenty of surf and sand and a carnival atmosphere. *Follow the Atlantic City Expwy. into town and you'll be able to see the casino towers, from the Bally's Grand on the right to the Showboat on the far left. Boardwalk access is through the casinos or the public walkways (Atlantic City Clerk's Office, tel. 609-347-5510).*

Swimming: Lots of ocean waves breaking near the shoreline. Rip currents can arise in stormy weather. Lifeguards on duty.

Sand: Medium fine, tan, moderately wide, with some blocks sloping more steeply into the water than others, backed by the boardwalk.

Amenities: Boardwalk and pier businesses offer virtually everything, including food and beach accessories. Rest rooms at New Jersey, New York, and Chelsea avenues and at Convention Hall.

Sports: Limited surfing, body boarding.

Parking: The casinos have parking garages, many charging only the $2 state tax. Other lots along Atlantic and Pacific avenues.

EAST OF THE CASINO STRIP

Between the Showboat Casino and Absecon Inlet is more than half a mile of beach devoid of crowds and the carnival atmosphere. The sand broadens considerably from New Hampshire to Maine avenues. The boardwalk contin-

Beauty	B
Swimming	C
Sand	B
Amenities	C

ues past, but few people follow it and the casino scene fades away entirely, supplanted by the ocean and the inlet. Fishing boats pass through the inlet, as do pleasure craft bound for the nearby Farley State Marina, Gardiner's Basin, and Harrah's and Trump Castle casinos. A jetty attracts the fishing crowd. *Take Atlantic Ave. north to the end, where it meets the sea.*

Swimming: The ocean surges in here, with rougher currents toward the inlet, where swimming is not allowed. One lifeguard may be on duty just north of Atlantic Avenue, but the rest of this section is unguarded.

Sand: Medium fine and light tan, spreading widely closer to the inlet. Erosion damage is evident in some narrow spots.

Amenities: None.

Sports: Fishing; windsurfers sometimes put in here.

Parking: It's possible to drive right up to this beach and park on the street near the boardwalk, but the area is deserted and has a spooky feel. If you're the cautious type, use a casino facility and walk to the beach.

VENTNOR

This beach is a far cry from the bustle of Atlantic City. It has its own boardwalk and a mile and a half of beach front, but the atmosphere is decidedly tamer, with local sunbathers at times outnumbering visitors. Up the beach you can see the

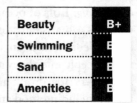

Beauty	B+
Swimming	B
Sand	B
Amenities	B

casinos rising in the distance, down the beach is the boardwalk backed by the low-rise town. *From Atlantic City, take Atlantic Ave. south to Ventnor (Ventnor City Clerk's Office, tel. 609-823-7904).*

Swimming: Ocean surf. Lifeguards on duty. Beach tags are required from Memorial Day through Labor Day.

Sand: Medium fine, light tan.

Amenities: Boardwalk shops and food stands. Rest rooms at Cambridge Avenue.

Sports: Fishing pier and volleyball at Cambridge Avenue, surfing.

Parking: In the street and in lots near the beach.

MARGATE

The beach at Margate draws a younger, flashy crowd distinguished by its beach-wear: thongs and skimpy bathing suits, on both men and women. The concentration of such fashion is at Washington Avenue, toward the western end of the

Beauty	B
Swimming	B
Sand	B
Amenities	B

130

beach. Lucy the Margate Elephant (*see* "Attractions") stands three stories high along the beach, overlooking the lifeguard headquarters with huge eyes that seem to take in the whole scene. *From Atlantic City, take Atlantic Ave. south through Ventnor to Margate (Margate City Clerk's Office, tel. 609-822-2605).*

Swimming: Rolling ocean surf. Lifeguards on duty. Beach tags required after late June.

Sand: Medium fine and tan.

Amenities: Refreshment stand next to Lucy the Elephant.

Sports: None.

Parking: In the street and in lots nearby.

HOTELS/INNS/B&BS

The casino-hotel towers dominate the skyline, but there are dozens of smaller properties in and around the city. Some are on the worn side, and others are quite decent hotels affiliated with national chains. The visitors bureau offers a brochure with a map that lists virtually all of them (tel. 800-262-7395). Several casino hotels have renovations or enlargements in the works; if you're making reservations, it's worth asking if any work will be in progress during your stay—insist on a room that doesn't have a crane outside your window.

◆ **Bally's Park Place Casino Hotel & Tower** (expensive). Bally's has 1,255 standard rooms and about 100 suites, plus nine restaurants. Entertainment venues include the Park Cabaret and the Grand Ballroom. Its huge spa offers a number of package plans. *Park Pl. and the Boardwalk, Atlantic City, NJ 08401; tel. 609-340-2000, 800-225-5977. 4 blocks north of Convention Hall, at Ohio Ave.*

◆ **Caesars Atlantic City Hotel/Casino** (expensive). Caesars has about 450 standard rooms, 200 suites, and ten restaurants. Live entertainment venues include the Circus Maximus Theater, the Venice Bar, and the Forum Lounge. It has rooftop tennis, an outdoor pool, miniature golf, an amusement arcade, a health spa, and a shopping arcade. *2100 Pacific Ave., Atlantic City, NJ 08401; tel. 609-348-4411, 800-443-0104. 2 blocks from Convention Hall, between Missouri and Arkansas Aves.*

◆ **Claridge Casino Hotel** (expensive). The Claridge has about 450 standard rooms and 60 suites, plus five restaurants and the Palace Theater. Indoor pool and health spa. *Boardwalk and Park*

Pl., Atlantic City, NJ 08401; tel. 609-340-3400, 800-257-8585.

◆ **Harrah's Casino Hotel** (expensive). Harrah's, one of two casinos located at the marina, away from the boardwalk strip, has about 500 standard rooms, 250 suites, eight restaurants, a health spa, and an indoor pool. The Broadway by the Bay Theater has shows like *Guys and Dolls. 777 Harrah's Blvd., Atlantic City, NJ 08401; tel. 609-441-5000, 800-427-7247.*

◆ **Merv Griffin's Resorts Casino Hotel** (expensive). About 640 standard rooms, 30 suites, seven restaurants, a spa, an indoor/outdoor pool, saunas, a game room, and a shopping arcade. Acts such as the Smothers Brothers and the Lovin' Spoonful appear at the Superstar Theater. *N. Carolina Ave. and the Boardwalk, Atlantic City, NJ 08401; tel. 609-344-6000, 800-336-6378.*

◆ **Sands Hotel & Casino** (expensive). The Sands has about 475 standard rooms, 60 suites, five restaurants, an indoor pool, a fitness center, and a food court. The Copa Room has musical reviews and comedy. *Indiana Ave. and Brighton Park, Atlantic City, NJ 08401; tel. 609-441-4000, 800-257-8580. On the boardwalk between Illinois and Indiana Aves.*

◆ **Showboat Casino-Hotel** (expensive). About 740 standard rooms, 60 suites, eight restaurants, a 60-lane bowling complex, and a video arcade. The Mardi Gras Showroom is where comics, dancers, singers, and illusionists perform. *801 Boardwalk, Atlantic City, NJ 08401; tel. 609-343-4000, 800-621-0200. At the boardwalk and Delaware Ave.*

◆ **The Grand Casino Resort** (expensive). About 370 rooms, 132 suites, five restaurants, a spa with indoor pool, and an amusement arcade. Live entertainment in the Cambridge Ballroom and Gatsby's. *Boston and Pacific Aves., Atlantic City, NJ 08401; tel. 609-347-7111, 800-257-8677.*

◆ **TropWorld Casino & Entertainment Resort** (expensive). TropWorld has 700 standard rooms, 300 suites, six restaurants, a two-and-a-half-acre indoor amusement park, and a shopping arcade with 15 stores. *Brighton Ave. and the Boardwalk, Atlantic City, NJ 08401; tel. 609-340-4000, 800-843-8767.*

◆ **Trump Plaza Hotel & Casino** (expensive). About 500 standard rooms, 75 suites, nine restaurants, a health spa, and an indoor pool. *Mississippi Ave. and the Boardwalk, Atlantic City, NJ 08401;*

tel. 609-441-6000, 800-677-7378.

◆ **Trump Taj Mahal Casino Resort** (expensive). More than 1,000 standard rooms, about 240 suites, nine restaurants, an indoor Olympic-size pool, and a health spa. Entertainment venues include the Mark G. Etess Arena, where you can see everything from the Village People to karate matches. *1000 Boardwalk, Atlantic City, NJ 08401; tel. 609-449-1000, 800-825-8786. On the boardwalk at Virginia Ave.*

◆ **Trump Castle Casino Resort** (expensive). Next to Farley State Marina, the hotel has about 570 standard rooms, 160 suites, eight restaurants, and a three-acre recreation deck, including tennis, pools, miniature golf, and a health club. *1 Castle Blvd., Atlantic City, NJ 08401; tel. 609-441-2000, 800-777-8477.*

HOUSE RENTALS

Vacation house rentals tend to be by the season—Memorial Day through Labor Day—although some monthlies pop up. Local ordinances discourage weekly rentals, but some boardwalk condominiums are available for $1,000 to $2,000 per week. Most rental homes are in Ventnor, Margate, and Longport, just to the south. Seasonal rentals go from a very modest $5,000 to $50,000 on the beach front.

◆ **Parkway Realty.** Seasonal and occasional monthly rentals. *9202 Ventnor Ave., Margate, NJ 08402; tel. 609-822-0533, 609-646-0015. Open daily.*

◆ **Premier Properties Real Estate.** Seasonal rentals, monthly minimum. *2401 Atlantic Ave., Longport, NJ 08043; tel. 609-822-3339. Open daily.*

RESTAURANTS

Each casino resort has several restaurants, including at least one that's open 24 hours, and often there's live entertainment within earshot. Caesars is home to a Planet Hollywood, with plenty of rock memorabilia to dine by.

◆ **Knife and Fork Inn** (expensive). This gabled classic has seafood, steaks, and an extensive wine list. The street-level porch dining area looks out on the busy intersection of Atlantic and Pacific avenues—and if you can snag the much-requested corner table, you'll be sitting where Burt Lancaster and Susan Sarandon

133

dined in the movie *Atlantic City. Atlantic and Pacific Aves., Atlantic City, NJ 08401; tel. 609-344-1133. Open for lunch and dinner Wed.-Sun. May-Jun., Tue.-Sun. Jul.-Sep., Wed.-Sun. Oct.-Nov., and Sat.-Sun. Dec.-Apr.*

◆ **Dock's Oyster House** (moderate). Many regard this as the city's best seafood restaurant; it's been in business since 1897. The service gets high marks, as does the casual atmosphere. Dishes like poached salmon, crab au gratin, and lobster are popular, as are the steaks and homemade pastas. *2405 Atlantic Ave., Atlantic City, NJ 08401; tel. 609-345-0092. Open for dinner Tue.-Sun. Apr.-Oct. Atlantic at Georgia Aves., near Convention Hall.*

◆ **Angelo's Fairmount Tavern** (inexpensive). This former speakeasy in the Ducktown section is a favorite among locals— and Frank Sinatra, when he's in town. Diners relish the meatballs, ravioli, and southern Italian specialties served up by Angelo "Sonny" Mancuso. *2300 Fairmount Ave., Atlantic City, NJ 08401; tel. 609-344-2439. Open daily for dinner and Mon.-Fri. for lunch.*

NIGHTLIFE

Atlantic City may have the best nightlife of any town its size in the country—thanks to the casino showrooms and their top-name performers. It also has numerous worthwhile night spots away from the boardwalk.

◆ **Six Shooters Rock Cafe.** This club features old and new rock and roll, including regional cover bands and, occasionally, nationally known acts. *201 S. New York Ave., Atlantic City, NJ 08401; tel. 609-347-0099. Open nightly.*

◆ **Studio Six.** The city's top gay dance club has a big outdoor area called the Surfside Deck Bar. *12 S. Mt. Vernon Ave., Atlantic City, NJ 08401; tel. 609-348-0192. Open nightly. Cover charge on the deck after 10 p.m.*

ATTRACTIONS

◆ **Gardiner's Basin.** A park on the edge of this historic boat basin, with period watercraft, an aquarium, and a museum. *800 N. New Hampshire Ave., Atlantic City, NJ 08401; tel. 609-348-2880. Off Absecon Inlet, near the Farley State Marina.*

◆ **Lucy the Margate Elephant.** This three-story elephant, a national historic landmark built in 1881, was a hotel and tavern in the early 1900s. It's one of the Atlantic City area's most enduring and endearing sites, with tours, a gift shop, and summer band concerts. *9200 Atlantic Ave., Margate, NJ 08402; tel. 609-823-6473. Open Mon.-Sat. 10-8 and Sun. 10-5 Jul.-Aug. and Sat.-Sun. 10-4:30 Apr.-Jun. and Sep.-Oct. Admission. Next to the beach at 92nd St. and Atlantic Ave.*

◆ **Miss America Pageant.** The Pageant is held each September, and tickets are sold for preliminary competition shows, the boardwalk parade, and the finals and crowning. Order forms are available, and phone orders are accepted beginning in early July. *Box 119, Atlantic City, NJ 08404; tel. 609-344-5278. Admission.*

SHOPPING

All the casino hotels have boutiques offering designer clothing, jewelry, and merchandise. On the boardwalk, the Shops on Ocean One (tel. 609-347-8086) is a full-scale mall with 120 stores on the pier across from Caesars.

BEST FOOD SHOPS

SANDWICHES: ◆ **White House Sub Shop.** *2301 Arctic Ave., Atlantic City, NJ 08401; tel. 609-345-1564. Open daily 10-11.*

SEAFOOD: ◆ **Capt. Ken Allen Fishing Center.** *432 N. Rhode Island Ave., Atlantic City, NJ 08401; tel. 609-345-0075. Open Mon.-Sat.*

FRESH PRODUCE: ◆ **Santori's Produce Outlet.** *520 N. Albany Ave., Atlantic City, NJ 08401; tel. 609-344-4747. Open daily.*

BAKERY: ◆ **Minos Bakery.** *4100 Ventnor Ave., Atlantic City, NJ 08401; tel. 609-344-8627. Open daily.*

ICE CREAM: ◆ **Stephanie's Ice Cream Parlor.** *2605 Boardwalk, Atlantic City, NJ 08401; tel. 609-344-5069. Open daily Feb.-late fall.*

WINE: ◆ **Bloom's Liquor Store.** *6430 Ventnor Ave., Ventnor, NJ 08406; tel. 609-822-1188. Open daily. Follow Atlantic Ave., which becomes Ventnor Ave.*

SPORTS
FISHING

Sport fishing party and charter boats are based in Gardiner's Basin and on the bayside of Margate.

◆ **Capt. Applegate's.** Party boat offers four-hour deep-sea fishing trips twice daily on a ship that holds up to 75 passengers. *Gardiner's Basin, Atlantic City, NJ 08401; tel. 609-345-4077, 609-652-8184. Departures daily at 8 and 1 May–Sep.*

SURFING

◆ **Heritage Surf & Sport.** Surfboards, wet suits, swimsuits, accessories, surf report. *9223 Ventnor Ave., Margate, NJ 08402; tel. 609-823-3331. Open daily.*

DIVING

◆ **Atlantic Divers.** Rentals of wet suits and other supplies; wreck dives; tour guides available. *2905 Fire Rd., Pleasantville, NJ 08234; tel. 609-641-7722. Open daily.*

BICYCLING

◆ **B & K Bike Rental.** Rentals for adults and children. *1743 Boardwalk, Atlantic City, NJ 08401; tel. 609-344-8008. Open Mar.–Nov.*

GOLF

◆ **Marriott's Seaview Golf Resort.** Thirty-six holes. Golf school. *Rte. 9, Absecon, NJ 08201; tel. 609-748-7680. On Reeds Bay, 6 mi. northwest of Atlantic City.*

◆ **Brigantine Golf Links.** Eighteen holes. *Roosevelt Blvd. and the Bay, Brigantine, NJ 08203; tel. 609-266-1388. Open daily. Admission.*

TENNIS

◆ **Atlantic Indoor Tennis.** One court, indoors and air-conditioned. *1225 W. Mill Rd., Northfield, NJ 08225; tel. 609-641-0372. Open daily. Admission. From Margate, take Rte. 563 across the channel to Northfield.*

◆ **Best Western Golf & Tennis World.** Three indoor courts and three outdoor Har-Tru courts, part of the 110-room Best Western Bayside Resort. *8029 Black Horse Pike, W. Atlantic City, NJ 08232; tel. 609-641-3546. Open daily. Admission. About 2 1/2 mi. from the boardwalk. Go west to the end of Pacific Ave., turn right onto Albany Ave., which becomes the Black Horse Pike.*

NATURE

◆ **Marine Mammal Stranding Center.** This center is part of a network that studies strandings and comes to the rescue whenever dolphins, whales, seals, and other sea life get into trouble. Founded in 1978, it handles scores of cases each year and maintains a recovery center as well as a museum. (The center was looking for a new home, so call first to confirm its location.) *Box 773, Brigantine, NJ 08203; tel. 609-266-0538. Open daily 11-5 Memorial Day-Labor Day and Sat.-Sun. 12-4 the rest of the year. Take the Brigantine Bridge (between Harrah's and Trump Castle) into Brigantine and continue 2 mi. on Brigantine Blvd.*

SAFETY TIPS

During stormy periods, the ocean along the boardwalk can develop rip currents that pull swimmers away from shore. During the hurricane-tainted summer of 1995, lifeguards had to rescue hundreds of swimmers. If you have any doubt about the conditions, ask a lifeguard.

Atlantic City's violent crime rate has dropped sharply in recent years, but as elsewhere in the state, nonviolent crime has risen, in part because of an unemployment rate that was about 14 percent in 1995. Violent crime usually takes place away from the boardwalk and does not involve visitors, but caution is in order. In the casino-rich atmosphere of losers, winners, and cash, there's always a scam or a theft unfolding somewhere.

TOURIST INFORMATION

◆ **Atlantic City Convention & Visitors Authority.** A tourist information center can also be found at Farley Plaza on the Atlantic City Expressway (tel. 609-965-6316). *2314 Pacific Ave., Atlantic City, NJ 08401; tel. 609-348-7100, 800-262-7395; fax 609-345-3685. Open Mon.-Fri. 9-5; open Sat. 9-5 for phone inquiries only.*

CHAPTER 14

Ocean City, NJ

Beauty	B
Swimming	B
Sand	B-
Hotels/Inns/B&Bs	B
House rentals	B+
Restaurants	B
Nightlife	C
Attractions	B
Shopping	C
Sports	B
Nature	A

*S*ince at least 1917, Ocean City, New Jersey, has billed itself as America's greatest family resort. This shore town ten miles south-west of Atlantic City is dry—no alcohol is sold, even in restaurants—and the formula has worked quite nicely in a place that got its start as a Methodist summer camp in the late 1800s.

The year-round population is more than 15,000, and during the peak season, mid-June through early September, that number swells to as many as 150,000. Part of the city's low-key character lies in its low-rise lodgings. Many vacationers stay in the stalwart three-story houses that were built early in the century and line many of the streets. There are almost no high-rises to overshadow the spacious eight-mile beach.

As on most barrier islands, getting around is easy. There are three routes leading onto the island, but they quickly hook into a simple grid laid out between the ocean and Egg Harbor Bay. The major north-south roads are West, Asbury, and Central avenues. The downtown area is toward the north, at about Asbury and Ninth, where City Hall is located.

But the heart of the resort beats at the city's two-and-a-half-mile boardwalk, in particular the portion between 5th and 15th streets, where most of the businesses are. The wooden walkway is packed with wholesome shops selling peanuts, saltwater taffy, fudge, burgers, pizza, lemonade, funnel cakes, pretzels, popcorn, frozen custard, and gifts. There's a movie theater, and a number of stores offer designer clothing and goods a cut above souvenir fare. Amusement rides, including a Ferris wheel and a water slide, front the boardwalk.

At Moorlyn Terrace, between 8th and 9th streets on the board-

HOW TO GET THERE

◆ From Philadelphia, Ocean City is about 1 1/4 hr. via the Atlantic City Expwy. and the Garden State Pkwy. From the Ben Franklin Bridge, follow Rte. 42 east until it becomes the Atlantic City Expwy. Then take the Garden State Pkwy. south to the first Ocean City exit.

◆ From New York, follow the Garden State Pkwy. south to the first Ocean City exit. In smooth traffic the drive takes about 2 1/4 hr.

◆ New Jersey Transit's bus route 319 leaves New York's Port Authority Bus Terminal and stops in Ocean City (tel. 215-569-3752).

walk, is the city's Music Pier, built in 1928 and considered the cultural centerpiece of the community. Performances of all kinds are staged here—dance, pageants, ballet, concerts by the Ocean City Pops Orchestra, and, occasionally, nationally known entertainers.

A number of professional athletes have owned homes in Ocean City, but the town's most enduring celebrity link is with the family of the late Grace Kelly, Princess of Monaco. The Kellys of Philadelphia summered in Ocean City, and to this day the family of Grace's sister Lizanne has property near the beach, just beyond the boardwalk.

The city is also known for a number of zany annual observances—including the Doo Dah Parade in April (lampooning the IRS), the Night in Venice Boat Parade in July, and the Miss Crustacean Hermit Crab Contest in August.

Starting in mid-June, trolleys run a loop from one end of town to the other (tel. 609-884-5230).

BEACHES

Many longtime visitors regard Ocean City's beach as the Jersey shore's best for gentle waves. Sand-replenishment programs keep the beach flush, but on occasion, vacationers renting homes near such projects have been affected by noise and obstructions: Ask if any replenishment is in the works before booking near the beach.

Beach badges are required from about mid-June through Labor Day. In recent years a season pass was $15; weekly, $6; and daily, $3. All are available at boardwalk booths, City Hall (9th St. and Asbury Ave.), or the Information Center (on the 9th St. Causeway).

Ocean City's beach front is long enough that its character varies considerably. *The beach runs the whole length of the city, with entry points at almost every perpendicular street.*

NORTH END

Near the boardwalk at 5th Street, the beach is narrower, with Wonderland Pier and its amusement rides close enough to exert a presence. Look north and the beach rises a bit, obstructing the view in that direction; from boardwalk

Beauty	C
Swimming	A
Sand	B
Amenities	A

level you can make out the Atlantic City casinos rising about ten miles away. From the sand looking south, you can see the Music Pier extending over the beach and the colorful boardwalk store fronts.

Swimming: Ocean waves break offshore, then glide in smoothly. Lifeguards on duty.

Sand: Fine and light tan, rising slightly to a fence-protected, scraggly dune just before the boardwalk.

Amenities: Rest rooms on the boardwalk at 6th Street and at the Music Pier at Moorlyn Terrace. Boardwalk vendors offer food and drinks.

Sports: Volleyball at 5th Street; surfing at 7th Street, fishing.

Parking: Municipal lot at 5th Street, street parking, and commercial lots.

SOUTH OF THE MUSIC PIER

At 12th Street, the beach is quite wide, with some pilings, jetties, and drainage pipes protruding into the water within sight. This section is near the heart of the boardwalk businesses and can be crowded in summer. Behind the board-

Beauty	B
Swimming	A
Sand	B
Amenities	A

walk rises the landmark Flanders Hotel, and to the south the ten-story, pink Port-O-Call Hotel is prominent. Also to the south, protruding over the water, is the Ocean City Fishing Club pier.

Swimming: Ocean waves break offshore, then glide in smoothly. Lifeguards on duty.

Sand: Fine and light tan, extending 100 yards or more at low tide to a fenced dune about three feet high along the boardwalk.

Amenities: Rest rooms on the boardwalk at the Music Pier and at 12th Street. Private shower facilities near the boardwalk at 13th Street.

Sports: Fishing.

Parking: Metered street parking and lots a short walk away.

SOUTH OF 21ST STREET

At about 15th Street, the boardwalk businesses drop off, although the board-walk continues south to 23rd Street. The beach grows considerably broader here and is less crowded in the summer. From the water's edge you can see the

Beauty	B
Swimming	A
Sand	B
Amenities	B-

boardwalk and beach panorama unfold to the north, while to the south the scene is simply surf, beach, boardwalk, and a long row of private two-story homes behind the beach as far as you can see. The beach is broad enough that the properties, mostly pastel with manicured backyards, are unobtrusive.

Swimming: Ocean waves break offshore, then glide in smoothly. Lifeguards on duty.

Sand: Fine and light tan, mixed with shells and pebbles near the boardwalk, stretching 150 yards or more at low tide from water's edge to a healthy, grass-topped dune about the height of the boardwalk.

Amenities: Few, away from the boardwalk. Rest rooms at 34th and 58th streets, private shower facilities at 34th Street near the beach. There is a cluster of eateries and other businesses a couple blocks west, within walking distance of the beach.

Sports: The beach at 29th Street is a designated sailboat put-in.

Parking: Street parking and commercial lots within walking distance.

HOTELS/INNS/B&BS

The city has a good range of motels, hotels, and B&Bs. The best-known hotel, the classic Flanders, was closed in May 1995, but the new owners say they plan to refurbish the hotel and reopen it (tel. 609-399-1000).

◆ **Port-O-Call Hotel** (expensive). This 100-room hotel on the boardwalk, among the city's biggest and tallest, is one of its nicest. Furnishings are standard but tasteful and well maintained. Ask for an upper room to get the best ocean views. Even the city-side views are excellent. *1510 Boardwalk, Ocean City, NJ 08226; tel. 609-399-8812, 800-334-4546. Take any of the island's north-south arteries to 16th St., from which you can see the 10-story hotel.*

◆ **New Brighton Inn** (moderate). This B&B is in a Queen Anne-style Victorian known as the "Marrying House" because its original occupant, a minister and Ocean City founding father, married hundreds of couples here. Decor includes antiques and period details. A third-floor room has a window seat and a cozy reading nook. Gourmet breakfasts are served on a sunny veranda. In-room AC and TV. Three blocks from the beach. *519 5th St., Ocean City, NJ 08226; tel. 609-399-2829. At Wesley Ave.,*

142

across from the Tabernacle grounds in the historic district.

◆ **Serendipity Bed & Breakfast** (moderate). This B&B offers six bedrooms, two with shared bath, nicely decorated in a shore-vacation motif of wicker and floral patterns. Rooms 4 and 5 are airy and spacious, with big, modern bathrooms. Room 5 is smaller and has a canopied bed and sheer rose curtains that give the room a rosy glow. AC and TV throughout. Innkeepers Clara and Bill Plowfield offer healthy breakfasts indoors or on a new veranda out back. From October through May, dinner is prepared by reservation. *712 9th St., Ocean City, NJ 08226; tel. 609-399-1554, 800-842-8544. 1/2 block from the boardwalk.*

HOUSE RENTALS

The city has a full range of rental properties, including bunga-lows, large homes bayside or oceanside, condos, and small and large complexes. A little place off the water might cost only $500 a week, whereas a five-bedroom on the ocean might go for up to $5,000. Seasonal rates range from $8,000 to $40,000.

◆ **Monihan Realty.** *3201 Central Ave., Ocean City, NJ 08226; tel. 609-399-0998, 800-255-0998. Open daily.*

◆ **Ocean City Board of Realtors.** The board publishes a list of its members. *405 22nd St., Ocean City, NJ 08226; tel. 609-399-0128; fax 609-399-2030.*

RESTAURANTS

Ocean City has a number of good restaurants, but the city's pro-hibition on alcohol makes it impossible to order wine with your meal. A lively and varied dining center has evolved across the 9th Street bridge in Somers Point, which has a number of large, festive restaurants and many smaller ones.

◆ **Cousin's Restaurant** (moderate). This local favorite offers fresh seafood, steaks, veal, pasta. *104 Asbury Ave., Ocean City, NJ 08226; tel. 609-399-9462, 800-286-1963. Open daily for dinner and 10-2 for Sun. brunch.*

◆ **The Crab Trap** (moderate). This harborside restaurant offers seafood, steak, and chicken dishes, including a popular seafood combo and lobster. *Broadway, Somers Point, NJ 08244; tel. 609-927-7377. Open daily for lunch and dinner. On the Somers Point circle.*

◆ **Chatterbox** (inexpensive). This longtime gathering spot—booths, tables, and a jukebox—serves a broad and basic diner menu of sandwiches, soups, chicken, steaks, and salads. A nostalgic mural of a student-packed soda fountain overlooks the dining room. The Fonz would feel at home. *9th St. and Central Ave., Ocean City, NJ 08226; tel. 609-399-0113. Open daily 24 hr. Memorial Day-Labor Day*

◆ **Luigi's** (inexpensive). This family-run restaurant has been in business since 1958, serving up pizza and Italian specials in a casual, booth-filled setting. *300 9th St., Ocean City, NJ 08226; tel. 609-399-4937. Open daily for lunch and dinner. It's on the right as you drive into town off the causeway.*

NIGHTLIFE

There's little nightlife beyond the boardwalk amusements and the Music Pier shows. People head across the causeway to Somers Point for a lively club and music scene, or to Atlantic City or the Wildwoods.

◆ **Anchorage Tavern.** Popular watering hole with two bars and several dining areas that appeal to all ages. *823 Bay Ave., Somers Point, NJ 08244; tel. 609-926-1778. Open daily.*

◆ **Brownie's By the Bay.** This dance club offers live music and DJs. *Bay Ave., Somers Point, NJ 08244; tel. 609-653-0030. Open daily.*

ATTRACTIONS

◆ **Historic District Walking Tour.** The city's historic district is bounded by 3rd and 9th streets from Atlantic to Central avenues. A 13-stop self-guided walking tour is described in a brochure from the Historic Preservation Commission that's available at the Chamber of Commerce Information Center. The brochure also has information on sites such as the Music Pier, City Hall, and the Flanders Hotel. *Box 157, Ocean City, NJ 08226; tel. 609-399-2629.*

◆ **Music Pier.** Year-round performances and exhibits, almost daily in summer. Call for a schedule of events. *Moorlyn Terrace and the Boardwalk, Ocean City, NJ 08226; tel. 609-525-9300. Between 8th and 9th Sts.*

◆ **Ocean City Historical Museum.** Founded in 1879, this museum includes Victorian furnishings and toys and items salvaged from the 1901 beaching of a four-masted barque at 17th Street. *17th St. and Simpson Ave., Ocean City, NJ 08226; tel. 609-399-1801. Open Mon.-Fri. 10-4 and Sat. 1-4 Jun.-Sep. and Tue.-Sat. 1-4 Oct.-May. In the Community Cultural Center.*

SHOPPING

Ocean City's shopping scene is sedate. Beachwear boutiques pepper the boardwalk, and the B&B Department Store is at 827 Asbury Avenue (tel. 609-391-0046). Atlantic City has more shopping, and there's a Macy's and other larger stores in Mays Landing, about 18 miles northwest of Ocean City.

BEST FOOD SHOPS

SANDWICHES: ◆ **Boyar's Sub and Grill.** *1338 Asbury Ave., Ocean City, NJ 08226; tel. 609-398-5466. Open daily.*

SEAFOOD: ◆ **Spadafora's Seafood Market.** *932 Haven Ave., Ocean City, NJ 08226; tel. 609-398-6703. Open daily in season. 1 block west of West Ave.*

ICE CREAM: ◆ **Tory's.** *3308 Asbury Ave., Ocean City, NJ 08226; tel. 609-391-7933. Open daily May-Sep. and Thu.-Sun. Oct.-Apr.*

BEVERAGES: ◆ **Acme Market.** *3428 Simpson Ave., Ocean City, NJ 08226; tel. 609-399-0546. Open daily.*

WINE: Alcohol sales are forbidden in Ocean City, so there are no liquor stores. A few minutes' drive across the 9th Street Causeway, at MacArthur Circle in Somers Point, Circle Liquor does a big business (tel. 609-927-2921). A cluster of large liquor stores is situated just off the island via 34th Street/Roosevelt Boulevard.

SPORTS

The Aquatic and Fitness Center is located in the city's Cultural and Community Center (18th St. and Simpson Ave., tel. 609-398-6900). Daily, weekly, and seasonal memberships are available, entitling members to fitness classes and use of the weight room and the six-lane, 25-meter pool.

FISHING

Surf fishing is permitted on nonbathing beaches, and there is a public fishing area on the Rush Chattin bridge between Ocean City and Strathmere. The Ocean City Fishing Club is at 14th Street and the beach (tel. 609-398-9800). Charter and party boats depart from numerous marinas along Great Egg Harbor Bay, including those along Bay Avenue in Ocean City, in Somers Point, and over the 34th Street bridge in Marmora.

◆ **Fin-Atics Marine Supply.** Marine supply and sportswear store has fishing and crabbing supplies. Rod-and-reel rentals. *1325 West Ave., Ocean City, NJ 08226; tel. 609-398-2248. Open daily.*

◆ **North Star.** Party boat offering four- and eight-hour daytime fishing trips, four-hour evening sails, and eight-hour overnight trips. *Palen Ave., Ocean City, NJ 08226; tel. 609-399-7588. Open daily. Between 9th and 10th Sts.*

BOATING

◆ **All Seasons Marina.** Power boat rentals for fishing, cruising, waterskiing. *551 Roosevelt Blvd., Marmora, NJ 08223; tel. 609-390-2516. Open year-round. Rentals May-Oct. Just over the 34th St. bridge.*

◆ **Waterfront Power Sports.** Power boat and Waverunner rentals. *312 Bay Ave., Ocean City, NJ 08226; tel. 609-926-1700. Open daily.*

SURFING

◆ **7th Street Surf Shop.** Surfing gear, clothing, skateboards. Surf reports (tel. 609-391-0041). The store also has a branch on the boardwalk (654 Boardwalk; tel. 609-391-1700). *654 Asbury Ave., Ocean City, NJ 08226; tel. 609-391-1700. Open daily. The designated surfing area is off 7th St. in Ocean City.*

BICYCLING

Numerous rental shops operate both on and off the boardwalk.

◆ **13th Street Bikes.** Bikes for children and adults, plus surrey rentals. *13th St. and the Boardwalk, Ocean City, NJ 08226; tel. 609-399-7121. Open Mar.-Nov.*

GOLF

◆ **Greate Bay Resort & Country Club.** An 18-hole, par-71 course. *901 Mays Landing Rd., Somers Point, NJ 08244; tel. 609-927-*

5071. Open year-round. Admission. Across the 9th St. bridge in Somers Point, 1/2 mi. down May's Landing Rd. on the right.

◆ **Ocean City Municipal Golf Course.** A par-3, 12-hole, 40-acre course. *26th St. and Bay Ave., Ocean City, NJ 08226; tel. 609-525-9233. Admission. Adjacent to the municipal airport, less than 1 mi. from the beach.*

TENNIS

◆ **Public courts.** Eight outdoor courts; pay fees at the clubhouse. *34th St. and Asbury Ave., Ocean City, NJ 08226; tel. 609-525-9294. Open daily. Admission. In Sand Castle Park.*

◆ **Public courts.** Courts outside the Sports & Civic Center. *6th St. and Atlantic Ave., Ocean City, NJ 08226; tel. 609-525-9307. Open daily. Admission.*

NATURE

Several cruise boat companies offer whale- and dolphin-watching trips.

◆ **Corson's Inlet State Park.** This designated nature area includes hiking trails, fishing, and a small boat launch. The Coastal Conservation Commission of Ocean City sponsors guided beach walks several times a week. *59th St. and Central Ave., Ocean City, NJ 08226; tel. 609-861-2404. Beach walks Tue. and Thu. at 9:30 and Wed. at 6:30 p.m. Jul.-Aug.; walks begin at the park entrance.*

TOURIST INFORMATION

◆ **Greater Ocean City Chamber of Commerce.** The chamber's main Information Center is on the causeway that becomes 9th Street. There also is an information office at the Music Pier on the boardwalk (tel. 609-525-9248) and an information window at City Hall (9th St. and Asbury Ave., tel. 609-399-6111). *Box 157, Ocean City, NJ 08226; tel. 609-399-2629, 800-232-2465. Open Mon.-Sat. 9-5 and Sun. 9-2 May-Sep. and Mon.-Sat. 10-5 and Sun. 10-2 Oct.-Apr. The causeway Information Center is on the right, 1 1/2 mi. from the Somers Point traffic circle, en route to Ocean City. If approaching from the opposite direction, a sign prohibits left turns into the parking lot, and violators are often ticketed in summer.*

◆ **Bed & Breakfast Guild.** This organization represents seven B&Bs, offering a brochure describing member properties. *401 Wesley Ave., Ocean City, NJ 08226; tel. 609-399-6071.*

CHAPTER 15

Sea Isle City

Beauty	B
Swimming	A
Sand	B
Hotels/Inns/B&Bs	B
House rentals	B
Restaurants	B
Nightlife	B
Attractions	B
Shopping	C
Sports	B
Nature	A

hen it was on the drawing board around 1879, Sea Isle City was envisioned as a city of canals and piazzas, fountains and public baths—a veritable Venice of the wetlands. A railroad was installed, the borough incorporated in 1882, and for a while it seemed as though it might outshine its booming neighbor to the north, Ocean City.

Alas, the railway washed out and heavy surf took

its toll on choice property. Sea Isle City never achieved its utopian promise, but it did flourish, and today its nearly 3,000 year-round residents shed no tears for piazzas unbuilt. They do, however, have a two-mile ocean-front Promenade and a secure reputation as a tranquil retreat.

The city covers most of Ludlam Island, one of the narrow barrier islands strung along the Jersey coast. Its population swells to 30,000 on hot summer weekends, absorbed by five miles of user-friendly ocean front and a compact central business district. Spend even a short time here and you're likely to hear testimony from families who have summered here for generations.

The southern mile or so of Sea Isle City is called Townsends Inlet, a section that enjoys its own cachet among regulars—something of a calm within the calm.

Sea Isle City shares its spit of quietude with tiny Strathmere at the northern tip, where the landmark Deauville Inn offers dining, drinking, entertainment, and a colorful history dating to bootlegging days.

BEACHES
Sea Isle City requires beach tags, although traditionally Wednesday has been a free day. The beach at Strathmere is free at all times.

HOW TO GET THERE
◆ From Philadelphia, Sea Isle City is less than 2 hr. via the Atlantic City Expwy. and the Garden State Pkwy. From the Ben Franklin Bridge, follow Rte. 42 east until it becomes the Atlantic City Expwy., then go south on the Garden State Pkwy. to the Sea Isle City exit.

◆ From New York, follow the Garden State Pkwy. south to the Sea Isle City exit.

◆ New Jersey Transit's bus route 315 leaves Philadelphia's Greyhound Bus Terminal and stops in Sea Isle City en route to Cape May (tel. 215-569-3752).

SEA ISLE CITY

The city's beach is long and pleasant with various backdrops, including boardwalk, beach houses, and inlet. From almost anywhere, the view up- and downshore on the medium-to-wide beach is a calm panorama of ocean,

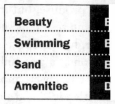

Beauty	E
Swimming	E
Sand	E
Amenities	D

sand, and low-rise homes. The Spinnaker condos, drab structures on the Promenade between 35th and 38th streets, loom like transplants from a megaresort. Near Townsends Inlet, around 91st Street, the beach is very wide, and there's a lot of water movement around the inlet. The tidal pools that collect here are great for kids to dabble in. Across the inlet, you can see Avalon to the south; to the north, you can make out Atlantic City. Moving north on the beach, jetties periodically protrude into the water. The beach near the Promenade is wide and flat, with waves breaking offshore in a long line before rolling in. *From Landis Ave., turn east to reach the beach.*

Swimming: Refreshing wave action. Lifeguard on duty.

Sand: Medium fine, light tan, rising to a low dune and, between 29th and 57th streets, the Promenade.

Amenities: Promenade businesses offer virtually everything you need. Rest rooms are at 33rd, 40th, and 44th streets on the Promenade and 85th Street at the beach.

Sports: Volleyball, limited surfing, body boarding.

Parking: Metered street parking.

STRATHMERE

Strathmere's allure is that what you see is what you get—unembellished beach, plain and simple. No beach badges, no bureaucracy, no amenities—something of an odd bird on the Jersey shore but much loved by those who know it. *From Ocean Dr., go east to reach the beach.*

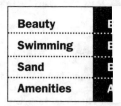

Beauty	E
Swimming	E
Sand	E
Amenities	A

Swimming: Refreshing wave action. No lifeguard.

Sand: Medium fine, light tan, rising to a low dune.

Amenities: No bathhouses or rest rooms. The town's few businesses are just off the beach.

Sports: None.

Parking: Limited street parking.

HOTELS/INNS/B&BS

◆ **Spinnaker Condominiums** (expensive). Built in the early 1970s, these two ten-story buildings are easily the island's biggest, housing 192 units, including about 60 that are on the rental market. All face the water and are individually furnished to their owners' tastes. Most are two bedrooms, a few three. Minimum rental is two weeks, and rentals are handled through any real-estate agent, not by the condo office. One agency that arranges rentals is Sea Winds Realty (26 38th St., Sea Isle City, NJ 08243; tel. 609-263-2390). *3500 Boardwalk, Sea Isle City, NJ 08243; tel. 609-263-6197. Entrance is off Landis Ave. or off the Boardwalk.*

◆ **The Colonnade Inn** (expensive). This remarkable 1890s inn, restored and redecorated in 1991, has something for everyone— B&B suites, B&B rooms, efficiency apartments—and handles up to 80 guests. The apartments are practically furnished; the suites are regal. The fourth-floor B&B rooms are tiny but deliciously cute. The top-of-the-line Golden Oaks Room has a king-size brass bed, a daybed alcove, antique dressers and tables, easy chair, love seat, fireplace, floral drapes, and Monet prints. The dark-wood sitting room is fit for Sherlock Holmes. *4600 Landis Ave., Sea Isle City, NJ 08243; tel. 609-263-0460. At 46th St.*

◆ **Sea Isle Inn** (expensive). Suites and efficiencies one block from the beach. *6400 Landis Ave., Sea Isle City, NJ 08243; tel. 609-263-4371.*

HOUSE RENTALS

◆ **Farina, Adgie & Boeshe Realtors.** *4315 Landis Ave., Sea Isle City, NJ 08243; tel. 609-263-2828, 800-213-2828. Open daily.*

◆ **Hoey Real Estate.** *27 JFK Blvd., Sea Isle City, NJ 08243; tel. 609-263-3006. Open daily.*

RESTAURANTS

◆ **Busch's** (moderate). This popular restaurant serves family-pleasing portions and is known for its seafood, particularly the she-crab soup (available only on certain days of the week). Many nights, there's entertainment on the menu too. *8700 Landis Ave., Sea Isle City, NJ 08243; tel. 609-263-8626. Open for dinner Fri.-Sun. mid-May-mid-Jun. and Tue.-Sun. mid-Jun.-Sep. South end of the island.*

◆ **Carmen's** (moderate). Open-air bayside seafood house that grew from a take-out shop to a local institution where shorts, T-shirts, and kids fit right in. *43rd St. & the Bay, Sea Isle City, NJ 08243; tel. 609 263-3471, 609-263-1634. Open daily for breakfast, lunch, and dinner Apr.-Oct.*

◆ **Garrity's Restaurant** (moderate). Long-time seafood and prime meat spot whose clientele has included former New Jersey Governor Jim Florio and the late Philadelphia Mayor Frank Rizzo. Stuffed shrimp is a specialty. Kids' menu, entertainment, and dancing. *85th St. & Landis Ave., Sea Isle City, NJ 08243; tel. 609-263-3164.*

NIGHTLIFE

The city and the tourism commission sponsor a "Concert Under the Stars" series of musical and other performances on Wednesday and Thursday evenings June through September on the Promenade at Kennedy Boulevard (tel. 609-263-8687).

◆ **Deauville Inn.** Landmark restaurant offers dancing and a variety of live music. *Willard Rd. at the Bay, Strathmere, NJ 08248; tel. 609-263-2080. Open daily. North end of the island.*

◆ **La Costa Motel & Cocktail Lounge.** Entertainment nightly in summer. *40th St. & Landis Ave., Sea Isle City, NJ 08243; tel. 609-263-3611. Open daily.*

◆ **Ocean Drive Lounge.** Also known as OD's, this club is a favorite of the rock crowd's. *40th & Landis Ave., Sea Isle City, NJ 08243; tel. 609-263-1000. Open nightly May-Sep. and weekends Mar.-Apr. and Oct.*

ATTRACTIONS

◆ **Fun City Amusement Park.** Rides, arcade, wheel games, snack bar, bumping boats. *33rd St. & the Boardwalk, Sea Isle City, NJ 08243; tel. 609-263-3862. Open daily late May-early Sep. Admission.*

SHOPPING

The city's shopping scene is beach-town basic—no designer outlets here. Stores are concentrated downtown at Kennedy

Boulevard and the Promenade and in the Spinnaker Seaside Shops between 35th and 38th streets on the Promenade.

BEST FOOD SHOPS

SANDWICHES: ◆ **Nickelby's.** *8301 Landis Ave., Sea Isle City, NJ 08243; tel. 609-263-1184. Open daily May-Sep. Townsends Inlet.*

SEAFOOD: ◆ **Mike's Fish & Seafood Market.** *4222 Park Rd., Sea Isle City, NJ 08243; tel. 609-263-3458. 2 blocks west of Landis Ave.*

BAKERY: ◆ **C Isle Bakery.** Breads and pastries. *4116 Landis Ave., Sea Isle City, NJ 08243; tel. 609-263-1888.*

ICE CREAM: ◆ **Yum-Yum Affair.** *31 JFK Blvd., Sea Isle City, NJ 08243; tel. 609-263-8578. Open daily Apr.-Oct.*

BEVERAGES: ◆ **Acme Market.** *63rd & Landis Ave., Sea Isle City, NJ 08243; tel. 609-263-9006. Open daily. South of the central business district.*

WINE: ◆ **Diamond's Liquor Store.** *4009 Landis Ave., Sea Isle City, NJ 08243; tel. 609-263-8411. Open daily.*

SPORTS
FISHING

◆ *Starfish.* This party boat offers daytime, evening, and night-time fishing excursions. *42nd St. & the Bay, Sea Isle City, NJ 08243; tel. 609-263-3800. Open daily. Day-trips depart at 8 and 1, evening trips Wed. and Fri.-Mon. at 6, and night trips Fri.-Sat. at 7.*

BOATING

Boating activities are based at the city marina at the bay end of 42nd Place (tel. 609-263-0009).

◆ **Sea Isle Water Sports Center.** Rents Waverunners, kayaks, and Sun Kat motorized lounge chairs. *329 43rd Pl., Sea Isle City, NJ 08243; tel. 609-263-9100. Open daily. At the causeway.*

◆ **Vitiello's Boat Rental.** Full- and half-day rentals of motorized fishing and crabbing boats. Speed boats rented by the hour and half-hour. Fishing and crabbing supplies. *317 43rd St., Sea Isle City, NJ 08243; tel. 609-263-7444. Open daily Apr.-Sep.*

SURFING

◆ **Heritage Surf & Sport.** Surfboard sales and rentals. Belly boards, wet suits, swimwear, and accessories. Surfing lessons and surf reports. *37th St. & Landis Ave., Sea Isle City, NJ 08243; tel. 609-263-3033. Open daily.*

BICYCLING

◆ **Vince's Bikes.** Cruiser and all-terrain bike rentals by the hour, day, or week, plus surreys and Rollerblades. *JFK & Pleasure Blvds., Sea Isle City, NJ 08243; tel. 609-263-3186. Open daily May-Sep.*

GOLF

There is no course on the island but several are within half an hour's drive, including the Ocean City Golf Club, the Greate Bay Country Club at Somer's Point, and the Avalon Golf Club (*see* Chapters 14 and 16, Ocean City and Stone Harbor).

TENNIS

◆ **Sea Isle City Recreation.** Lighted public courts at Dealy Field are $8 an hour on weekdays before 1 p.m. and on weekends. Reservations must be made in person with the attendant no more than two days in advance. Free play Monday through Friday after 1 p.m. *63rd St. & Central Ave., Sea Isle City, NJ 08243; tel. 609-263-6163. Open daily.*

NATURE

◆ **Beachcomber Walks.** Guided tours of the beach focusing on shells, birds, and tides. Participants also share what they've found on the beach in a "shell and tell" session. *29th St. & the Beach, Sea Isle City, NJ 08243. Tours Tue. and Thu. Admission. Walks start at the 29th St. beach.*

◆ *Cruis'n One.* Tour boat offers dolphin-watching, sunset nature cruises, and morning sightseeing and moonlight cruises. *42nd St. & the Bay, Sea Isle City, NJ 08243; tel. 609-263-1633, 800-278-4761. Departures daily mid-Jun.-mid-Sep. Admission.*

TOURIST INFORMATION

◆ **Sea Isle City Tourism Commission.** Brochures and tourist information are available daily May through September at the Beach Badge Office (125 Kennedy Blvd. near Landis Ave.; tel. 609-263-1771). The Tourism Commission also has information. *121 42nd St., Second Fl., Box 622, Sea Isle City, NJ 08243; tel. 609-263-8687. Open Mon.-Fri. 9-5.*

CHAPTER 16

Stone Harbor

Beauty	B
Swimming	A
Sand	B
Hotels/Inns/B&Bs	B
House rentals	B
Restaurants	B
Nightlife	C
Attractions	C
Shopping	B
Sports	B
Nature	A

*M*ore than most South Jersey barrier island communities, Stone Harbor projects an atmosphere of ordered gentility, with row after row of handsome contemporary houses and a trim business district whose stores offer above-average shopping. That orderliness extends a few blocks east to the three-mile beach, its dunes fortified by tidy bulkheads and a shoreline segmented by jetties that more or less keep the sand and surf in compliance with the town's wishes.

Most of the island is just three blocks wide, with First Avenue running closest to the ocean beach. Third Avenue, also known as Ocean Drive, crosses from north to south, intersecting the flower-bedecked business district at 96th Street (which, going west, becomes Stone Harbor Boulevard and leads across Great Bay to the Wetlands Institute and the Garden State Parkway).

The beach is uniformly straight, while on the west side the island has a contorted shoreline of no less than eight bays, basins, and harbors that beckon boaters on the Intracoastal Waterway.

Both Stone Harbor, with about 1,100 year-round residents, and its northern neighbor, Avalon, with about 2,000, have a sedate and upscale flavor—you won't find any group houses filled with yelping twentysomethings. The communities also have strong links to environmentalism.

In 1969 the World Wildlife Fund met in Stone Harbor to address the threat to marshes and tidelands brought by the area's development in the 1960s. The conference, attended by Charles Lindbergh, led to the founding of the Wetlands Institute, an environmental study center that runs a museum and educational programs.

At its south end, Stone Harbor has a bird sanctuary for

HOW TO GET THERE

◆ From Philadelphia, Stone Harbor is less than 2 hr. via the Atlantic City Expwy. and the Garden State Pkwy. From the Ben Franklin Bridge, follow Rte. 42 east until it becomes the Atlantic City Expwy., then go south on the Garden State Pkwy. to the Stone Harbor exit.

◆ From New York, follow the Garden State Pkwy. south to the Stone Harbor exit.

◆ New Jersey Transit's bus route 315 leaves Philadelphia's Greyhound Terminal and stops in Stone Harbor en route to Cape May (tel. 215-569-3752).

herons, egrets, and ibis, and Avalon has a bird area as well. Avalon is also known as the town that posted "turtle crossing" signs in an effort to spare diamondback terrapins along Ocean Drive. Another program salvaged eggs from stricken turtles, incubated them, and returned the hatchlings to the water.

BEACHES

Avalon and Stone Harbor are connected by Seven Mile Beach and recognize each other's beach badges.

STONE HARBOR

The beach runs north-south for about 42 blocks. Near the southern end, at 111th Street, it's backed by upscale, mostly two-story homes that are just behind a dune neatly buttressed by wooden walls and reinforced with jetty

Beauty	B
Swimming	B
Sand	B
Amenities	C

stones. The large estate rising just south of 111th Street is Villa Maria by the Sea, a convent. To the north, the beach is partitioned by jetties every few blocks, and at 101st Street there's a small public gazebo.

While the whole beach is good, the blocks between 80th and 83rd streets are most scenic, with no structures rising behind this relatively wide stretch. A well-maintained dune is high enough to block the view of the parking area and the adjoining park. A few low-rise motels are to the north, and homes continue up the coastline, but they intrude little on the beach. *From Ocean Dr. (also known as Third Ave.), follow almost any street east to the beach.*

Swimming: Good. Water is sometimes serene, with waves that rise close to shore and fold gently. Swimming tags needed. Lifeguard on duty.

Sand: Fine, light tan, rising to a well-maintained dune.

Amenities: Rest rooms at 96th and 122nd Streets. Downtown businesses west on 96th Street.

Sports: Volleyball at 81st Street.

Parking: Each beach block has a handful of diagonal spaces. Parking for more than 100 cars at 83rd Street and First Avenue.

157

AVALON

This wide beach has an undeveloped atmosphere. Beach homes and the boardwalk rise behind it, but the boardwalk is noncommercial, and the beach is big enough that the houses don't intrude. The beach is busiest in the blocks

Beauty	B
Swimming	B
Sand	B
Amenities	B

on either side of 30th Street, which is where the town's community center and a big parking lot are located.

From the beach at 28th Street, the view north is all wide sand, with beach houses hunkering behind the dune. In the other direction, through the timbers of a long fishing pier, the shoreline arcs south past Stone Harbor until it fades from sight in the beach haze. *From Ocean Dr. (known in Avalon as Third Ave.), turn east for 3 long blocks.*
Swimming: Good, with waves that break about 50 yards out, then roll a few times before gliding smoothly onto a gently sloping beach. Beach tags required. Lifeguard on duty.
Sand: Fine, light tan, strewn with shells and dune grass in places, rising to a medium dune.
Amenities: Rest rooms at the community hall near the boardwalk at 30th Street. On the boardwalk at 30th is a cluster of shops (ice cream, beachwear, and arcades) and Terranova's, a second-floor pasta and seafood restaurant overlooking the water.
Sports: Surfing at 30th Street, rafting and catamarans at designated beaches.
Parking: Big lot at 30th Street.

HOTELS/INNS/B&BS

Most motels on the island are clustered near the Stone Harbor-Avalon borough line, around 80th Street, on or within two blocks of the beach.
◆ **Golden Inn** (expensive). One of the few lodgings open year-round, this hotel has a restaurant and a lounge. *7849 Dune Dr., Avalon, NJ 08202; tel. 609-368-5155.*
◆ **Avalon Inn** (moderate). This 44-room hotel offers modern accommodations with AC, TV, heated and kiddie pools, sun decks, and patio. *Dune Dr. at 79th St., Avalon, NJ 08202; tel. 609-368-1543, 800-452-8256. Closed Nov.-Mar. and Sun.-Thu. Oct.*
◆ **Windrift** (moderate). This motel has a prime location on the

158

beach, across from the park tennis courts. Restaurant and lounge, with nightly music and dancing. *Ocean front at 79th St., Avalon, NJ 08202; tel. 609-368-5175, 800-453-7438. Closed Nov.-Mar. and Sun.-Thu. Mar.-mid-May and Oct.*

◆ **The Sea Lark** (inexpensive). Avalon's only B&B has seven guest rooms, four with private bath. A new, air-conditioned one-bedroom apartment on the third floor, the Artists' Loft, features original art. Other rooms have ceiling fans only and are individually furnished with early-American antiques. Breakfast is served on the wraparound porch. Room 1, the most popular, has a private entrance. *3018 First Ave., Avalon, NJ 08202; tel. 609-967-5647. Open. Mar.-early Jan. and weekends Jan.-Feb.*

HOUSE RENTALS

The island has many houses and other units for rent—most available by the week. A one- or two-bedroom house can rent for as little as $600, while a big, place on the water could cost $6,000 plus.

◆ **Avalon Real Estate Agency.** *30th St, at Dune Dr., Box 10, Avalon, NJ 08202; tel. 609-967-3001. Open daily.*

◆ **Coldwell Banker/James C. Otton Real Estate.** *2825 Dune Dr., Box 325, Avalon, NJ 08202; tel. 609-368-2156, 800-355-9990, 800-220-4004. Open daily.*

RESTAURANTS

◆ **Mimi's Amore** (expensive). This one-room restaurant boasts that it offers "gourmet dining without the gourmet price," and the dining experience is convincing. An upscale ambience is matched by dishes such as Chicken Georgia (chicken breasts topped with walnuts, fresh peaches, and a cream-peach sauce). Desserts are made on the premises. Plank walls are decorated with wicker baskets and copper dessert molds. BYOB. *330 96th St., Stone Harbor, NJ 08247; tel. 609-368-5800. Open daily for dinner.*

◆ **Fish Tales** (moderate). This one-room seafood restaurant seats 48 and is decorated with colorful paintings. Owner-chef Gregory Biederman changes the menu periodically, offering such dishes as red snapper stuffed with shrimp mousse. The bouillabaisse is also popular. No liquor license, so BYOB. *99th St. at Third Ave., Stone Harbor, NJ 08247; tel. 609-967-3100. Open daily for dinner Jun.-Oct. and Thu.-*

Sun. Apr.-May and Nov.-Dec. Across from St. Paul's Catholic Church.

◆ **Marabella's Seafood House** (moderate). Marabella's has both a seafood restaurant and an Italian restaurant, located next to each other and both spawned by the hugely successful eatery of the same name in Philadelphia. They're known for "designer dishes," grilled foods, and inventive selections that delight grazers. *2409 Dune Dr., Avalon, NJ 08202; tel. 609-368-3352. Open daily for dinner May.-Nov. and Wed.-Sun. the rest of the year. The Seafood House is at 24th St. and Dune Dr.; the Italian restaurant is at 25th St. and Dune Dr.*

◆ **Terranova's** (moderate). At first sight, it's tempting to dismiss this restaurant perched above the Avalon boardwalk as just another sandwich shop, but the food is splendid. It's named for the owner-chef's ancestral home town in southern Italy. The family recipes on parade here include the chef's signature *zuppa di pesce*, chicken *scapparelle*, and a killer chocolate ravioli dessert. BYOB. *Boardwalk and 29th St., Avalon, NJ 08202; tel. 609-368-4500. Open daily for dinner and Sat.-Sun. for breakfast. Above the cluster of boardwalk shops near the Avalon community center.*

NIGHTLIFE

Nightlife revolves around a few clubs, including lounges in the Windrift and the Golden Inn (*see* "Hotels/Inns/B&Bs").

◆ **Fred's Tavern.** Live music on weekends. *314 96th St., Stone Harbor, NJ 08247; tel. 609-368-5591. Open daily.*

◆ **Henny's Driftwood Dining Room.** Live music or karaoke on weekends in season. *9628 Third Ave., Stone Harbor, NJ 08247; tel. 609-368-2929. Open Tue.-Sun. Mar.-Dec. and Thu.-Sun. Feb.*

SHOPPING

Stone Harbor has a good choice of stores on its downtown shopping strip, including Pappagallo, Island Girl, the Happy Hunt, and Eagles Eye Company Store.

BEST FOOD SHOPS

SANDWICHES: ◆ **Shore Bites.** *9500 Third Ave., Stone Harbor, NJ 08247; tel. 609-368-2323. Open daily.*

FRESH PRODUCE: ◆ **Grandpa's Produce.** *Harbor Square Mall, Stone Harbor, NJ 08247; tel. 609-967-5252. Open daily Memorial*

Day-Labor Day. In the open mall on 96th and 97th Sts. downtown.
BAKERY: ◆ The Bread & Cheese Cupboard. *246 96th St., Stone Harbor, NJ 08247; tel. 609-368-1135. Open daily May-Oct. Also another location in Avalon (3254 Dune Dr.; tel. 609-967-5335).*
ICE CREAM: ◆ Springer's Homemade Ice Cream. *9420 Third Ave., Stone Harbor, NJ 08247; tel. 609-368-4631. Open daily.*
WINE: ◆ Fred's Liquor Stores. *314 96th St., Stone Harbor, NJ 08247; tel. 609-368-5591. Open daily. Fred's also has a store in Avalon (2258 Dune Dr.; tel. 609-967-4121).*

SPORTS
FISHING
◆ Smugglers Cove. Fishing-boat rentals, bait-and-tackle shop, marine supplies. *370 83rd St., Stone Harbor, NJ 08247; tel. 609-368-1700. Open daily. At the floating docks across from the public boat ramp.*

BOATING
An attended boat-launching ramp is located at 81st Street and the bay, and catamaran sailors can launch from the beach south of 122nd Street with a permit from the borough clerk.
◆ Avalon Anchorage Marina. Boat rentals for fishing, crabbing, sightseeing. Individual, group, and custom charters. *885 21st St. and the Bay, Avalon, NJ 08202; tel. 609-967-3592. Open daily.*
◆ Island Watersports. Rentals of Sunfish, Windsurfers, Waverunners. *97th St. and the Bay, Stone Harbor, NJ 08247; tel. 609-368-6114. Open daily. There's also a location in Avalon (tel. 609-967-5466).*

SURFING
◆ Faria's. Rentals of surfboards, body boards, wet suits. *3246 Dune Dr., Avalon, NJ 08202; tel. 609-368-0400. Open daily.*

BICYCLING
◆ Harbor Bike & Beach Shop. Rentals, sales, and service. *9828 Third Ave., Stone Harbor, NJ 08247; tel. 609-368-3691. Open daily Apr.-Nov. and Sat.-Sun. Dec.-Mar.*

GOLF
◆ Avalon Golf Club & Driving Range. An 18-hole course; public

driving range next door. *1510 Rte. 9 N., Swainton, NJ 08210; tel. 609-465-4653. Open daily. Admission. Across the bay from Avalon.*

TENNIS

◆ **Avalon Public Tennis Courts.** Six outdoor courts ($12 per hour or $16 for 90 minutes; half price early afternoon on week-days. *Avalon Recreation Dept., tel. 609-967-3066. Open daily. Admission. At Second Ave. and 7th St.*

◆ **Stone Harbor Public Tennis Courts.** Eleven tennis courts at 82nd Street and Second Avenue (tel. 609-368-1210) and five at 97th Street and Second Avenue (tel. 609-368-1287). An extensive lessons program is offered in summer. *Tel. 609-368-1210. Open daily. Admission.*

NATURE

◆ **Stone Harbor Bird Sanctuary.** Said to be the only municipally operated bird sanctuary in the country, this refuge has herons, egrets, ibis, and many other species. *c/o Borough of Stone Harbor, 9508 Second Ave., Stone Harbor, NJ 08247; tel. 609-368-5102. Between 111th and 116th Sts. and Second and Third Aves.*

◆ **Wetlands Institute and Museum.** Surrounded by wetlands, the institute offers educational exhibits, bird-watching, trails, an observation tower, marsh walks, and a gift shop. Each September it sponsors the Wings 'n' Water Festival. *1075 Stone Harbor Blvd., Stone Harbor, NJ 08247; tel. 609-368-1211. Open Mon.-Sat. 9:30-4:30 mid-May-Sep. and Tue.-Sat. 9:30-4:30 Oct.-early May. Between the Garden State Pkwy. and the island.*

TOURIST INFORMATION

◆ **Avalon Chamber of Commerce.** The chamber operates an information center. *30th St. and Ocean Dr., Avalon, NJ 08202; tel. 609-967-3936. Open daily May-Oct.*

◆ **Stone Harbor Chamber of Commerce.** Booklets, maps, brochures available at chamber offices. *212 96th St., Stone Harbor, NJ 08247; tel. 609-368-6101. Open year-round for phone and mail inquiries. Walk-in office open daily 10-2 and 4-9 Jun.-Oct. and weekends in May. Near the water tower.*

CHAPTER 17

The Wildwoods

Beauty	B
Swimming	A
Sand	B+
Hotels/Inns/B&Bs	A
House rentals	A
Restaurants	B+
Nightlife	B+
Attractions	B
Shopping	B
Sports	B
Nature	B

The five miles of beach lining North Wildwood, Wildwood, and Wildwood Crest are the widest in New Jersey—among the widest in the whole Middle Atlantic—and the colorful frenzy of boardwalk life is celebrated here with great gusto. The three resort towns share the umbrella of The Wildwoods and, like nowhere else in South Jersey, are synonymous with summer fun for the young and the young at heart.

While Wildwood Crest, a dry town with a family bent, has a tamer personality, North Wildwood and Wildwood share a two-and-a-half-mile boardwalk and a freewheeling reputation that has recently undergone some rewriting.

In the 1960s, Bobby Rydell sang, "Oh those Wildwood days. Wild, wild Wildwood days. Every day's a holiday, and every night is Saturday night." The song found a ready audience in his home town of Philadelphia, less than two hours away, and for decades high schoolers have made Wildwood part of their rite of passage. For about three weeks each June, new graduates celebrate "seniors week"—a farewell to childhood with a post-graduation fling.

While the tradition continues, it's been tempered in recent years as officials crack down on underage drinking and try to cultivate a more wholesome image.

North Wildwood has passed laws limiting tattoo parlors and the display of T-shirts with raw messages in boardwalk storefronts. Wildwood, meanwhile, wants to open a Native American casino—under the aegis of a Delaware Indian tribe that was driven out of the area in the late 1800s. That effort is expected to meet opposition from Atlantic City.

The Swedish fishermen who worked these waters before 1880 would be amazed at the amusement piers with water slide

HOW TO GET THERE

◆ From Philadelphia, the Wildwoods are about a 95-min. drive. From the Ben Franklin Bridge, follow Rte. 42 east until it becomes the Atlantic City Expwy., then go south on the Garden State Pkwy. to Exit 6 for N. Wildwood or Exit 4B for Wildwood and Wildwood Crest.

◆ From New York, follow the Garden State Pkwy. south to the Wildwood exits.

◆ New Jersey Transit's daily bus route 319 from New York City's Port Authority Bus Terminal stops in Wildwood (tel. 215-569-3752).

and roller coaster silhouettes etched high against the sky. But they would be right at home with the deep-sea and surf fishing.

Wildwood was named for the wild, wind-gnarled trees that line the beach, but somehow these specimens have become less typical of the resort than the artificial palm trees that inhabit the hotel parking lots and entrances. In the blocks that parallel the water front, hundreds of low-rise motels and hotels simulate tropical resorts with ersatz palms and pastel paint jobs. Along the water front are some larger hotels, but unlike Miami Beach, this is no high-rise heaven.

When filled to capacity, the Wildwoods are a happening place indeed. The range of restaurants, night clubs, and hotels makes this an attractive destination. When all is said and done, though, the most stunning draw is the beach—in places the length of three football fields from boardwalk to surf line. For many visitors, it becomes the beach against which they measure all others.

BEACHES

The Wildwoods don't require beach badges, and there are plenty of public rest rooms.

NORTH WILDWOOD

There are ten blocks of boardwalk in North Wildwood, and the entertainment piers there loom distractingly—or enticingly, for some—over the beach. But north of those piers is some of the most delicious ocean front in the

Beauty	A
Swimming	A
Sand	B+
Amenities	B

Middle Atlantic. Not only is the beach immense at 13th Avenue, stretching hundreds of yards to the sea, but it's backed by a double line of dunes: one thick and heavily covered with tall grass and shrubs, the other broken yet towering, reminiscent of a Badlands butte. They possess a wind-swept wildness that may come as a surprise in a place so thoroughly developed.

Looking south from this beach you see the amusement piers and, beyond them, the continuing sweep of Wildwood's big beach. Look to the north and the view is almost totally beach, sea, and dunes. Ironically, many people avoid this stretch because it takes several minutes of walking to reach, parking isn't as convenient, and it doesn't have the nearby amenities that the boardwalk offers. *From Ocean Dr., turn east on any avenue from 2nd to 26th.*

Swimming: Ocean waves break about 100 yards out in a long line, then several times before rolling in smoothly. Lifeguard on duty.

Sand: Fine, light tan, stretching hundreds of yards back to the bulwarklike dune along JFK Beach Drive.

Amenities: The boardwalk begins at 16th Avenue. North of that, there are no amenities, although in summer a tram along JFK Beach Drive connects with the boardwalk.

Sports: Surfing in designated areas, Boogie boarding, volleyball in designated areas, fishing.

Parking: Metered parking along JFK Beach Drive and elsewhere and many commercial lots.

WILDWOOD

Wildwood's beach is humongous. When you step off the boardwalk, this sweeping expanse of sand would seem like a desert if it weren't for that ocean. The piers interrupt the view, but from near the Civic Center the vista south is

Beauty	B+
Swimming	A
Sand	A
Amenities	A

especially impressive because there are no piers in adjacent Wildwood Crest. Although there are many motels within sight, once you've walked several minutes to get to the water's edge, their presence fades. *From any north-south road in town, turn east to reach the beach.*

Swimming: Ocean waves break about 100 yards out in a long line, then several times before rolling in smoothly. Lifeguard on duty.

Sand: Fine, light tan, stretching 300 yards or more to the boardwalk.

Amenities: Everything you need is on the boardwalk, including the information booth and rest rooms in the 3600 block (Lincoln Avenue). Showers for a fee at the boardwalk and Poplar, Baker and Ocean avenues.

Sports: Boogie boarding, volleyball in designated areas.

Parking: Municipal and private lots line Ocean Avenue along the boardwalk.

WILDWOOD CREST

Wildwood Crest's beach begins where the Wildwood boardwalk ends, narrowing somewhat but remaining wide. There's no boardwalk traffic, but three- to six-story motels back the beach in a somewhat helter-skelter line.

Beauty	B+
Swimming	A
Sand	A
Amenities	B

The sand extends for 150 yards or more, rising slightly to form irregular dunes a few feet high in front of the motels. Just north of the beach patrol headquarters at Rambler Road is a nice section of larger dunes that is part of a dune grass project administered by the city and the Crest Memorial School Class of 1997. These dunes occupy an undeveloped area several blocks wide and afford a break in the continuous line of motels and boardwalk. *From any north-south road in town, turn east to reach the beach.*

Swimming: Ocean waves break about 100 yards out in a long line, then break several times before rolling in smoothly. Lifeguard on duty.

Sand: Fine, light tan, stretching back to low dunes.

Amenities: Hotels and other businesses are a short walk from the beach. Rest rooms at Rambler Road. No boardwalk.

Sports: Surfing and Boogie boarding in designated areas.

Parking: Commercial lots and street parking near Ocean Avenue.

HOTELS/INNS/B&BS

The Wildwoods have more hotels, motels, cottages, B&Bs, and other lodgings than any city in New Jersey. The Greater Wildwood Hotel-Motel Association publishes a 200-page lodging guide, available for $3.50 (Box 184, Dept. D, Wildwood, NJ 08260).

◆ **Montego Bay** (expensive). With a spring 1996 opening, this hotel is one of the area's newest, offering all two-room suites with full kitchens, private ocean-front balconies, heated pool, and laundry. On the boardwalk. *1800 Boardwalk, N. Wildwood, NJ 08260; tel. 609-523-1000, 800-962-1349.*

◆ **Port Royal Hotel** (expensive). This large white hotel sits perpendicular to the water, so most of the balconies have views up or down the beach. *6801 Ocean Ave., Wildwood Crest, NJ 08260; tel. 609-729-2000. Open Mother's Day-Columbus Day.*

◆ **The Craig House** (moderate). This 13-room British B&B in a 1902 Victorian home has a mix of rooms on three floors, each with a differing theme and decor. Most popular is the Scottish Room, in a turret with five windows. Operators Doreen and Alex McKechnie, who hail from England and Scotland, are very friendly and keep the place spotless. Home baking. Two blocks from the boardwalk in a family part of town. *2704 Atlantic Ave., Wildwood, NJ 08260; tel. 609-522-8140. Between Juniper and Poplar Aves.*

HOUSE RENTALS

While motels dominate the main drags, the area also has many homes, apartments, cottages, and condos for rent by the week, month, or season. Prices range from $400 a week for a one-bedroom off the water to $2,000 a week for a three-bedroom ocean-front unit.

◆ **Calloway Realty.** *7601 Pacific Ave., Wildwood Crest, NJ 08260; tel. 609-522-7777. Open daily.*

◆ **Hoffman Agency.** *6301 Pacific Ave., Wildwood Crest, NJ 08260; tel. 609-522-8177, 800-999-8177. Open daily.*

RESTAURANTS

◆ **Captain's Table** (moderate). This ocean-front restaurant has, predictably, a nautical decor, with fine views and family dining. *Hollywood Ave. & the Beach, Wildwood Crest, NJ 08260; tel. 609-522-0325. Open daily for breakfast, lunch, and dinner.*

◆ **Garfield's Giardino Ristorante** (moderate). Seafood, pasta, chicken, and veal round out the menu. Among the popular dishes are the orange roughy topped with scallops, sun-dried tomatoes, and capers and the chicken saltambucca. *3800 Pacific Ave. Mall, Wildwood, NJ 08260; tel. 609-729-0120. Open daily for dinner Apr.-Nov. and Thu.-Mon. Dec.-Mar. In the Holly Beach Mall.*

◆ **Russo's** (moderate). This well-established restaurant offers Italian fare and seafood. *4415 Park Blvd., Wildwood, NJ 08260;*

tel. 609-522-7038. Open daily for dinner.

◆ **Two Mile Inn and Crab House** (moderate). These water-front establishments offer seafood and steaks with a view. *Box 1528, Wildwood Crest, NJ 08260; tel. 609-522-1341. Open daily for lunch and dinner Apr.-Nov. On Ocean Dr. between Wildwood Crest and Cape May.*

NIGHTLIFE

◆ *Delta Lady* **Inland Cruises.** Banjo cruises in a variety of musical styles, including Dixieland, country, fifties, rock, and show tunes. Reservations suggested. *Wildwood Marina, Wildwood, NJ 08260; tel. 609-522-1919. Cruises daily at 10:30 and 2 and nightly at 7 and 10 May-Sep. Admission. At Rio Grande and Susquehanna Aves., near the Boat House Restaurant.*

◆ **Seasons Restaurant & Lounge.** The lounge offers DJ, music, dancing, karaoke, and other entertainment. *222 E. Schellenger Ave., Wildwood, NJ 08260; tel. 609-522-4400. Opens daily at 3.*

◆ **The Playpen.** Sprawling club offers a range of live bands and other acts. *3400 Pacific Ave., Wildwood, NJ 08260; tel. 609-729-3566.*

ATTRACTIONS

The area is a hotbed of arcades, go karts, batting cages, and other family amusements.

◆ *Delta Lady* **Inland Cruises.** Paddlewheel replica departs on regular sightseeing cruises to the inland waterways of Cape May County, Cape May Canal, bird and wildlife sanctuaries, marinas, and other points of interest (for more information, *see* listing under "Nightlife," above).

◆ **George S. Boyer Museum.** This museum has exhibits on the history of the Wildwoods and houses the National Marbles Hall of Fame. Admission is free. *3907 Pacific Ave., Wildwood, NJ 08260; tel. 609-523-0277. Open Mon.-Fri. 9:30-2:30 and Sat.-Sun. 10:30-2:30 May-Sep.; open Thu.-Sun. 10:30-2:30 the rest of the year. In the Holly Beach Mall.*

◆ **Hereford Inlet Lighthouse.** This 1874 lighthouse, which resembles a large, red-roofed house more than it does a typical lighthouse tower, is open for tours. It also contains the North Wildwood information center. *154 Central Ave., N. Wildwood,*

NJ 08260; tel. 609-522-4520. Open daily in summer and weekends in winter. At 1st and Central Aves. in N. Wildwood.

◆ **Mariner's Landing.** This big amusement pier includes a giant 40-car Ferris wheel, the Sea Serpent roller coaster, a 1,200-foot monorail, a carousel, a water park, and many other rides. *Schellenger & the Boardwalk, Wildwood, NJ 08260; tel. 609-729-0586. Open daily Memorial Day-Labor Day and weekends Apr.-May and Sep.*

◆ **Morey's Pier.** This amusement pier has dozens of rides and amusements, including a 60-mph roller coaster, log flumes, and a carousel. *25th Ave. & the Boardwalk, N. Wildwood, NJ 08260; tel. 609-522-5477. Open daily Memorial Day-Labor Day and weekends Apr.-May and Sep. Admission.*

BEST FOOD SHOPS

SEAFOOD: Many vacation home renters shop for seafood at the Lobster House Fish Market in Cape May (tel. 609-884-3064). (For more information, *see* Chapter 18, Cape May).

BAKERY: ◆ **Twenty-sixth Street Bakery.** *2600 New York Ave., Wildwood, NJ 08260; tel. 609-729-2611. Open Mar.-Dec.*

ICE CREAM: ◆ **Sea Shell Ice Cream.** *300 E. Rio Grande Ave., Wildwood, NJ 08260; tel. 609-522-7822. Open daily May-Oct.*

WINE: ◆ **Green's Liquor Store.** *5301 Pacific Ave., Wildwood, NJ 08260; tel. 609-522-9463. Open daily.*

SPORTS
FISHING

◆ *Sea Raider.* Party boat offers six-hour deep-sea fishing trips for flounder, weakfish, sea bass. *Wildwood Fishing Center, Wildwood, NJ 08260; tel. 609-522-1032. Daily sailings at 10 a.m. May-Oct. At Rio Grande and Susquehanna Aves.*

BOATING

◆ **Kayak Rentals.** One- and two-passenger kayaks; canopy boats also available for fishing, crabbing, sightseeing. *18th and Delaware Aves., N. Wildwood, NJ 08260; tel. 609-522-7676. Open daily.*

◆ **Mocean Water Safaris.** Rentals of jet, pontoon, and water-skiing boats, Sun Kats, Waverunners, and Jet Skis. *560 W. Rio Grande Ave., Wildwood, NJ 08260; tel. 609-522-3017. Open daily.*

At the foot of the George Reading Bridge, between Urie's and the Boat House restaurants.

◆ **Ocean Water Sports.** Waverunner rentals for one or two passengers. *Spencer Ave. & the Beach, Wildwood, NJ 08260; tel. 609-729-6660. Open daily May–Sep. In front of the Fun Pier.*

◆ **Pier 47 Marina.** Boat rentals, including skiffs and pontoon boats, for fishing, crabbing, sightseeing. Bait and tackle also available. *3001 Wildwood Blvd., Wildwood, NJ 08260; tel. 609-729-4774. Open daily. On Rte. 47, between the Wildwood bridge and Exit 4B off the Garden State Pkwy.*

BICYCLING

Cycling is allowed on the boardwalk until 11 a.m. on weekdays and until 10:30 a.m. on weekends. Many rentals are available on and off the boardwalk.

GOLF

◆ **Wildwood Golf & Country Club.** Eighteen holes. *1170 Golf Club Rd., Cape May Court House, NJ 08210; tel. 609-465-7823. Open daily. Admission. From Wildwood, take Rte. 47 west, and go north on Rte. 9 to the county seat, Cape May Court House.*

TENNIS

In North Wildwood, courts are in the Allen Recreation Park at 22nd and Delaware avenues. In Wildwood Crest, they are between Columbine and Wisteria at Atlantic Avenue (tel. 609-523-0202).

NATURE

◆ **Captain Schumann's Whale Watching.** An 80-foot sightseeing boat makes two-and-a-half-hour trips in search of marine mammals. Three cruises daily; the best bet for whales is the afternoon cruise. Naturalist on board. *4500 Park Blvd., Wildwood, NJ 08260; tel. 609-522-2919. Daily departures at 10:30, 2, and 7 May–Oct. Admission.*

TOURIST INFORMATION

◆ **Greater Wildwood Chamber of Commerce.** Its boardwalk visitors center has information on North Wildwood, Wildwood, and Wildwood Crest. *Box 823, Wildwood, NJ 08260; tel. 609-*

729-4000. Open daily 8:30 a.m.-10 p.m. late May-mid-Sep. and Mon.-Fri. 8:30-4:30 mid-Sep.-May. The visitors center is in the 3600 block of the boardwalk, just south of Mariner's Landing pier.

◆ **Greater Wildwood Hotel-Motel Association.** The association has a staffed welcome center with many brochures on Route 47, on the way into Wildwood from the Garden State Parkway. It also publishes an annual guide to motels and hotels, available for $3.50. *Box 184, 1 S. Rte. 47, Dept. D, Wildwood, NJ 08260; tel. 609-522-4546, 800-786-4546. Welcome center open daily 9-9 May-Sep. and Mon.-Fri. 9-5 Oct.-Apr. From Exit 48 off the Garden State Pkwy., drive east on Rte. 47 (Wildwood Blvd.). The welcome center is on the right.*

◆ **North Wildwood Tourism Commission.** *Box 499, N. Wildwood, NJ 08260; tel. 609-522-7722, 800-882-7787. Open daily 9 a.m.-10 p.m. Memorial Day-Labor Day and Mon.-Fri. 10-4 the rest of the year. Located at 22nd Ave. and the boardwalk.*

◆ **Wildwood Crest Tourist Information.** *Beach and Rambler Rd. E., Wildwood Crest, NJ 08260; tel. 609-522-0221. Open May-Sep.*

CHAPTER 18

Cape May

Beauty	A
Swimming	B
Sand	B-
Hotels/Inns/B&Bs	A
House rentals	B-
Restaurants	A
Nightlife	B-
Attractions	B
Shopping	C
Sports	B
Nature	A

ape May is the shin-ing jewel of New Jersey shore towns. Some have broader beaches or bawdier nightlife, but none brings all the ele-ments of a beach holiday together with more panache. Victoriana thrives, but not as some contrived amusement park theme. The town is a National Historic Landmark, with 600-plus Victorian buildings—including dozens of ornate and charming inns—creating an ambience at once seductive and

173

fantastic. The city's location at the tip of the Cape May peninsula gives it a land's-end quality that enhances the vacation atmosphere. On one side lies the Atlantic; on the other, burly Delaware Bay.

Cape May's earliest settlers took advantage of its strategic location, first as a whaling outpost and then during the Revolution, when privateers targeted British merchant ships as they sailed by.

By the mid-1800s, Cape May's hotels bulged with visitors from the big northeastern cities. Then came a surge of colorful

HOW TO GET THERE

◆ Cape May is just under 3 hr. from New York City, 5 hr. from Washington, D.C., using the Lewes-Cape May Ferry, and about 2 hr. from Philadelphia. Its location at the southern end of the Garden State Pkwy. makes it easy to find.

◆ From New York, cross into New Jersey and take the Garden State Pkwy. south the whole way.

◆ From Washington, take U.S. 50 toward Annapolis, MD, and across the Bay Bridge. Continue south on Rte. 50 to MD Rte. 404 west, then west on U.S. 9 to Lewes, DE, for the 70-min. ferry ride.

◆ From Philadelphia, take the Atlantic City Expwy. in New Jersey east to the Garden State Pkwy., then follow the parkway south to Cape May.

◆ The Cape May-Lewes Ferry makes the 70-min. trip between Cape May and Lewes frequently during the summer. Each of the 5 ferries carries 100 cars and up to 800 people. For information, call 800-64-FERRY; for reservations, call 800-717-SAIL.

174

residential buildings that today give the city its cock-of-the-walk appearance. The Civil War was a setback for the resort, but by 1865 entrepreneurs were reviving tourism with a rail line from Philadelphia, horse racing, and the budding game of baseball. The idea was to stir interest in summer contests among teams hailing from Philadelphia and New York. Civic leaders also encouraged President Ulysses S. Grant to make Cape May his summer White House; Grant did visit in 1874, but he never fulfilled the dreams of town fathers.

Besides good looks, Cape May boasts fine dining and diversions. It has some of the state's best restaurants, and activities abound, particularly outdoor and nature-related recreation. Deep-sea and surf fishing, golf, whale-watching, and hiking are all nearby, and Cape May Point is one of the country's renowned bird-watching locations.

The city's water front is lined with wave-washed sand. A narrow dune with spotty dune grass separates the beach from a paved, leveelike promenade (with a few arcades and eateries) that extends for about one and a half miles. What Cape May lacks—the spirited frenzy of a big-time boardwalk—can be found at North Wildwood, a couple of parkway exits to the north.

Cape May's Achilles' heel is parking. On a midsummer day, when more than 30,000 vacationers have swarmed the town, the competition for beachside spaces is intense, and traffic backs up. Some experienced visitors find an unmetered space and leave the car there for the duration of their trip.

BEACHES
CITY BEACHES

Beach Drive runs relatively straight, east to west, along Cape May's downtown water front, and the beaches there go by more than a dozen names, often linked to the closest street intersecting Beach Drive. Near the main

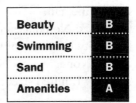

Beauty	B
Swimming	B
Sand	B
Amenities	A

part of town, stone jetties extend into the water every three blocks or so, providing a partitioning effect.

At high tide some of these beaches are narrow, and even

at low tide they are only moderately wide. East of downtown, the beach becomes more expansive, and there is a spacious feel as the promenade ends and the distance between the surf and the big Victorians on Beach Drive grows considerably.

Swimming: Good, with plenty of wave action. The water is clean and inviting. Using the beach requires a beach tag, available at a beachside concession window, City Hall, Washington Mall, or Convention Hall. Lifeguard on duty.

Sand: Moderately fine and tan. Beach width varies with tide and location.

Amenities: Bath houses and concessions.

Sports: Body board rentals from beach concessionaire.

Parking: There is 12-hour metered parking on Beach Drive and side streets; 50 cents per hour.

BAY BEACH

At the west end of Beach Drive, Bay Beach has evolved as the most natural of the city's strands—formed recently from sand washed down from the replenished beaches nearby. That natural building action gives it a gentle slope. The jetty around which the wandering sand has

Beauty	B
Swimming	B
Sand	B
Amenities	D

swept also acts to tame the waves.

This beach arcs gracefully to the west, to Cape May Point State Park and its lighthouse, perhaps a mile away. You can walk the whole way on the beach, passing a bird preserve on the way.

Swimming: Good swimming in gentle water. Lifeguard on duty.

Sand: Fine, tan.

Amenities: No concessions, but it's only a block from the Cape May City beach amenities.

Sports: None.

Parking: Limited street parking at west end of Beach Drive.

East End Beach

At the east end of Beach Drive, where it meets Wilmington Avenue, the beach front continues, wider and farther from the city crowds.

POINT BEACHES

The beach at Cape May Point State Park is scenic, with its landmark lighthouse nearby, but the water is too turbulent for swimming. The beach gets a lot of foot traffic from people on their way to the lighthouse and the bird-watching site.

Beauty	B-
Swimming	D
Sand	C-
Amenities	C

An old military gun platform just offshore also draws pedestrians, sometimes turning the small beach into a throughway.

Nearby are a string of point beaches with secluded ambience that contrasts with the city beaches. Most are suitable for swimming, and some have lifeguards in season.

The beaches are all protected by a high dune with heavy vegetation. The area nearby is residential—beach houses and private homes and no commercial development. Well-marked wooden walkways lead from the street to the beaches. The street names change frequently, but it is not difficult to find the beach entrances by keeping close to the dune. *From Cape May, take Sunset Blvd. west to Rte. 629 (Lighthouse Ave.). Turn left and follow the signs to the park.*
Swimming: Most of the beaches are good for swimming, with varying degrees of wave activity. A couple are too rough, and warnings are posted. Between Wildin and Coral Aves., a 900-ft. concrete reef is submerged for erosion control. Beach tags are required Memorial Day to Labor Day, and can be bought from an attendant. Lifeguard on duty at some beaches.
Sand: Moderately fine brown.
Amenities: No vending facilities. Rest rooms near the lighthouse.
Sports: Fishing. No organized activities.
Parking: Cape May Point State Park has a large free lot. Parking for most of the other beaches is limited to a small number of free spaces on side streets.

SUNSET BEACH

Sunset Beach is a modest yet overhyped stretch of sand, but it does have its charms. People go there for great sunsets, to get a glimpse of the odd shipwreck protruding offshore, and to col-

Beauty	B
Swimming	D
Sand	C
Amenities	C

lect "Cape May diamonds." The shipwreck is not worth the trip, but the sunsets and the diamonds are. Actually milky quartz crystals buffed by the action of the waves curling around Cape May Point, the diamonds can be polished and faceted to resemble the real thing.

In summer, the sunset is accompanied by a flag-lowering ceremony often attended by hundreds of visitors. The shipwreck is the S.S. *Atlantus*, a World War I-era concrete ship that broke loose in a storm in 1926, got stuck, and has been deteriorating ever since. A trailer-size chunk of ragged concrete is all that can be seen above the water. *About 2 1/2 mi. west of the Washington Mall on Rte. 606 (Sunset Blvd.); tel. 609-884-7079.*

Swimming: Beach falls off sharply. Many people simply wade in, searching for Cape May diamonds.

Sand: Small beach with coarse brown sand giving way to marble-size stones at the water line.

Amenities: Nearby are a few gift and apparel shops and the Sunset Beach Grill, a snack bar with an outdoor deck. Rest rooms available.

Sports: Fishing.

Parking: A couple of free parking lots, plus free roadside parking. For sunsets, come early if you want a spot close to the beach.

Higbee Beach

Part of the Higbee Beach Wildlife Management Area, about 15 minutes from central Cape May, it's one of the state's few with nude sunbathing, although it's not sanctioned. The strip of fine brownish sand arcs about a mile along the bay, between the Cape May Canal inlet and Sunset Beach. A sandy path leads from a small parking lot through brush to the beach. A larger lot is about a mile away. *From Cape May, take Rte. 606 (Sunset Blvd.) toward Cape May Point. Turn right onto Rte. 607, then left onto Rte. 641 (New England Rd.), which ends at the beach lot.*

HOTELS/INNS/B&BS

Cape May's Victorian inns and B&Bs are its showpieces. Many are open almost year-round, except in January. Expect to pay $100 to $200 per night most of the year. Ask if your room will have a private or shared bath, how many flights of stairs you'll be climbing, and about the availability of air-conditioning. The city also has a range of more modern hotels that, depending on amenities and distance from the beach, are $75 to $150 per night in summer.

◆ **Marquis de Lafayette** (very expensive). A bit fortresslike on the outside, luxurious inside. A modern hotel across from the beach with suites furnished in lush Victorian style, all balconied. On the top floor, a restaurant and club look out over the ocean. Those sensitive to noise should avoid fifth-floor rooms beneath the restaurant and club. Sauna and pool. Package plans include meals. *501 Beach Dr., Cape May, NJ 08204; tel. 609-884-3500, 800-257-0432.*

◆ **Coachman's Motor Inn & Beach Club** (moderate). A sprawling, 65-unit, three-level motel with standard rooms, efficiencies, and suites, well-maintained and -equipped. It's the only place in town with its own tennis courts. For best beach views, request a room on the third floor. Rooms 33 and 63 are more spacious corner units. The penthouse has two rooms and a full kitchen. *205 Beach Dr., Cape May, NJ 08204; tel. 609-884-8463.*

◆ **Hotel Macomber** (moderate). This solid, 44-room, shingle-style mansion offers Victorian ambience for less than many of the city's B&Bs. Most rooms have private bath and air-conditioning. Its age shows, but the family-run atmosphere goes a long way. Rooms 1 and 2 share a private second-floor porch great for reviewing the water front and Beach Drive parade. *727 Beach Dr., Cape May, NJ 08204; tel. 609-884-3020. Open weekends only Mar.-Apr. and Nov.-Dec. Closed Jan.-Feb. Across from the Convention Center.*

◆ **The Chalfonte** (moderate). Cape May's oldest and most celebrated hotel savors tradition, and many guests return year after year. Its 100 rooms border on the spartan, with wood floors and minimal furnishings. Rates include Southern-style breakfast and dinner in the spacious dining room. Snag one of the three Chalfonte cottages for seclusion; you'll still have the convenience of the hotel restaurant. *301 Howard St., Cape May, NJ 08204; tel. 609-884-8409. Closed Nov.-Apr. Three blocks from the beach.*

◆ **The Inn of Cape May** (moderate). A giant B&B with 77 rooms decked out in white wicker. Wandering the lobby is like wandering

179

an antiques store, and sure enough, it's all for sale. No air-conditioning, so in hot weather ask for a breeze-catching oceanside room or one with windows on two sides. Two-thirds of the rooms have their own bath. *Beach Dr. and Ocean Ave., Cape May, NJ 08204; tel. 609-884-3500, 800-257-0432. Closed mid-Oct.-mid-May.*

HOUSE RENTALS

Rental homes and units are best reserved early in the year. In Cape May, expect to pay $1,500 a week for a several-bedroom Victorian near the ocean, $1,100 for a two-bedroom ocean-front condo, $600 for homes near the village green. In Cape May Point, homes go from $1,800 ocean front to $800 inland.

◆ **Coastline Realty.** *1400 Texas Ave., Cape May, NJ 08204; tel. 609-884-5005, 800-377-7843. Open daily. Closed Sun. late May-Jan.*

◆ **Tolz Inc. of Cape May.** *Box 498, Cape May, NJ 08204; tel. 609-884-7001, 800-444-7001. Open daily.*

RESTAURANTS

◆ **Mad Batter** (expensive). A celebrated restaurant, its sophisticated dishes boldly blend Caribbean, French, New Orleans, and other cuisines to deliver original and satisfying dishes. The atmosphere soars as well. When the weather is fine, request a table on the open front porch, with its view of Jackson Street's other Victorian buildings. *19 Jackson St., Cape May, NJ 08204; tel. 609-884-5970. Open daily for breakfast, lunch, and dinner. At the Carroll Villa Hotel.*

◆ **The Lobster House** (moderate). Crowds swarm this restaurant for good seafood dining and wharfside ambience. There are indoor dining rooms and an outdoor raw bar with seating on the pier and the smell of the sea air. Dinner reservations may save you a wait. *Fisherman's Wharf, Cape May, NJ 08204; tel. 609-884-8296. Open daily for lunch and dinner. Driving into Cape May, it's on the left just after you cross the harbor bridge.*

◆ **The Magnolia Room at the Chalfonte** (moderate). Southern dinners are the house specialty, with signature dishes such as Dot's Southern Fried Chicken and Miss Helen's Crab Cakes, and the menu varies daily. The spacious dining room on the first floor of the Chalfonte is country elegant and can be down-home friendly. Diners sometimes are seated with other parties. There's a separate kids-only room for children six and under. Men don't need jackets, but collared shirts are required. *301 Howard St., Cape May, NJ 08204; tel. 609-884-8409. Open daily for breakfast and dinner late May-early Sep.*

◆ **Mangia Mangia** (inexpensive). A recently opened restaurant, it specializes in affordable family-style Italian with plenty of pasta and specialties like rigatoni and mushroom sausage. No reservations. *110 N. Broadway, Cape May, NJ 08204; tel. 609-884-2429. Open daily for dinner.*

◆ **McGlades on the Pier** (inexpensive). Location is this casual restaurant's calling card—it sits above the beach—but the menu is offbeat and interesting, with selections like crabmeat-and-cheese omelettes and Uncle Guido's Chili. The shaded wooden deck is ideal for taking in the surf while dining. *722 Beach Dr. at Stockton St., Cape May, NJ 08204; tel. 609-884-2614. Open daily for breakfast, lunch, and dinner May-Oct.; breakfast and lunch only Tue. On the promenade, next to the Convention Center, behind Morrow's Nut House.*

NIGHTLIFE

◆ **Blackbeard's.** This restaurant/night club offers dinner theater, DJ, dance music, and other entertainment. *1045 Beach Dr. at Philadelphia Ave., Cape May, NJ 08204; tel. 609-884-5611. Open nightly Mar.-Dec. In the Grand Hotels Oceanfront.*

◆ **Cape May Stage.** Professional equity theater company draws excellent reviews. *405 Lafayette St., Cape May, NJ 08204; tel. 609-884-1341. Performances often run 5 nights a week in the summer, less often at other times. Admission.*

◆ **The Henry Sawyer Room at the Chalfonte.** Cabaret, professional theater, folk music, and concerts by candlelight. *301 Howard St., Cape May, NJ 08204; tel. 609-884-8409. Open nightly Memorial Day-Labor Day. Admission.*

◆ **The Shire.** Restaurant and bar with live blues, jazz, salsa, and reggae. *315 Washington Mall, Cape May, NJ 08204; tel. 609-884-4700. Bands play 7 nights a week 10 p.m.-2 a.m. Memorial Day-Labor Day; weekends in the off-season. Admission varies.*

ATTRACTIONS

History is a constant theme in Cape May, where the Victorian presence is never more than a glance away. Tours include the horse-drawn carriage variety and guided visits to Victorian inns.

◆ **Emlen Physick Estate.** This 18-room house, built in 1879, was designed by Frank Furness and today includes a museum that illustrates family life during that era. Its carriage house is home to the Cape May County Art League. *1048 Washington St., Cape May, NJ 08204; tel. 609-884-5404, 800-275-4278. Call for tour schedule. Admission. Drive into Cape May on Washington St. and the Physick Estate is on the left, set back slightly from the road.*

◆ **Historic Cold Spring Village.** A 19th-century farm village with stroll-around exhibits on iron- and tinware, weaving, baking, pottery, spinning, and other crafts. Country store, restaurant, and bakery. *720 Rte. 9, Cape May, NJ 08204; tel. 609-898-2300. Open weekends 10-4:30 Memorial Day-Father's Day, daily Father's Day-Labor Day, and Sat.-Sun. in Sept. Admission. On Rte. 9, 3 mi. north of Cape May City. From the Garden State Pkwy., take Exit 4A and follow the signs. From Beach Dr. in Cape May, take Broadway north, which continues as Seashore Rd. over the Cape May Canal to Rte. 9. The village is on the right.*

SHOPPING

Washington Mall is Cape May's central shopping area, with dozens of specialty stores interspersed among dining and snack spots. Victoriana and the sea are prevailing themes. To shop the outlet malls in Rehoboth Beach, Delaware, take the 70-minute ferry ride to Lewes and catch the free shuttle into Rehoboth. The ferry terminal is in North Cape May, 10 to 15 minutes from central Cape May. There are 11 or more daily round-trips June through September, fewer at other times of the year.

◆ **Tradewinds.** Cultural art, jewelry, carving, crafts from Latin America and Africa. A break from Victoriana. *304 Washington Mall, Cape May, NJ 08204; tel. 609-884-6720. Open daily.*

◆ **Uniquely Yours.** Victorian hats, fashions, jewelry, baby gowns. *308 Carpenter's Lane, Cape May, NJ 08204; tel. 609-884-0002, 800-307-2552. Open daily. Closed Jan.*

◆ **Whale's Tale.** Gift shops with jewelry, shells, books, bric-a-brac, cards, games, and Victorian frames. *312 Washington Mall, Cape May, NJ 08204; tel. 609-884-4808. Open daily.*

BEST FOOD SHOPS

SANDWICHES: ◆ **Zoe's.** Fresh roast turkey and beef, hoagies, plus veggie choices. *715 Beach Dr., Cape May, NJ 08204; tel. 609-884-1233. Open daily for breakfast, lunch, and dinner.*

SEAFOOD: ◆ **The Lobster House Fish Market.** The fishing boats literally pull up to the back door of this fish market, located at the wharfside restaurant bearing the same name. *Fisherman's Wharf, Cape May, NJ 08204; tel. 609-884-3064. Open daily 8 a.m.-7 p.m. Sun.-Thu., 8 a.m.-8 p.m. Fri.-Sat. The wharf is on your left as the Garden State Pkwy. ends and you cross the canal into Cape May.*

FRESH PRODUCE: ◆ **Broadway Farm Market.** For more than a quarter of a century this roadside stand has offered daily-picked produce that must pass the muster of proprietor Alice Emmons. Regular customers reserve the rare beach-plum jelly well in advance. *Broadway at Central, Cape May, NJ 08204. Open Mon.-Sat. 7-7 late Jun.-late Oct. From Washington Street Mall, follow W. Perry out of central Cape May. Turn right onto Broadway. The stand is a few miles up the road on the left, at Central.*

BAKERY: ◆ **Cape May Bakers.** Breads, pastries, cookies, muffins, and a multitude of other baked delights. *482 W. Perry St., Cape May, NJ 08204; tel. 609-884-7454. Open Mon.-Sat. 7:30-5, Sun. 7:30-3. Closed Mon. during the off-season.*

ICE CREAM: ◆ **Gazebo Restaurant & Ice Cream Cafe.** Over 24 flavors, 12 toppings, plus frozen yogurt and no-fat choices. Try the Cappuccino Crunch. *Washington Mall, Cape May, NJ 08204; tel. 609-884-4832. Open daily 11 a.m.-11:30 p.m. Apr.-Nov.*

BEVERAGES: ◆ **Acme.** Soda by the case. *Victorian Plaza, Cape May, NJ 08204; tel. 609-884-7900. Open daily 7 a.m.-9 p.m.; 7 a.m.-8 p.m. during the off-season. Between Washington and Lafayette Sts. near the east end of Washington Mall.*

WINE: ◆ **Collier's.** Good selection of wines, liquors, setups, and beer. *202 Jackson St., Cape May, NJ 08204; tel. 609-884-8488. Open daily.*

SPORTS
FISHING

Cape May is one of the state's busiest commercial fishing ports and thrives as a sport-fishing destination. Scores of party and charter boats operate from Fisherman's Wharf and vicinity. Party boats carry a large number of people and charge per person. Charter boats include captain, mate, and equipment, usually for groups of up to six people.

◆ **Party & Charter Boat Association.** Represents dozens of charter, party, and sightseeing boats in Cape May County. Ask for the group's brochure, "Let's Go Fishing," from the tourist office. *Box 1065, Cape May, NJ 08204.*

◆ **South Jersey Fishing Center.** Home to about 20 charter operators and numerous private boats. *1231 Rte.109, Box 641, Cape May, NJ 08204; tel. 609-884-3800. Open daily. In the harbor.*

BICYCLING

◆ **Village Bicycle Shop.** Rents cruisers, mountain bikes, racing bikes, and surreys. Repairs. *2 Victorian Plaza, Cape May, NJ 08204; tel. 609-884-8500. Open daily Mar.-Nov. In the Acme parking lot, next to the horse carriage boarding site.*

GOLF

◆ **Cape May National Golf Club.** *Box 2369, Cape May, NJ 08204; tel. 609-884-1563. Admission. 2 mi. south of Rte. 47 on Rte. 9, at Rte. 9 and Florence Ave.*

TENNIS

◆ **William J. Moore Tennis Center.** Only public courts in Cape May; very reasonable rates; two-week and monthly contracts are available, otherwise on a first-come, first-served basis. 12 Har-Tru and 4 all-weather courts, all unlighted. *1020 Washington St., Cape May, NJ 08204; tel. 609-884-8986. Open daily 8 -7 Memorial Day-Nov.; 9-5 Dec.-Memorial Day. Admission. Go south on Washington St., past the Emlen Physick Estate, and turn left onto Madison Ave. The entrance is immediately on your left.*

NATURE

The Cape May peninsula is a nature lover's paradise, rich with coastal and wetland species, bird sanctuaries, whale and dolphin activity, wildlife management areas, and many opportunities for hiking, biking, and exploring. Several organizations offer instruction.

◆ **Cape May Bird Observatory.** Bird-watching programs, workshops, and tours, plus a birding shop with books and equipment. *707 E. Lake Dr., Cape May Point, NJ 08204; tel. 609-884-2736; birding hotline, 609-884-2626. Open daily 9-5. From Cape May, drive west on Sunset Blvd. Turn left onto Lighthouse Dr. It's on the right, just off Lighthouse Dr.*

◆ **Cape May Point State Park.** The park, site of the Cape May Lighthouse, also has 180 acres of wildlife preserve, including sand dunes, nature museum, nature trails and programs, and the Cape May Migratory Bird Refuge. *Box 107, Cape May Point, NJ 08204; tel. 609-884-2159. Grounds open daily sunrise-sunset; museum open daily, call for hours. Follow Sunset Blvd. from downtown Cape May for about five min. Turn left at Lighthouse Ave., where a sign indicates the way to Cape May Point.*

◆ **Cape May Whale Watch & Research Center.** Whale-, dolphin-, and bird watching. *1286 Wilson Dr., Cape May, NJ 08204; tel. 609-898-0055. Open daily 9-6 Apr.-Oct.; Wed., Sat., and Sun. in Nov. Admission.*

◆ **Jersey Cape Nature Excursions.** Back-bay birding and wildlife tours, spring and fall shorebirds, seabird colonies. *Box 254, Cape May, NJ 08204; tel. 609-884-3712. Tour times vary. Closed Dec.-Jan. Admission. Located at the Miss Chris Marina in the wharf area next to the large blue* Cape May Whale Watcher. *The dock is at Third Ave. and Wilson Dr.*

TOURIST INFORMATION

◆ **Cape May Welcome Center.** In addition to the center, an information booth at the east end of the Washington Mall sells tickets for most tours, including children's guided trolley tours, Physick Estate tours, historic district walking tours, and evening trolley tours and rides. *405 Lafayette St., Cape May, NJ, 08204; tel. 609-884-9562. Open daily 9-4:30.*

◆ **Cape May County Chamber of Commerce.** *Box 74, Cape May Court House, NJ, 08210; tel. 609-465-7181. Open Mon.-Fri. 8:30-4:30.*

◆ **Chamber of Commerce of Greater Cape May.** Offers beautiful book on the Victorian inns and B&Bs. *Box 556, Cape May City, NJ, 08204; tel. 609-884-5508. Open Mon.-Fri. 9-8 and Sat.-Sun. 9-5 Apr.-Oct. and Mon.-Fri. 9-5 and Sat.-Sun. 11-3 Nov.-Mar.*

◆ **Cape May County Tourism.** *Box 365, Cape May Court House, NJ, 08210; tel. 609-886-0901, 800-227-2297. Open Mon.-Fri. 8:30-4:30.*

CHAPTER 19

Lewes/Cape Henlopen

Beauty	A
Swimming	A
Sand	A
Hotels/Inns/B&Bs	A
House rentals	B
Restaurants	B+
Nightlife	C
Attractions	B
Shopping	B
Sports	B-
Nature	A

Drive off the big ferry at Lewes, Delaware, and a right turn carries you past the long, golden arc of the town's Delaware Bay beach front, about half a mile west of the ferry pier. It's an eye-catching strip of sand, uniform in breadth and texture, nuzzled by the bay with barely a splash. Just beyond is downtown Lewes (pronounced *LEW-ehs*), with its busy fishing wharf and Victorian shopping district.

A left turn from the ferry takes you into Cape Henlopen State Park, whose Atlantic shore front is as wild and invigorating as the Town Beach is tame. This one-two combination alone would make Lewes appealing, but the town offers another inducement. It has class.

Sitting at the northern tip of Delaware's 28-mile coastline, Lewes is just off the beaten path of Delaware Route 1 and the headlong rush of holidaymakers bound for Rehoboth Beach, Dewey Beach, and Ocean City, Maryland. Unlike the towns farther south, Lewes does not have a boardwalk or a honky-tonk aspect and distinguishes itself from other shore communities by crafting its reputation as a "town with a beach, not a beach town." It is best known as the southern terminus of the Cape May-Lewes Ferry, but many ferry users bypass the downtown area on the way to someplace else.

Lewes has cultivated its history, which dates back to the town's founding by Dutch whalers in 1631, and proudly proclaims itself the "first town in the first state." For a look at some

HOW TO GET THERE

◆ Driving from Philadelphia to Lewes takes about 2 1/4 hr. in smooth traffic. Go south on I-95 to DE Rte. 1 and U.S. Rte. 13 south, then follow Rte. 1 all the way to the Lewes turnoff at U.S. Rte. 9.

Driving from Washington, DC, to Lewes takes about 3 1/4 hr. Take U.S. 50 to Annapolis, crossing the Bay Bridge and following U.S. 50 to Rte. 404 and then Rte. 9 into Lewes.

◆ The Cape May-Lewes Ferry takes 70 min. for the 17-mi. journey and operates year-round, with nearly a dozen round-trips a day during summer. Each ferry carries up to 100 cars and 800 passengers (information, 800-64-FERRY; reservations, 800-717-SAIL).

of the area's historic homes, stroll through Shipcarpenter Square, a 3-acre commons surrounded by 11 acres of historic homes dating from 1720 to 1880. These colonial, federal, and Victorian homes, now privately occupied and located near the Historical Society complex, were moved from different locations, all within 40 miles of Lewes (not available for touring).

Lewes's location has made it a strategic point for shipping. When merchant vessels began sailing up the Delaware Bay for the important ports of Philadelphia and Wilmington, they had to take on local pilots to navigate the area's tricky shoals. Lewes-based pilots competed vigorously for that business, often racing to sea to meet approaching ships. During an 1888 hurricane, several pilot-boarding schooner crews threw caution to the wind and were lost in the storm, and the tragedy led to the formation of the Delaware River and Bay Pilots Association. To this day, it provides pilots for boats in and out of the Delaware Bay region.

Other seafaring dramas occupy Lewes's history, including many shipwrecks. One of the best known was the H.M.S. *DeBraak*, a British brig whose sinking in 1798 gave rise to stories that gold was aboard. Treasure hunters finally found the wreckage in 80 feet of water in 1984—but recovered no gold.

Lewes is strategically located where the bay channel and east-west and north-south sea lanes converge. During the Civil War, the Lewes area was the only part of Delaware to side with the Union. It wanted to keep its trading ties with the North.

Cape Henlopen's location subjects it to some harsh forces. A 60-foot lighthouse built in about 1765 toppled into the ocean in 1926, the victim of erosion that had eaten away a quarter mile of land to reach it. Even today, in Cape Henlopen State Park, a section of "walking dunes" testifies to those same forces as wind continually shifts their position.

Because of its seafaring past, the harbor remains active, with its own commercial and sportfishing fleet. Situated on the Lewes & Rehoboth Canal, the harbor is ringed by restaurants, lodgings, and sightseeing and fishing operations. The canal leads to the Delaware Bay in one direction, Rehoboth Bay in the other.

While Lewes promotes a quiet reputation, it has at least one rollicking event. On the first weekend of November, tens of thousands of people descend for the annual World Championship Punkin' Chunkin' contest, in which teams use catapult devices to hurl leftover Halloween pumpkins for distance and accuracy. In recent years, the winning distance has exceeded 2,000 feet.

BEACHES
BEACH NO. 1 AND BEACH NO. 2

Lewes's town beach front stretches for more than a mile along the Delaware Bay and consists of Beach No. 1 and Beach No. 2. Beach No. 2 runs from a dune near the east end of the parking lot to the long stone jetty that marks

Beauty	B
Swimming	B-
Sand	B
Amenities	C+

the ferry dock. Beach No. 1 runs in the opposite direction and is much longer.

Beach No. 2 is backed by a medium-high grassy dune, with new two-story condos visible at a distance. Behind Beach No. 1 is the parking lot, then, farther along its arc, are two- and three-story beach houses and a residential area.

Everything about these beaches seems tame. The bay water laps the shore, but there is no significant wave action in good weather. On Beach No. 1 in particular there's an atmosphere of regulation, what with the huge, metered parking lot, calm water with buoys marking the swimming limits, and signs prohibiting Jet Skis, boating, and fishing in the swimming area. For families with young children, this seems to be an especially friendly beach, with easy, level access from the parking lot. *From central Lewes, the town beach is 1 1/5 mi. north on Savannah Rd.*

Swimming: Calm, clear, shallow water. Lifeguard on duty.

Sand: Medium fine, light tan, mixed with pebbles near the water line.

Amenities: Rest rooms at the beach patrol headquarters; food sales; and beach chair, Boogie board, raft, and sand-accessible wheelchair rentals from a shack at the edge of the parking lot.

Sports: No water sports.

Parking: Large parking lot with metered spaces.

CAPE HENLOPEN STATE PARK BEACH

The state park beach is a gorgeous stretch of undeveloped coastline, on a par with what you expect to find at a national seashore. From the beach the only man-made objects in sight are the Cape Henlopen Lighthouse and a distant water tower to the south.

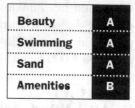

Beauty	A
Swimming	A
Sand	A
Amenities	B

The bathhouse off the parking lot is the main beach entry, but there are several other access points through the dunes in the area, both north and south. Driving north from the main pavilion you'll find another lot, and just before that, an access road for off-road vehicles. The radar installation protruding above the treeline belongs to the Cape Henlopen Ship Reporting Station. Just beyond the radar, another lot accesses the bay side of the point, an area that is off-limits for much of the summer because of nesting shorebirds. To reach beach points south of the bathhouse, walk the beach or, driving, turn right onto the road just before the park's entrance booth. The road winds past several old military structures, including a tower that from the top gives an excellent view of the rolling dune topography. In the sand you may see giant "graffiti" spelling out epithets such as "Tom and Sue Forever" in handfuls of pine needles.

Two miles up this road from the entrance booth is Herring Point overlook, which has a pedestrian dune crossing down to the beach and offers a good view of the 80-foot Great Dune to the north. *From the ferry dock, Cape Henlopen State Park Beach is less than 1 mi. east on Henlopen Dr.*

Swimming: Good, with steady waves. Lifeguard on duty.

Sand: Light brown and very fine, almost powdery, building to a grassy dune.

Amenities: Bathhouse with rest rooms, showers, and snack bar. Beach vendor rents umbrellas, chairs, and Boogie boards.

Sports: Boogie boarding, fishing.

Parking: Large parking area at bathhouse, smaller parking lots to the north and at Herring Point overlook. Vehicle fee.

HOTELS/INNS/B&BS

The number of charming inns and B&Bs exceeds what you

might expect in a town this size, and you can even rent a house-boat moored in the harbor. Near the harbor are a handful of motels catering to fishermen. But overall, the number of rooms available is limited. In summer, reserve early. If Lewes is booked up, Rehoboth Beach to the south has more rooms (*see* Rehoboth Beach chapter).

◆ **The Inn at Canal Square** (expensive). A landmark at harbor's edge, the inn has 19 rooms and three suites looking out on fish-erman's wharf. Rooms are spacious and smartly furnished with reproduction antiques. Ask for one of the five rooms on the third floor for the best sunrise/sunset views. Moored outside and available for rent is a two-bedroom, two-floor houseboat, the only one licensed for lodging in the state. It comes with AC, fireplace, marine toilet— and the chance the fishing boats may wake you before dawn. *122 Market St., Lewes, DE 19958; tel. 302-645-8499, 800-222-7902; fax 302-645-7083. Just off Savannah Rd. near the canal bridge.*

◆ **The New Devon Inn** (expensive). A historically registered build-ing, this inn has 24 rooms and two suites in the historic shop-ping district. It was renovated in 1989 in elegant fashion. Corner units—like Room 108, which looks out on both Market and Second streets—are the largest of the standard rooms. The building also has shops and a well-regarded restaurant, The Buttery. *Box 516, Lewes, DE 19958; tel. 302-645-6466, 800-824-8754. Three blocks west of Savannah Rd. on Second St. at Market St.*

◆ **Wild Swan Inn** (expensive). This inn has only three guest rooms but is a Victorian standout both inside and out. A gaze-bo on the front porch is good for sitting but is just feet from busy Kings Highway. Out back is a 35- by 17-foot swimming pool. The interior is a cornucopia of Victoriana and other col-lectibles, from wreaths and mirrors to an Edison record player and a collection of swan curios. Bedrooms have antique chan-deliers and authentic Victorian decor. Private baths. *525 Kings Hwy., Lewes, DE 19958; tel. 302-645-8550. From downtown Lewes, go south on Savannah Rd. Turn left onto Kings Hwy. and fol-low it about 1 mi. The inn is opposite the library.*

◆ **Blue Water House** (moderate). This B&B a few blocks from the town beach opened in 1993 and has trim, modern lines with a wraparound second-floor balcony and enclosed third-floor lookout with sweeping views. Ask for a room opening onto the balcony. Rooms are large and simply furnished. Breakfast is homemade breads, fruit, and cereal. The B&B supplies Boogie boards and other beach amenities, and the owners operate day-trips on their 32-foot fishing boat. Five minute walk to beach. *407 E. Market St., Lewes, DE 19958; tel. 302-645-7832, 800-493-2080. Near the canal bridge in central Lewes, turn onto Angler's Rd., then make a right onto E. Market St.*

◆ **The Beacon Motel** (moderate). This chain-style motel has 66 basic, balconied rooms, some of them obviously used by smokers (nonsmoking rooms are not available). Rooms lack charm but are clean. This is about the only middle ground between the pricier inns and the motels catering to the fishing crowd. For more space, request one of the 20 rooms equipped with two double beds. *514 Savannah Rd., Lewes, DE 19958; tel. 302-645-4888, 800-735-4888. Open late Mar.-Nov. About halfway between the town beach and Fisherman's Wharf.*

HOUSE RENTALS

◆ **Lewes Realty.** *418 E. Savannah Rd., Lewes, DE 19958; tel. 302-645-1955, 800-705-7590. Open daily.*

RESTAURANTS

Lewes's restaurants offer the requisite seafood you expect in a port town, but you can also find a British pub atmosphere, tasty French pastries, and first-rate Italian dining.

◆ **Rose & Crown Restaurant and Pub** (expensive). This place delivers pub flavor with a flair, and the brickwork and dark woods combine in a variety of dining areas to offer both formal and informal atmosphere, including a high-ceilinged, skylit section. Popular are the tournedos Parisienne, broiled seafood combination, shrimp in white clam sauce, and shrimp Milano. *108 Second St., Lewes, DE 19958; tel. 302-645-2373. Open daily for lunch and dinner.*

◆ **Gilligan's Harborside Restaurant and Bar** (moderate). From the outside it looks fishy, built into the hull of a fishing boat seemingly grounded along the harbor shore. But inside it's quickly clear this is no crab shack. Dishes like crispy flattened chicken and *penne mare e monti* have propelled the place into the upper ranks under the care of chef Larry Abrahms, formerly of the Striped Bass in Philadelphia. The crab cake on sourdough is a favorite. A bar and deck out back overlook the harbor action. *Canal Sq., Lewes, DE 19958; tel. 302-645-7866. Open daily for lunch and dinner Mar.-Sept.; open Mon. for lunch, Thu.-Sat. for lunch and dinner, Sun. for brunch Oct.-Dec. Closed Jan.-Feb. At First St. and Canal Sq., next to the Inn at Canal Sq.*

◆ **Kupchick's** (moderate). It may no longer be sole holder of the title of best restaurant in town, but it remains a contender, with seafood and steak dishes that pack the place. Live music from a central foyer can be heard on both the formal and less formal sides of the restaurant. *3 E. Bay Ave., Lewes, DE 19958; tel. 302-645-0420. Open daily for dinner. At the town beach.*

◆ **La Rosa Negra** (moderate). This friendly and casual restaurant with a black-and-white motif succeeds with its authentic Italian cuisine, including appetizers like seafood focaccia and crabmeat & artichoke hearts. Winning entrées include shrimp marsala and sautéed salmon in a port wine and sun-dried tomato butter sauce. Owner-chef Jim Evans vacationed in Lewes as a child, and his wife and co-owner, Denise Evans, has a big reputation for baked desserts. *128 Second St., Lewes, DE 19958; tel. 302-645-1980. Open Mon.-Sat. for lunch and daily for dinner.*

◆ **Lighthouse Restaurant** (moderate). This casual wharfside restaurant has a lighthouse look, dominating the harbor near the Lewes drawbridge. It has several seating areas and a predictable menu of seafood offerings. The indoor dining rooms have lots of glass for harbor views, and there's a big wooden deck outdoors for waterside ambience as the fishing and tour boats move along the canal. *Box 623, Lewes, DE 19958; tel. 302-645-6271. Open daily for breakfast, lunch, and dinner. Just off Savannah Rd. on Angler's Rd.*

NIGHTLIFE

As befits a town whose slogan is "busy days, quiet nights," there's not much going on after dark here besides eating and drinking. A few restaurants have live music, especially on weekends, including the Rose & Crown and Kupchick's.

ATTRACTIONS

Many of Lewes's attractions are related to its history—much of which is related to its nautical heritage.

◆ **Cannonball House Marine Museum.** This house was struck by a cannonball in the War of 1812, during a bombardment by the British. A sign marks the spot in the front. The museum has nautical exhibits. *Front and Bank Sts., Lewes, DE 19958; tel. 302-645-7670.*

◆ **Historical Society Complex.** Half a dozen historic buildings occupy this complex, including the Thompson Country Store, Ellegood House, Blacksmith Shop, Rabbit's Ferry House, Burton-Ingram House, Plank House, and Doctor's Office. Guided and self-guided tours are available. *Shipcarpenter and Third Sts., Lewes, DE 19958; tel. 302-645-7670. Open. Tue.-Fri. 10-3, Sat. 10-12:30 mid-June-Labor Day. Admission.*

◆ **St. Peter's Episcopal Church.** This church, built around 1858, has a cemetery with many interesting graves, including that of James Drew, captain of the ill-fated H.M.S. *DeBraak,* which sank offshore. *Second and Market Sts., Lewes, DE 19958; tel. 302-645-8479. Open daily.*

◆ **Swaanendael Museum.** The town museum takes its name from the Dutch whaling fishery founded in 1631 as Zwaanendael, near the site that later became Lewes. The museum was built in 1931 to commemorate those settlers and its Dutch colonial revival style is patterned after a typical Dutch town hall. Inside are displays documenting the evolution of Lewes from the original colony through today. *Savannah Rd. and Kings Hwy., Lewes, DE 19958; tel. 302-645-1148. Open Tue.-Sat. 10-4:30, Sun. 1:30-4:30. Closed Mon.*

SHOPPING

The shopping district is a compact area bounded by Front Street, Savannah Road, and Second and Market streets. The mix and quality of the shops are good, with little of the souvenir-type merchandise that plagues many tourist towns. Several have antique, Americana, or seafaring themes, but there is little duplication of merchandise. More shopping is nearby at the factory outlets of Rehoboth Beach (*see* Rehoboth Beach chapter).

◆ **Carolina Moon.** Antiques and collectibles, including stained glass, architectural items, iron pieces, quilts, old toys, and reproductions. *123 Second St., Lewes, DE 19958; tel. 302-645-5300. Open daily. Closed Jan.-Feb.*

◆ **Lewes Mercantile Antique Gallery.** Under one roof, 35 vendors offer a variety of prints, furniture, antique boxes, paintings, chandeliers, and many other collectible items in a tasteful, orderly setting. *109 Second St., Lewes, DE 19958; tel. 302-645-7900. Open daily.*

◆ **Preservation Forge.** Blacksmith John Ellsworth forges gates, chandeliers, fireplace pokers, plant hangers, and other ironwork from his barn shop. The big doors swing open to welcome observers. About 90 percent of his business is custom work, and he's been doing it in town for about 20 years. *114 W. Third St., Lewes, DE 19958; tel. 302-645-7987. Closed Sun. and Wed.*

BEST FOOD SHOPS

SANDWICHES: ◆ **A Taste of Heaven Cafe.** Tantalizing sandwiches on baguettes or croissants, plus other light fare. *115 Savannah Rd., Lewes, DE 19958; tel. 302-644-1992. Open daily.*

SEAFOOD: ◆ **Lewes Fishhouse.** *1130 Rte. 1, Lewes, DE 19958; tel. 302-644-0708. Open daily May-Oct. Closed Mon.-Tue. Nov.-Apr.*

FRESH PRODUCE: ◆ **Homestead Market.** *1019 Kings Hwy., Lewes, DE 19958; tel. 302-644-0708. Open daily late May-early Sep.*

BAKERY: ◆ **Bayside Bake Shoppe.** Everything is lovingly made from scratch by Julius Paoli, including the pies, the pastries, and the sourdough, pesto, whole wheat, English sunflower, and five-grain breads. *1004 Kings Hwy., Lewes, DE 19958; tel. 302-645-5610. Open daily. South of downtown on Kings Hwy.*

ICE CREAM: ◆ **Kings Homemade Ice Cream.** Homemade ice cream and frozen yogurt, plus a killer brownie ice cream sandwich. *201 Second St., Lewes, DE 19958; tel. 302-645-9425. Open daily. Closed late Oct.-mid-Mar.*

BEVERAGES: ◆ **Lloyd's IGA.** *611 Savannah Rd., Lewes, DE 19958; tel. 302-645-6589. Open daily.*

WINE: ◆ **Henlopen Beverage Mart.** *410-412 Savannah Rd., Lewes, DE 19958; tel. 302-645-8741. Closed Sun.*

SPORTS

FISHING

Fisherman's Wharf is packed with head boats and charter boats, and many part-day and all-day trips are available. Surf fishing is also popular.

◆ **Fisherman's Wharf.** Full day, half-day, night-fishing, and charter boats are available here, as well as a variety of marine mammal, nature, and sunset cruises. *By the Drawbridge, Lewes, DE 19958; tel. 302-645-8862, 302-645-8541. Open daily. Fishing tapers off Dec.-Mar.*

SURFING

Lewes has a few shops that sell Boogie boards, but serious surfers head south to Rehoboth and Dewey beaches and the Indian River Inlet.

BICYCLING

◆ **Lewes Cycle Sports.** All kinds of bikes and beach cruisers for sale or rent. Repairs. *526 Savannah Rd., Lewes, DE 19958; tel. 302-645-4544. Open daily 8-6. Between the town beach and downtown Lewes, next to the Beacon Motel.*

TENNIS

◆ **Cape Henlopen State Park.** Four tennis courts in modest condition; first-come, first-served basis. *42 Cape Henlopen Dr., Lewes, DE 19958; tel. 302-645-8983. Daylight hours. Park admission during the season; no extra charge for tennis courts. After entering the park, go past the Seaside Nature Center. The courts are on the right.*

◆ **Lewes town courts.** Two courts; first-come, first-served basis. *Front St. at Shipcarpenter St., Lewes, DE. Lights operate from sunset-11 p.m. daily. Alongside the boat-launching area.*

NATURE

◆ **Cape Henlopen State Park.** This 4,000-acre park is packed with natural diversions, including the one-and-one-fifth-mile Pinelands Nature Trail, which begins across from the park's Seaside Nature Center. The center has marine aquariums and audio-visual programs. Check at the center for its daily schedule. Birding and fishing are popular, and camping is available. The Gordon's Pond Wildlife Area at the park's southern end is more easily reached via an entrance near Rehoboth Beach (*see* Rehoboth Beach chapter). *42 Cape Henlopen Dr., Lewes, DE 19958; tel. 302-645-8983. Open daily Apr.-early Oct. Park admission during the season. Cape Henlopen Dr. runs right into the park.*

◆ **Fisherman's Wharf Marine Center.** Marine mammal sightseeing cruises depart regularly; dolphin- and whale-watching cruises. *Savannah Rd. by the Drawbridge, Lewes, DE 19958; tel. 302-645-8862. Open daily May-Oct. Admission.*

◆ **Prime Hook National Wildlife Refuge.** This 8,800-acre refuge ten miles northwest of Lewes has trails for wildlife observation and photography, plus facilities for hunting, fishing, canoeing, and boating. *RD 3, Box 195, Milton, DE 19968; tel. 302-684-8419. Take Rte. 1 north to Broadkill Beach Rd., which leads to refuge headquarters.*

SAFETY TIPS

Traffic—not crime—is the biggest headache for Lewes's police in the summertime. Parking in the shopping district is limited and the town encourages visitors to walk, not drive, whenever possible. In Cape Henlopen State Park cars are broken into occasionally; lock up and keep valuables out of sight.

TOURIST INFORMATION

◆ **Lewes Chamber of Commerce and Visitors Bureau.** *Box 1, Lewes, DE 19958; tel. 302-645-8073; fax 302-645-8412. Open Mon.-Fri. 10-4, Sat. 9-3, Sun. 10-2 May-Oct.; Mon.-Fri. 10-4 Nov.-Apr. In the Fisher-Martin House at 120 Kings Hwy., behind the town museum, where Savannah Rd. and Kings Hwy. intersect.*

CHAPTER 20

Rehoboth Beach

Beauty	B
Swimming	B
Sand	B
Hotels/Inns/B&Bs	B
House rentals	B
Restaurants	A-
Nightlife	B
Attractions	A
Shopping	A
Sports	B
Nature	B

Rehoboth Beach is the beefiest of the shore towns along Delaware's 28-mile Atlantic coast, laying claim to the longest boardwalk, the most motel rooms, and the greatest choice of restaurants. Swarms of tourists converge here from Washington, Baltimore, Philadelphia, and Wilmington. While Rehoboth prides itself on being a family destination, it has its sophisticated and honky-tonk sides too. Late into the night, the cacophony of its boardwalk arcades mingles with the crash of waves and the sounds of beach volleyball under the lights.

Rehoboth's credentials as a holiday resort date back more than a century, to 1891, when the state legislature approved a charter for "the providing and maintaining of a permanent seaside resort," but the groundwork was laid two decades earlier when Methodists established the Rehoboth Beach Camp as a place for summer religious gatherings. In 1873 came the first boardwalk and in 1878 a railroad line began bringing more visitors. The flow of holidaymakers grew, and the religious meetings were discontinued. The area's future as a resort was set.

Today, no trains roll into town, but Delaware Route 1 provides an easy if sometimes packed gateway. Aside from those who make Rehoboth their home base, many vacationers from Cape May, New Jersey, to Ocean City, Maryland, regard Rehoboth as a necessary day-trip, either for its restaurants or its shopping. Because Delaware has no state sales tax, Rehoboth's sizable and fast-growing factory-outlet malls are particularly appealing to bargain-hungry shoppers.

The city's growth as a shopping mecca followed an earlier transition from sleepy shore town to hip restaurant town. The change was fueled during the 1980s by an influx of gay visitors and business people. Rehoboth emerged as the Northeast's most

HOW TO GET THERE

◆ From Washington, DC, in smooth traffic, Rehoboth Beach is 3 hr. away. Take U.S. Rte. 50 east to Annapolis, cross the Bay Bridge, and take Rte. 404 east to Rte. 1 south.

◆ From Philadelphia, the trip takes just over 2 hr. In smooth traffic. Follow I-95 south past Wilmington to DE Rte. 1 (at times U.S. 13), which goes south all the way to Rehoboth Beach.

gay-friendly resort outside of Fire Island, New York, and Provincetown, Massachusetts, with restaurants and dance clubs where gays felt at home. Several blocks of beach attract mainly gay sunbathers, and the gay community's style and financial clout have had a great deal of influence. But not all of Rehoboth greets the gay scene with open arms, and there is political tension between those who see the city as all-embracing and those who cling to the traditional "family resort" concept. Still, Rehoboth is destined to remain one of a handful of U.S. resorts with entrenched and highly visible gay communities.

The city's main drag is Rehoboth Avenue, with cherry trees along its grassy median, leading to a turnaround at the boardwalk. Near the turnaround is a band shell for nightly concerts, and dozens of eateries and beach shops catering in summer to masses of vacationers. Rehoboth is big enough for you to wear yourself out walking. To help, the Jolly Trolley makes its rounds between Rehoboth and nearby Dewey Beach (*see* Dewey Beach chapter). There's also a Park & Ride bus that operates on Rehoboth Avenue between the boardwalk turnaround and City Hall at Third Street.

The town's playful soul resides on the broad boardwalk, which stretches for one mile along a tight line of shops, arcades, eateries, miniature golf courses, and motels, especially in the blocks on either side of Rehoboth Avenue. The boardwalk sees traffic from dawn, when bikers and joggers turn out, to past midnight, when the late-night crowd hangs out, trying to make the day last just a little bit longer.

BEACHES
REHOBOTH BEACHES

The beach at Rehoboth stretches for two miles from Dewey Beach on the south to Cape Henlopen State Park to the north. With its boardwalk and nearby businesses, the beach is citified, but it's broad enough to accommodate a lot

Beauty	B
Swimming	B
Sand	B
Amenities	A

of people and activity. For crowd relief, walk or drive north to the state park's undeveloped shoreline. Several blocks of beach at the south end of Rehoboth attract a gay crowd. *From Rte. 1, turn*

east on 1A, which leads to Rehoboth Ave. and the boardwalk area.
Swimming: Clear water with waves that break close to the shore-line. Lifeguard on duty.
Sand: Moderately fine, light tan, sloping slightly in a moderately wide swath from boardwalk to water.
Amenities: No bathhouse. Boardwalk rest rooms at Maryland and Delaware avenues. Many businesses along the boardwalk.
Sports: Body boarding, skim boarding, and volleyball on the beach between Rehoboth and Olive avenues.
Parking: Metered parking, in lots and on streets around town, effective daily 10 a.m. to midnight.

CAPE HENLOPEN STATE PARK BEACH

This beach, at the south end of the state park, is a nice contrast to the developed beach front along the boardwalk at Rehoboth. Crossing through a dune at the far end of a parking lot you come out at a rock jetty and, except for a cou-

Beauty	A
Swimming	B
Sand	A
Amenities	C

ple of WWII observation towers, can see little but sand and surf for a mile north up the coast toward Cape Henlopen. To the south, the shoreline goes even farther, to Rehoboth and beyond. (*See* Lewes-Cape Henlopen chapter for information on another beach accessible from the park's main entrance near the Lewes ferry terminal.) *Go south on Rte. 1 and then east onto Rte. 1A. Make a left onto Columbia Ave., then a left onto Surf Ave. Turn right onto Dunway, which becomes Ocean Dr. and leads to parking lot.*
Swimming: Clear water with strong wave action. Lifeguard on duty.
Sand: Moderately fine, light brown sand. Somewhat rolling beach backed by a low grassy dune.
Amenities: Portable toilets in the parking lot. Shack near entrance of beach for chair and umbrella rentals.
Sports: Designated surfing area.
Parking: Large parking lot. Day-use fee.

HOTELS/INNS/B&BS

◆ **Boardwalk Plaza Hotel** (very expensive). This large, modern hotel has 84 rooms, suites, and efficiencies furnished in grand

Victorian style, including armoires and floral curtains. Its four floors of pink wedding-cake exterior make it the most prominent place on the boardwalk, both in size and appearance. Indoor-outdoor spa. Best rooms have balconies that open over the boardwalk. *2 Olive Ave., Rehoboth Beach, DE 19971; tel. 302-227-7169, 800-332-3224.*

◆ **Sea Witch Manor** (expensive). A rarity among Victorian B&Bs, it's brand new. Owners Joan and Dennis Santangini completed the three-story, turreted Victorian in 1994 and filled it with antiques collected locally. The Sunrise Room has a king-size brass bed and a small private balcony. Anna's Room has a big bed and a clawfoot tub. Gourmet breakfast, plus afternoon tea served on the wraparound front porch. *71 Lake Ave., Rehoboth Beach, DE 19971; tel. 302-226-9482. At Rehoboth Ave. and Fourth St.*

◆ **Rehoboth Beach Inns and B&BS.** More than a dozen inns and B&Bs are listed in the "Southern Delaware Visitors Guide & Vacation Planner," published by the Sussex County Convention & Tourism Commission. *Box 240, Georgetown, DE 19947; tel. 302-856-1818, 800-357-1818.*

HOUSE RENTALS

A variety of homes, condos, apartments, and town houses are available, with rentals usually for a minimum of one week in July and August. A two-bedroom three or four blocks from the ocean runs $800 to $1,000 per week, with comparable oceanfront or ocean-view units going for $1,400 to $2,000. A five-bedroom house near the water is $2,500 to $3,500.

◆ **Coldwell Banker Rehoboth Resort Realty.** *4157 Hwy. 1, Rehoboth Beach, DE 19971; tel. 302-227-5000, 800-800-4134. Open daily.*

◆ **O'Conor, Piper & Flynn Realtors.** *4421 Hwy. 1, Rehoboth Beach, DE 19971; tel. 302-227-6151, 800-441-8090. Open daily.*

RESTAURANTS

Rehoboth Beach underwent a restaurant renaissance in the 1980s, and the dining scene continues to thrive. Seafood is popular, but many menus reflect an uncommon cultural diversity. Several of the city's hottest restaurants are along Wilmington Avenue.

◆ **La La Land** (expensive). There's nothing understated about this first-rate restaurant, where the flamboyant decor—purple and turquoise, stencils and collages—goes hand in hand with the imaginative menu. Appetizers like the roasted mignon of eggplant with goat cheese and roasted peppers are tasty preludes to such entrées as swordfish with pineapple relish, halibut sautéed in porcini mushroom powder, and chili-rubbed tenderloin of beef with jalapeño jack cheese polenta. The wine list is also superb. *2 Wilmington Ave., Rehoboth Beach, DE 19971; tel. 302-227-3887. Open daily for afternoon tapas and dinner and Sun. for brunch late May-Sep.*

◆ **The Back Porch Cafe** (expensive). Refined yet casual, this restaurant is simply and tastefully furnished, with ferns and stained glass. A diverse menu includes lunch choices such as grilled tenderloin of beef salad southwestern, summer-vegetable lasagna, and seared cornmeal-encrusted soft-shell crab with black bean pureé and mango relish. The crab-cake sandwich is delicious. Dinner items may include roast rack of lamb au jus, herbed goat cheese soufflé, or pan-seared red snapper. *59 Rehoboth Ave., Rehoboth Beach, DE 19971; tel. 302-227-3674. Open daily for lunch and dinner late May-Sep. and for dinner Fri.-Sun. late Mar.-May and Oct.; brunch on Sun.*

◆ **The Cultured Pearl** (expensive). This upscale sushi bar and seafood restaurant has Japanese and American selections, ranging from veal Chesapeake and dijon-encrusted salmon to shrimp tempura and seafood one-pot, plus dozens of sushi selections. Among sushi rolls are the Rehoboth (yellowtail, tuna, salmon, avocado, flying-fish egg, and scallion), the Ocean City (cooked tuna with cream cheese), and the Philly (crab stick, shrimp, and cream cheese). *19A Wilmington Ave., Rehoboth Beach, DE 19971; tel. 302-227-8493. Open daily for dinner.*

◆ **Chez La Mer** (moderate). This well-regarded restaurant with three dining areas offers a wide range of interesting seafood and meat dishes, such as the roast pork loin stuffed with spinach, apricots, and walnuts and the sautéed shrimp with bowtie pasta, leeks, tomatoes, spinach, and saffron sauce. It also has a vegetarian menu and a good wine selection. When Al and Tipper Gore ate here one Memorial Day weekend, they had swordfish and soft-shell crabs. *210 Second St., Rehoboth Beach, DE 19971;*

tel. 302-227-6494. Open for dinner Apr.-Nov.

◆ **Dogfish Head Brewing & Eats** (moderate). This high-ceilinged restaurant with a long bar and plenty of elbow room between the tables opened in 1995 as Delaware's first microbrewery. The menu has a good selection of burgers, sandwiches, and salads, plus creative hickory-wood-grilled pizza, grilled entrées such as tuna steak and salmon fillet, and a daily vegetarian special. Some evenings there's live entertainment. *320 Rehoboth Ave., Rehoboth Beach, DE 19971; tel. 302-226-2739. Open daily for lunch and dinner Apr.-Oct.; abbreviated hours at other times.*

◆ **Sir Guy's Restaurant & Pub** (moderate). This comfortable pub-style restaurant serves shepherd's pie and bangers (sausages) at lunch, steak and kidney pie at dinner, plus an assortment of sandwiches, salads, and meat and seafood entrées. *243 Rehoboth Ave., Rehoboth Beach, DE 19971; tel. 302-227-7616. Open daily for lunch and dinner.*

NIGHTLIFE

◆ **Arena's.** Live music most nights. *Rehoboth Beach, DE 19971; tel. 302-227-1272. In the Village by the Sea Shoppes.*

◆ **Fran O'Brien's Beach House.** Live music most evenings, followed by DJs on Fridays and Saturdays. *59 Lake Ave., Rehoboth Beach, DE 19971; tel. 302-227-6121. Open nightly in season.*

◆ **Irish Eyes Pub & Restaurant.** There's often something on the evening entertainment menu here during the summer, including live comedy on Mondays, live rock and roll Tuesdays and Wednesdays, and live Irish music Thursday through Sunday. Late-night food menu available until 1 a.m. *15 Wilmington Ave., Rehoboth Beach, DE 19971; tel. 302-227-2888. Open daily.*

◆ **Sydney's Blues & Jazz Restaurant.** Live blues and jazz in an old schoolhouse. Dinner, grazing, and café menus, plus a Sunday jazz brunch. *25 Christian St., Rehoboth Beach, DE 19971; tel. 302-227-1339. Open daily May-Nov. and Thu.-Sun. Dec.-Apr. At Rehoboth Ave. intersection.*

SHOPPING

The outlet malls along Route 1 are among the busiest in the country. Traffic backs up badly along Route 1 on weekends and rainy days, and turning left across the traffic can seem almost impossible. Consider plotting your route to allow a right-hand turn into the mall lots.

◆ **Ocean Outlets.** This outlet group has about 100 stores in two complexes, one called Seaside, the other Bayside. Seaside includes Reebok, Eddie Bauer, Bugle Boy, Oshkosh B'Gosh, and Oneida. Bayside includes Champion/Hanes, Van Heusen Direct, Westport Woman, American Tourister, and Book Warehouse. *1600 Ocean Outlets, Rehoboth Beach, DE 19971; tel. 302-226-9223. Open daily. On Rte. 1 between Rtes. 9 and 1A.*

◆ **Rehoboth Outlet Center.** More than 50 stores, including Ann Taylor, L. L. Bean, Jones New York, Nautica, Coach, Danskin, Liz Claiborne, and Benetton. *Rte. 1 at Midway, Rehoboth Beach, DE 19971; tel. 302-644-2600. Open daily.*

BEST FOOD SHOPS

SANDWICHES: ◆ **Delaware Sub Shop.** Cheese steaks, subs, gyros, and other sandwiches. *First St. and Wilmington Ave., Rehoboth Beach, DE 19971; tel. 302-227-0440. Open daily in season.*

SEAFOOD: ◆ **Rehoboth Seafood Market.** *4147A Rte. 1, Rehoboth Beach, DE 19971; tel. 302-227-3551. Open daily in season. On Rte. 1 just south of Rehoboth Ave.*

BAKERY: ◆ **Di Bonaventure's Italian Bakery.** *220 Rehoboth Ave., Rehoboth Beach, DE 19971; tel. 302-226-0176. Open Wed.-Mon.*

ICE CREAM: ◆ **The Ice Cream Store.** *Rehoboth Ave. and the Boardwalk, Rehoboth Beach, DE 19971; tel. 302-227-4609. Open daily mid-Feb.-early Nov.*

BEVERAGES: ◆ **Super Soda Center.** *605 Rehoboth Ave., Rehoboth Beach, DE 19971; tel. 302-227-2625. Open daily.*

WINE: ◆ **Ocean Wines & Spirits.** *4313 Rte. 1, Rehoboth Beach, DE 19971; tel. 302-227-7700. Open Mon.-Sat.*

SPORTS

Besides water sports, volleyball is popular in Rehoboth Beach, with nightly volleyball in summer from 7 to 11 on the beach between Rehoboth and Olive avenues. Health clubs include the Midway Fitness Center, the Firm Health Club, the Sussex Family YMCA, and the Body Shop Fitness Center. The Midway Shopping Center on Route 1 has a skating rink, and behind the shopping center is the Midway Bowling Center.

FISHING

Surf fishing is popular along the coast in nonswimming areas. Charter boat and headboat fishing trips depart from Fisherman's Wharf in Lewes and the Indian River Inlet marina south of Dewey Beach (*see* Lewes and Dewey Beach chapters).

SURFING

The best surfing in the area is near the Indian River Inlet, a few miles south of Rehoboth (*see* Dewey Beach chapter). Surfers also gather just north of Rehoboth Beach at the southern end of Cape Henlopen State Park.

DIVING

◆ **Old Inlet Dive Shop.** A 45-foot charter boat carries divers to Atlantic wreck sites in 60 to 90 feet of water, departing at about 7 a.m. and returning early to midafternoon. *3407 Rte. 1, Rehoboth Beach, DE 19971; tel. 302-227-0999. Open daily Apr.-mid-Nov.*

BICYCLING

◆ **Marilee Bike Rental.** Bike rentals for adults and children, including surrey bikes. *70 Rehoboth Ave., Rehoboth Beach, DE 19971; tel. 302-227-5534. Open daily May-Sept., weekends Oct.-Apr.*

GOLF

◆ **Old Landing Golf Course.** This 18-hole, par-70 course is the only full public course in Sussex County. *300 Old Landing Rd., Rehoboth Beach, DE 19971; tel. 302-227-3131. Open daily. Admission. From central Rehoboth Beach, go north on Rte. 1, turn left onto Rte. 274, and follow it for 2 1/2 mi.*

TENNIS

◆ **Rehoboth City Courts.** Four courts; $7 per hour; reservations accepted in person—no phone reservations. (Other courts are available at Rehoboth Junior High School on State Road.) *Surf Ave., Rehoboth Beach, DE 19971. Open daily 7-7. Admission.*

Located between Rehoboth Beach and North Shores, along one of the beach parking lots; somewhat obscured by vegetation.

NATURE

◆ **Twin Capes Nature Tours.** Outdoor tours include the Rehoboth Beach nature walk, the Cape Henlopen nature tour, and the waterfowl decoy and sanctuary tour. Also sells tickets for kayak tours, whale- and dolphin-watching trips, and the Cape May-Lewes ferry. *49 Baltimore Ave., Rehoboth Beach, DE 19971; tel. 302-227-5850, 800-227-5850. Open daily. Admission. Tours leave from the office near Second St. and Baltimore Ave.*

SAFETY TIPS

Rehoboth Beach can draw up to 60,000 people on a busy weekend, so there is the inevitable smattering of property crime that comes with transient crowds. In June 1995, police reports showed four burglaries, 41 thefts, 23 traffic accidents, and 330 traffic arrests.

TOURIST INFORMATION

◆ **Rehoboth Beach-Dewey Beach Chamber of Commerce.** *501 Rehoboth Ave., Rehoboth Beach, DE 19971; tel. 302-227-2233, 800-441-1329. Open Mon.-Fri. 9-5 and Sat.-Sun. 9-12 May-Sep. Closed Sun. Oct.-Apr.*

◆ **Sussex County Convention & Tourism Commission.** Sussex County includes all of Delaware's Atlantic Ocean resort towns, Rehoboth Beach among them. The Tourism Commission offers a visitors guide, maps, group itineraries, and other information. *Box 240, Georgetown, DE 19947; tel. 302-856-1818, 800-357-1818. Open Mon.-Fri. 8-4:30. Located in the International Center at the Delaware Technical College in Georgetown.*

Dewey Beach

Beauty	B
Swimming	B
Sand	B-
Hotels/Inns/B&Bs	B
House rentals	A
Restaurants	B
Nightlife	C
Attractions	C
Shopping	C
Sports	A
Nature	B

*T*ucked neatly between ocean and bay, Dewey Beach became Delaware's newest incorporated city in 1982. But, long before that, it earned a reputation as an inviting beach where revelers buried beer kegs—taps protruding from the sand—and the brew flowed freely for anyone who happened along. "Every night was Saturday night," recalls one native son. The good old days yielded to a more restrained present, and although the city retains its cachet as a weekend party town in summer, it's also become a family-friendly destination. Today as then, Dewey is often mentioned in the same breath as its bigger sibling to the north, Rehoboth Beach. The Jolly Trolley runs between them every 30 minutes like clockwork. But Dewey has its own personality, a good range of motels and rental properties, noteworthy restaurants, and its own diversions. State Route 1, the backbone of all Delaware beach cities, runs for 20 blocks through town, bisecting it into oceanside and bay-side. In most places you can walk from one shoreline to the other in a matter of minutes.

From either side, the view is soothing. Dolphins frequently arc along the undeveloped beach on summer afternoons, and sailboards and Jet Skis glide across the wide Rehoboth Bay. The only sour note is sounded in signs that read: "Quiet! Residential area. Loud noise and disorderly behavior prohibited. Violators will be prosecuted."

The Ruddertowne dining, shopping, and entertainment

HOW TO GET THERE

◆ In smooth traffic, Dewey Beach is 2 hr. from Philadelphia International Airport and 2 1/2 hr. from Baltimore-Washington International and Washington National airports. In peak weekend traffic, add another 30 to 45 min.

◆ From Philadelphia, follow I-95 south past Wilmington to DE Rte. 1 (at times U.S. 13), which goes south all the way to Dewey Beach. Watch for speed traps in Odessa, DE.

◆ From Baltimore and Washington, go to Annapolis, MD, cross the Bay Bridge, go south on U.S. 50, east on MD 404 and DE 404, east on U.S. 9 to DE Rte. 1, and then south to Dewey.

complex at Dickinson Street is Dewey's largest gathering point. Its restaurants, as well as the Waterfront restaurant a few blocks away, are favorites for watching the sun set over the calm water.

BEACHES
OCEANSIDE

The ocean front is undeveloped. There is no boardwalk, only a narrow dune separating the beach from two- and three-story houses, condos, and motels. Barrels for recycling and trash are set at regular intervals, but the beach is not

Beauty	B
Swimming	B
Sand	C
Amenities	C

regularly groomed. A few beach shacks rent umbrellas and sell snacks. A jeep roves the sand offering drinks, and a strolling ice cream vendor may happen by.

Guaranteed to make an appearance is the Dewey Beach Patrol, a youthful and smartly dressed summer corps with a reputation for aggressively enforcing the city's ban on drinking alcohol in public. Dewey lore has many accounts of the beach patrol inspecting coolers in search of banned beverages—sometimes for no apparent reason, which leaves sandcastle lawyers crying foul.

Swimming: Water is relatively clear, though sometimes seaweed is present. The beach shelf slopes gradually, but the drop-off can change overnight depending on surf conditions. The shore is usually free of dangerous currents or undertows. Lifeguard on duty.

Sand: Moderately fine brown sand mottled with shell remnants, building into a low, grassy dune.

Amenities: Dewey Beach has no rest rooms or changing stations. Rte. 1 businesses are a block or two away. Motels discourage nonguests from using rest rooms.

Sports: Skim-boarding (*see* Sports) is big, as is volleyball, on weekends. Fishing and crabbing in surf and tidal waters.

Parking: On the streets leading to the beach. Parking permits are required from 10 a.m. to 5 p.m. Purchase daily, weekly, and seasonal permits at the Town Hall. Permits must be posted in the car—strictly enforced. Motels limit guests to one vehicle.

BAYSIDE

With its wide, smooth water, Rehoboth Bay offers an excellent counterpoint to the ocean surf for learning or practicing sailing and sailboarding, as well as Jet Skiing and waterskiing.

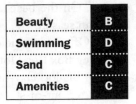

Beauty	B
Swimming	D
Sand	C
Amenities	C

A few splotches of sand have been dumped at the Rusty Rudder and the Waterfront restaurants, but just south of Dewey on the bay itself there are a couple of small beaches along Route 1, at Tower Road and nearby at Bay Road.

From parking lot to waterline the beaches are only a few yards deep and not very wide, but they are popular launching points for sailboarders, and the water is shallow and gentle.

The Tower Road beach is rather bland; the Bay Road beach is bigger, with dunes to one side and tall grass to the other. Both are backed by parking lots.

Swimming: Calm water safe for swimming but not diving. It remains shallow a long way into the bay. No lifeguard.

Sand: Moderately fine brown.

Amenities: Portable toilets. Bay Road has a boat ramp and a few picnic tables and grill.

Sports: Windsurfing, boating, crabbing.

Parking: Parking lots at each site. Day-use fee is $2.50 for Delaware vehicles, $5 for out-of-state.

TOWER ROAD: OCEANSIDE

On the ocean side of Route 1 at Tower Road is a broad, excellent beach that is part of Delaware Seashore State Park, complete with facilities but minus the clutter of the city. The parking lot holds hundreds of cars, and a boardwalk leads

Beauty	A
Swimming	A
Sand	B
Amenities	B-

from the big bathhouse over a dune to the beach, which has a slight roll to it. A World War II observation tower stands just north of the central beach area.

Swimming: Good surf swimming. Lifeguard on duty.

Sand: Fine brown.

Amenities: Full bathhouse with showers, toilets, and food concession. On the beach, a vendor rents chairs, umbrellas, body boards in season.

Sports: Off-road vehicle surf fishing to the south, with access from Key Box Road lot.

Parking: Big lot. Day-use fee is $2.50 per car for Delaware vehicles, $5 for out-of-state.

INDIAN RIVER INLET

About four miles south of Dewey on Route 1, the Indian River Inlet area of the Delaware Seashore State Park throbs with activity, including swimming on sizable beaches on both sides of the inlet. Ocean water rushes between

Beauty	B
Swimming	B
Sand	B
Amenities	A

the two barrier islands into Indian River Bay, where a busy marina has a full lineup of fishing and sightseeing.

The swift water, the constant movement of fishing boats, and the arrival and departure of vehicles from Route 1 into the park area creates a kinetic atmosphere. The beaches seem raw and refreshing, although the inlet bridge traffic and man-made bustle detract from the natural setting.

The north side of the inlet is a designated surfing beach, but surfers tout the south side, too, depending on the season. Getting to the north beach can take several minutes of walking from the huge parking lot and under the Route 1 bridge.

The south side beach also has a huge lot, with a big bathhouse opening onto the beach. The beach ends abruptly at the nearby inlet jetty but sprawls southward as far as the eye can see.

Swimming: Good, although the surf can be rough at times. Lifeguard on duty.

Sand: Fine, tan sand.

Amenities: South beach has full bathhouse with showers, rest rooms, and food concession. On the beach, a vendor rents chairs, umbrellas, body boards in season. Campgrounds on both sides of the inlet.

Sports: Surfing, surf fishing. Boats, fishing equipment for rent at the marina. Fishing, dolphin, and whale-watching charters.

Parking: Big lots. Day-use fee is $2.50 per car for Delaware vehicles, $5 for out-of-state.

HOTELS/INNS/B&BS

Dewey Beach is a low-rise town with roughly 450 rooms, most in motels of a few dozen rooms or less, with only a couple of B&Bs. Many of the motels have been built in the last 15 years, providing a good supply of modern rooms, a number with kitchen facilities. Motels usually require a two-day minimum stay for weekends, three days for holidays, and most are closed after the April to October tourist season.

♦ **Best Western Gold Leaf** (expensive). Dewey's biggest is basic balconied beach-style, four stories, 72 rooms, a block off the beach, with garage parking, rooftop pool. Modern, nondescript furnishings. Half the rooms have views of ocean and bay, the others—fronting busy Rte. 1—look out on the hopping Ruddertowne complex at bayside. *1400 Rte. 1, Dewey Beach, DE 19971; tel. 302-226-1100, 800-422-8566; fax 302-226-9785.*

♦ **The Surf Club** (expensive). One of Dewey's newest lodgings, with 45 luxury efficiency units, outdoor pool, hot tub, and sauna; VCRs and bicycles available. Rooms are airy and spacious, with tile floors and Southwestern decor. Whereas most motels ban taking their towels to the beach, the Surf Club provides beach towels. *1 Read St., Dewey Beach, DE 19971; tel. 302-227-7059, 800-441-8341.*

♦ **Atlantic View Motel** (moderate). On the beach. Half the three-story motel's 35 units have ocean views; all have balconies or decks. Rooms are spacious, light, and basic. Those with a king-size bed also have a sofa bed. *2 Clayton St., Dewey Beach, DE 19971; tel. 302-227-3878, 800-777-4162; fax 302-226-2640. Open Easter- Halloween. 3-night minimum for weekends in season.*

♦ **Barry's Gull Cottage** (moderate). A Nantucket-style cornucopia of white wicker, antiques, quilts, and stained glass, wrapped in lush vegetation and guarded by cats. Three rooms, tightly set, with bamboo-shaded patio garden and fountain. Player piano and video library. Named after the cottage in *The Ghost and Mrs. Muir.* Superlative breakfasts. Five-minute walk to the beach. *116 Chesapeake St., Dewey Beach, DE 19971; tel.*

302-227-7000, 302-227-0547. Closed Nov.-Apr.; 2-night mini-mum on weekends. On Dewey's northernmost residential street, just off Rte. 1A, before Silver Lake.

◆ **Bellbuoy Motel** (moderate). An unobtrusive three-story motel in a quiet setting, it has 16 rooms with either one king or two double beds; light-wood paneling, good lighting, refrigerators and some microwaves. One full-size apartment with kitchen and living room. On the beach block. *21 Van Dyke St., Dewey Beach, DE 19971; tel. 302-227-6000. Closed mid-Oct.-Mar.*

◆ **Southwinds Motel Efficiencies** (moderate). Modern and clean with stainless-steel kitchenettes in all units. Some have high sloping ceilings with skylights. All have large balconies. Must cross Rte. 1 to reach the beach a block away. *1609 Rte. 1, Dewey Beach, DE 19971; tel. 302-227-7800, 800-392-8507. Closed mid-Oct.-mid-Apr.*

HOUSE RENTALS

Dewey Beach has about 800 rental properties, evenly divided between condos and houses. Weekly rates in season (roughly Easter to Columbus Day) range from $500 for a one-room apartment to $3,500 for an ocean-front town house. Many have a one-week minimum. Houses in the northern third of town date back to the 1960s; most town houses and condos to the south postdate 1980. All agencies for Dewey rentals also book the rest of the Delaware shore.

◆ **Century 21 Mann and Moore Associates Inc.** *4343 Rte. 1, Rehoboth Beach, DE 19971; tel. 302-227-9477, 800-255-8200. Open daily.*

◆ **Coldwell Banker.** *4157 Rte. 1, Rehoboth Beach, DE 19971; tel. 302-227-5000, 800-800-4134. Open daily.*

RESTAURANTS

Crab shacks and sandwich spots hug Rte. 1, but Dewey has a good assortment of more elaborate eateries as well.

◆ **Two Seas Restaurant** (expensive). Remarkably good seafood. Located on the second floor, it has sophisticated dishes in a comfortable setting that avoids beach-town clichés. For a special or romantic meal, this is the place. Try the soft-shell crabs

214

or the snapper crusted in red onion. Stroll up to the rooftop deck for a Dewey overview. *Van Dyke & Rte. 1, Dewey Beach, DE 19971; tel. 302-227-2610. Open daily for dinner from late May- Oct. or Nov.*

◆ **Captain's Table** (moderate). Classic surf and turf in a place where effort goes into the food, not the decor. *Rte. 1, Rehoboth Beach, DE 19971; tel. 302-227-6203. Open daily for lunch and dinner. Closed Sun. during the off-season. On Rte. 1 just north of Dewey; it's easy to overlook on the ride between Dewey and Rehoboth.*

◆ **Rusty Rudder** (moderate). Laid-back dining on the bayside deck or in the dining room. Specialties include seafood and ribs, with a hefty buffet three nights a week. *113 Dickinson St., Dewey Beach, DE 19971; tel. 302-227-3888. Open daily for lunch and dinner. Ruddertowne, at the bay.*

◆ **Coconuts Seafood House** (inexpensive). High-volume lobster and shrimp specials make this a good seafood value, with family night and other deals that hook hordes. Expansive dining-hall atmosphere on the bay; no outdoor seating. *Dagsworthy St. at the bay, Dewey Beach, DE 19971; tel. 302-227-3317. Open daily for dinner Apr.-Sep. Next to the Waterfront, its sibling on the bay.*

◆ **Gary's Surf Spray Cafe** (inexpensive). Healthy food in a beach-bar setting on Rte. 1, indoor or outdoor seating. Try the turkey burger with Gary's special seasoning. Fuller meals are also on the menu, including vegetable lasagna and Cajun catfish. *2000 Rte. 1, Dewey Beach, DE 19971; tel. 302 227-8519. Open daily for breakfast, lunch, and dinner mid-May-mid-Sep. No credit cards. Ocean side of Rte. 1 at New Orleans St.*

◆ **Grotto Pizza** (inexpensive). Traditional pizza, which can be wolfed down at the counter or savored in the adjacent sit-down restaurant. The Grand, a stuffed slice with cheese, topping, onion, and garlic, takes the edge off your appetite after an afternoon of skim-boarding. *Rte. 1 and Reed St., Dewey Beach, DE 19971; tel. 302-227-3407. Open daily for lunch and dinner late May-late Nov.*

NIGHTLIFE

Dewey's nightlife is largely limited to dining, drinking, and swaying to the music at a handful of bars and restaurants. Beyond that, Dewey vacationers head for Rehoboth's more varied waters.

◆ **Bottle & Cork.** Rock and roll bar with live music, including the occasional nationally known act. *1807 Rte. 1, Dewey Beach, DE*

19971; tel. 302-227-8545. Open nightly May-Sep.

◆ **Ruddertowne Pier.** Families go night crabbing with the kids off this wooden pier that extends far along the shallow water. Take your own crab pots or string line and chicken necks. *Dickinson St. at the bay, Dewey Beach, DE 19971; tel. 302-227-3888. Spotlights illuminate the pier well into the wee hours.*

◆ **Rusty Rudder.** Ruddertowne's anchor business hops with live rock and reggae bands and, especially on weekends, big crowds on the large outdoor deck. *113 Dickinson St., Dewey Beach, DE 19971; tel. 302-227-3888. Open daily.*

◆ **Starboard Restaurant.** Smoky lounge area has low ceilings, TVs, and dart boards. Many Dewey regulars insist on having last call here. Weekend mornings, check out the Bloody Mary bar, with a choice of 60 vodkas. *2009 Rte. 1, Dewey Beach, DE 19971; tel. 302-227-4600. Open nightly St. Patrick's Day-Labor Day, Thu.-Mon. Labor Day-mid-Oct.*

◆ **The Waterfront.** DJs blast away nightly on the sandy deck. The signature drink is the high-octane Dewey Devil, made of rums, blackberry brandy, orange juice, strawberries, and cream, and topped with whipped cream and a cherry. *135 McKinley St., Dewey Beach, DE 19971; tel. 302-227-9292. Open nightly.*

SHOPPING

Big-time shopping is just minutes away in Rehoboth's outlet malls north of Dewey along Rte. 1, but Dewey has a few notable shops of its own.

◆ **Peppers.** Mecca for hot sauce lovers. With over 2,000 varieties, it claims the world record. Definitely worth a stop, if only to read labels like Hot Buns at the Beach and Hell in a Bottle. Part of the Starboard Restaurant. *2009 Rte. 1, Dewey Beach, DE 19971; tel. 302-227-4608, 800-998-3473; fax 302-227-4603. Open daily 8 a.m.-1 a.m. May-Sep. and 10-6 the rest of the year.*

◆ **Shops at Ruddertowne.** *Dickinson St. at the bay, Dewey Beach, DE 19971. Open daily.*

BEST FOOD SHOPS

SANDWICHES: ◆ **Dagsworthy Deli.** *1808 Rte. 1, Dewey Beach, DE 19971; tel. 302-227-8580. Open daily. In the Sea Spot Shops on the* *east side of Rte. 1 at Dagsworthy St.*

FRESH PRODUCE: ◆ **Bozie's Produce.** On the north edge of Dewey Beach, with drive-up stands on both sides of Route 1. *Rte. 1, Rehoboth Beach, DE 19971; tel. 302-227-6370. Open daily Apr.-mid-Oct.*

ICE CREAM: ◆ **Ben & Jerry's.** *1905 Rte. 1, Dewey Beach, DE 19971; tel. 302-227-7552. Open daily early Jun-Labor Day. At New Orleans St. in the Ocean Winds group of stores.*

BEVERAGES: ◆ **Dewey Beach Liquors.** Liquor, beer, wine, and soda by the case. *1807 Rte. 1, Dewey Beach, DE 19971; tel. 302-227-3191. Closed Sun.*

SPORTS

Dewey Beach's sports scene really percolates for a town this size, with lots of biking and running and a full range of water sports, including skim-boarding—a tricky maneuver practiced mostly by teenage guys. Even if it's not up your alley, it's entertaining to watch skim-boarders as they stand on the beach with their circular boards, waiting for the leading lip of a wave to spread smooth and shallow. At just the right moment, they run diagonally toward the wave, flinging the board ahead of them, then leap atop it as it skims across the water-lubricated sand. Their momentum carries them into the oncoming wave, which they curl into before coming to a splashing halt. Volleyball is also big here—nets go up each weekend all along Dewey Beach. For those who'd rather jog, Seashore Striders regularly organizes runs. Call the running club hot line for a schedule (tel. 302-684-1512).

FISHING

Charter boat and surf fishing are both popular. No license is required for fishing in tidal waters, which includes Rehoboth Bay. The season starts in early April with mackerel. Blue fishing continues into December. Inland waters have sea bass, sea trout, tautog, kingfish, mackerel, black drum, and croakers, plus striped bass, or rockfish, from March to December. Big fish—marlin, tuna, mako shark, swordfish, dolphin—run from late spring to early autumn. Charter boats cost from $250 to $1,000 per day (*see* Lewes and Ocean City, Maryland, chapters). For surf fishing, Indian River Inlet is a popular site.

◆ **Captain K's.** Half-day fishing and crabbing trips on the bay and rentals of 16-foot runabouts and 23-foot pontoon vessels. *1117 Rte. 1, Rehoboth Bay Marina, Dewey Beach, DE 19971; tel. 302-945-3345, 302-226-2012. Open daily May-Oct.*

◆ **Herb's Bait & Tackle.** Bait, rod-and-reel rentals, tackle, and advice. Official weigh station. *1905 Rte. 1, Dewey Beach, DE 19971; tel. 302-227-0631. Open daily May-Oct.*

◆ *Judy V* **Fishing Boat.** This 65-foot boat leaves from Indian River Inlet at south end of the park for half-day fishing trips in the morning, dolphin cruises in the early afternoon. *Delaware Seashore State Park, Dewey Beach, DE 19971; tel. 302-422-8940. Fishing charters depart 8 a.m., dolphin cruises from 1-3 p.m. Open daily Apr.-Oct; call for winter hours.*

BOATING

◆ **Ocean Wind Watersports.** Parasailing and Jet Ski rentals on Rehoboth Bay. Look for coupons in beach publications. *Collins St. at the bay, Dewey Beach, DE 19971; tel. 302-227-4359. Open daily 8 a.m. until dusk in season. Rehoboth Bay Marina, one block south of Ruddertowne.*

SURFING AND SKIM-BOARDING

Surfing is best near the Indian River Inlet, site of the Delaware State Surfing Championships, in early morning and evening. Dewey prohibits surfing near crowded beaches.

◆ **Dewey Beach Surf and Sport.** This shop's skim-boards put Dewey on the map, where it remains with its annual skim-board competition. The shop has every other water device, too. Surfboards, body boards, skim-boards, rafts, fins, and wet suits by the hour, day, or week. *1904 Rte. 1, Dewey Beach, DE 19971; tel. 302-227-8288. Open daily.*

◆ **East of Maui.** Surf boards, Boogie boards, and Windsurfers for sale or rent. *2400 Rte. 1, Dewey Beach, DE 19971; tel. 302-227-4703. Open Sun.-Fri. 10-6; Sat. 10-7 Apr.-Nov. In the wedge where Rtes. 1 and 1A intersect.*

DIVING

◆ **Old Inlet Dive Shop.** A 45-foot charter boat carries divers to

Atlantic wreck sites in 60 to 90 feet of water, departing (daily when demand is high) at 7 a.m. and returning early to mid-afternoon. *3407 Rte. 1, Rehoboth Beach, DE 19971; tel. 302-227-0999.*

GOLF

None of lower Delaware's dozens of golf courses are in Dewey Beach. The Salt Pond Golf Club is in Bethany Beach (*see* Bethany Beach chapter).

TENNIS

Two public tennis courts are available between Dagsworthy and McKinley streets, near Coconuts restaurant at the bay. First-come, first-served; no water fountain.

NATURE

◆ **Delaware Seashore State Park.** Burtons Island Nature Trail, located at the north end of the marina, is 1.5 miles long; insect repellent is recommended. Dolphin and whale-watching cruises leave from the marina. Also at the park: boating, boat rentals, camping, fishing, picnicking, and swimming. *Rte. 1, Dewey Beach, DE 19971; tel. 302-227-2800, 302-227-3071. Open daily May-Oct. and Mon.-Fri. the rest of the year. Admission. 4 mi. south of Dewey Beach.*

SAFETY TIPS

Dewey is a place where crime *does* take a vacation. Parking enforcement and rowdy-party complaints make up most police actions. Take common-sense precautions, such as not leaving valuables on the car seat.

TOURIST INFORMATION

◆ **Dewey Beach Town Hall.** *105 Rodney Ave., Dewey Beach, DE 19971; tel. 302-227-6363. Open daily 9-5 Memorial Day-Labor Day and Mon.-Fri. 9-5 the rest of the year.*
◆ **Rehoboth Beach-Dewey Beach Chamber of Commerce.** *501 Rehoboth Ave., Box 216, Rehoboth Beach, DE 19971; tel. 302-227-2233; 800-441-1329. Open Mon.-Fri. 9-5 and Sat. 9-12 year-round; open Sun. 9-12 May-Sep.*

CHAPTER 22

Bethany Beach

Beauty	B
Swimming	A
Sand	B
Hotels/Inns/B&Bs	C
House rentals	B
Restaurants	B-
Nightlife	D
Attractions	D
Shopping	C
Sports	C
Nature	B

ethany Beach is the Delaware shoreline's last outpost of quietude, a town of a few hundred people whose companionable board-walk is measured in blocks, not miles, and where the restaurants cater to families rather than singles.

While all of the state's beach cities tout themselves as family-friendly, Bethany vigorously embraces the theme. Along with nearby South Bethany Beach and the community of Fenwick Island, Bethany calls itself one of "the quiet resorts," sandwiched between boisterous Ocean City, Maryland, to the south and Rehoboth-Dewey Beach to the north.

Bethany got its start in 1894 as a summer camp for the Christian Missionary Society of Washington, D.C., and a decade later had grown enough to get a post office branch and its first boardwalk. The resort expanded at a measured pace, and it wasn't until 1976 that house numbers were assigned. The boardwalk has been replaced or repaired several times over the years because of storm damage, most recently in 1992.

While the city may be low-rise and compact, it's not really a remote burgh. On its southern edge, the 11 lofty towers of the huge Sea Colony development rise along the water, and other Sea Colony town houses and garden apartments sprawl to the west, totaling about 1,700 units.

For the most part, Bethany delivers on its promise to be a quiet beach town. Besides robust beaches on the Atlantic, the area boasts water sports and natural attractions on nearby Little Assawoman Bay, including Delaware's Fenwick Island State Park, with facilities on both the ocean and the bay. Fresh- and saltwater fishing are popular, and off-road-vehicle beach access is nearby for surf fishing.

Bethany's seven-block ocean-front boardwalk has few businesses on it and not a single arcade or "whack-a-mole" game in

HOW TO GET THERE

◆ From Washington, D.C., in smooth traffic, the drive to Bethany Beach is about 3 hr. Take U.S. Rte. 50 east to Annapolis, cross the Bay Bridge, take Rte. 404 east to Georgetown, DE, then U.S. Rte. 113 south to Rte. 26 east.

◆ From Philadelphia, the trip takes about 2 1/2 hr. in smooth traffic. Follow I-95 south past Wilmington to DE Rte. 1 (at times U.S. 13), which goes south all the way to Bethany Beach.

sight. Instead, two- and three-story condos rise along much of the boardwalk, with contented vacationers looking down from their decks on pedestrians just feet away. People stroll in close quarters, and there is a sense of community even among strangers. The ocean surges near to the boardwalk, especially at high tide, giving the beach front an intimate feel. Everyone on the sand would be within shouting distance if it weren't for the roar of the surf.

Bethany's main business street is Garfield Parkway, which runs a few short blocks from Delaware Route 1 to the boardwalk. There are changing rooms, rest rooms, and beach patrol offices, plus a stage with benches for regularly scheduled summer performances on the boardwalk.

Local politicians vigilantly work to maintain Bethany's quiet demeanor. Even with just a handful of restaurants serving liquor, the Town Council in 1995 voted to cut off alcoholic drink sales at 11:30 p.m.—a compromise after restaurant owners complained bitterly about the original plan to make last call 10:30.

Fenwick Island, five miles south on Route 1, has numerous motels and restaurants but is largely residential. Still, its lack of a central business district and proximity to Ocean City rob it of the coziness of Bethany.

BEACHES
BETHANY BOARDWALK BEACH

The beach along the boardwalk is caressed by waves heavy with foam, and it extends far beyond the boardwalk at both ends, so there is room to spread out even at high tide, when the beach is not particularly wide. The sand is only a

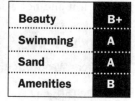

Beauty	B+
Swimming	A
Sand	A
Amenities	B

few steps off the boardwalk, and there are also access points over a low dune at streets that run perpendicular to the shore. The proximity of the boardwalk and a string of buildings behind the beach mean it doesn't have the wild, wide-open feel of a totally undeveloped beach front, but it's convenient to have everything close at hand.

Swimming: Water is clean, with enough wave action to make even wading lively. Beware of the stone jetties that are submerged except at low tide. Lifeguard on duty in summer.

Sand: Evenly spread, moderately fine, and tan. The beach has been replenished.

Amenities: At the main boardwalk entrance there are rest rooms and a bathhouse. Snack bars and shops are close by. Chair rentals available.

Sports: Boogie boarding is allowed, but surfing (like most other sports) is prohibited when lifeguards are on duty. After guards are off, surfing is allowed north of Campbell Place.

Parking: Nearby meters are 75 cents per hour. Permits required for side streets close to the beach.

FENWICK ISLAND STATE PARK

Three miles of barrier island beach front make this park particularly attractive. There is some private property along a portion of the ocean-front beach, but much of it has an away-from-it-all feel.

Beauty	A
Swimming	A
Sand	A
Amenities	B

There is a small beach for launching water-sports craft across Route 1 from the park's main entrance. The concessionaire, Bay Sports, rents Waverunners, sailboats, pedal craft, kayaks, and Windsurfers (tel. 302-539-7999). There's a small dirt parking lot (no charge). *The park entrance is on Rte. 1, about 4 mi. south of Bethany Beach; tel 302-539-9060.*

Swimming: The beach resembles Bethany Boardwalk's—minus the boardwalk and development behind the dune, so it's actually much bigger and more scenic. Lifeguard on duty.

Sand: Moderately fine, light tan, building to a wide and grassy dune.

Amenities: Big, modern bathhouse with rest rooms, showers, and food concession. Beach-equipment rentals from cabana on beach. Boardwalk crosses dune from bathhouse to beach.

Sports: Swimming, saltwater fishing, Boogie boarding; also a designated surfing area. Nearby, along Rte. 1, are several entry points for off-road vehicles posting surf-fishing permits.

Parking: Large lot. The park charges a per-car day-use fee: $2.50 for Delaware license plates; $5 for out-of-state.

FENWICK ISLAND

Fenwick Island's beachline doesn't exactly have a wilderness feel; there are plenty of low-rise beach homes and a few motels just behind the dune that runs along most of the beach. Yet it doesn't seem commercial either.

Beauty	B+
Swimming	B
Sand	A
Amonitios	D

There's no boardwalk or sea-front business district, and the beach is wide enough to satisfy anyone who'd rather not be in the shadow of buildings.

Look north and the beach goes on and on; look south and Ocean City, Maryland, rises not far away, and you can easily see how Delaware's rules have succeeded in keeping development back from the beach, while just across the state line in Ocean City the hotels are perched at water's edge. *From Rte. 1, turn east on any street south of the visitors center, from Lewes St. to Atlantic Ave.*

Swimming: Clear, clean water with wave action. Lifeguard on duty.
Sand: Fine and tan, with occasional black streaking from minerals.
Amenities: No bathhouse.
Sports: Surf fishing, body boarding. On the bay side, Jet Ski rentals and parasailing are available.
Parking: Parking from Bunting Avenue to the dune requires a permit (limited to residents), but property owners sometimes provide permits to renters. Other street parking is free.

HOTELS/INNS/B&BS

Bethany Beach doesn't have many full-service motels, so it's best to reserve far in advance. Otherwise, during the busy season, you'll have to get lucky and catch a cancellation. Hundreds of rental units are available in the huge Sea Colony condo development bordering Bethany. More motels are a few miles south in Fenwick Island.

◆ **The Addy Sea** (expensive). Spectacular lodging in a beachfront house that was Bethany Beach's first. The 13 rooms pay homage to the Victorian era without putting starch in a casual holiday. Some rooms have private bath, some half bath, some shared. Rooms 6 and 7 have large corner picture windows and seating areas that look out to sea. A large downstairs bedroom, the Captain's Quarters, was originally the office of builder John Addy. *Box 275, Bethany Beach, DE 19930; tel. 302-539-3707. Closed Nov.-Mar. At Atlantic Ave. and Ocean View Pkwy.*

◆ **Bethany Arms** (moderate). This motel has 52 rooms in five buildings. Two of the buildings, E and D, front the boardwalk. Almost all rooms have ocean views, and Room 36, an end room on the third floor, has a clear balcony view down the coast. Rooms are well laid out and furnished in earth tones and have kitchen facilities. *Box 1600, Bethany Beach, DE 19930; tel. 302-539-9603. Closed mid-Oct.-Feb. At Atlantic Ave. and Hollywood St.*

◆ **Blue Surf Motel** (moderate). The Blue Surf has about 40 rooms next to the boardwalk, a few of them actually attached to the boardwalk. Most are spacious, with fully furnished kitchens. The motif is dark-wood paneling, but the rooms are nicely equipped, with air-conditioning, two double beds, telephone, and TV. The three ocean-front annex rooms offer more privacy and a good vantage point of the boardwalk without being too close. Room 126's balcony overlooks the boardwalk bandstand. *Box 999, Bethany Beach, DE 19930; tel. 302-539-7531. At Garfield Pkwy. and the boardwalk. Open Apr.-mid-Oct.*

◆ **Journey's End** (inexpensive). For those who crave authentic lodgings and don't mind no-frills. This traditional guesthouse hasn't changed much since it opened in 1927. It has shared rest rooms, no AC or TV, and outdoor showers. The eight rooms are furnished family style and are neat and clean. The atmosphere is simple and friendly. A block from the beach. Anti-aircraft defense crews boarded here in WWII. *101 Parkwood St., Bethany Beach, DE 19930; tel. 302-539-9502. Closed Oct.-mid-May. On Atlantic Ave., 3 blocks south of Garfield Pkwy.*

◆ **Westward Pines Motel** (inexpensive). This ten-room, family-run motel is a real switch from the usual beach fare. Located several blocks away from the water on a quiet plot with towering trees and a split-rail fence, it's more like a mountain cabin. The rooms, with modern decor, are meticulously maintained and have ceiling fans and AC; some have king-size beds. One room has a fireplace, one has a Jacuzzi, two have decks. No credit cards accepted. *10 Kent Ave., Bethany Beach, DE 19930; tel. 302-539-7426. From Rte. 1, turn west on Jefferson Bridge Rd.*

and left onto Kent Ave. It's is set back from the road, on the left.

HOUSE RENTALS

Condos and beach homes are plentiful in Bethany-Fenwick Island, with bayside rentals available in the Fenwick area. A two-bedroom house a couple of blocks from the beach may rent for $650 a week, while a five-bedroom oceanfront home could go for more than $4,000. A four-bedroom condo on the boardwalk at Bethany may cost $2,000.

◆ **Connor Jacobsen Realty.** *8 N. Pennsylvania Ave., Bethany Beach, DE 19930; tel. 302-539-9300, 800-543-5550. Open daily.*

◆ **Sea Colony.** A landmark development with ocean-front high-rise units plus town houses and garden apartments in wooded areas west of Route 1. The ocean-front towers are called the beach community; the other sections are called the tennis community. About one-third of the 1,700 units can be rented. *Drawer L, Bethany Beach, DE 19930; tel. 302-539-6961, 800-732-2656. Open daily. Rte. 1 at West Way, just south of Rte. 26.*

RESTAURANTS

◆ **Sedona** (expensive). The southwestern cuisine makes waves beyond Bethany Beach, with vacationers and residents from up and down the coast reserving a place in the dining room or bar. Popular openers are the El Paso sausage and Santa Fe pork taco and the warm curried butternut squash soup. Top entreés are blue-corn-dusted Sedona crab cakes, grilled lamb eye loin or tuna steak, and a wild game selection that has included elk, antelope, buffalo, kangaroo, and emu. *26 Pennsylvania Ave., Bethany Beach, DE 19930; tel. 302-539-1200. Open daily for dinner Apr.-Nov.*

◆ **Tom & Terry's Seafood Restaurant and Bar** (expensive). A sterling seafood spot with fine food, a comfortable modern setting, and soothing views over Assawoman Bay, whose green wetlands border the restaurant. Stuffed lobster tail, jumbo backfin crab cakes, prime rib, and char-grilled swordfish and tuna steaks are mainstays of the dinner menu. An expanse of glass gives the indoor dining rooms that outdoor feel, and then there's Tom & Terry's more casual section, Flamingo's Bar and (outdoor) Deck Grille. *Rte. 54 and the Bay, Fenwick Island, DE 19944; tel. 302-*

436-4161. *Open daily for lunch and dinner. From Rte. 1, go west 1 1/2 mi. on Rte. 54.*

◆ **Dream Cafe** (inexpensive). This espresso bar and gourmet shop has creative salads, deli sandwiches, bagels, croissants, Belgian waffles, and sweets, plus a children's menu. A natural place for beginning or ending a Sunday stroll. *Pennsylvania Ave. and Campbell Pl., Bethany Beach, DE 19930; tel. 302-539-1588. Open daily 7 a.m.-10 p.m.*

◆ **The Frog House** (inexpensive). Family restaurant with a basic menu of seafood, steaks, pasta, sandwiches, and salads. Big servings. *116 Garfield Pkwy., Bethany Beach, DE 19930; tel. 302-539-4500. Open for breakfast, lunch, and dinner Apr.-Oct.; breakfast and lunch Nov., Jan.-Mar. Closed Dec.*

NIGHTLIFE

The nightlife is slim in Bethany. Boardwalk strolling is big, and in summer, concerts and musical events are held at the bandstand on Friday and Saturday evenings. For nightclubs and live music, head to Ocean City, Rehoboth Beach, or Dewey Beach.

ATTRACTIONS

◆ **Viking Golf, Go Karts & Waterslide.** *Rtes. 1 and 54, Fenwick Island, DE 19944; tel. 302-539-1644. Open daily 9 a.m.-midnight for golf and 9 a.m.-10 p.m. for go karts and water slide May-Oct. Admission.*

SHOPPING

Bethany Beach has several stores beyond the average beach variety. For a big excursion, hit the outlet malls (*see* Rehoboth Beach chapter), or Ocean City, just south.

◆ **Area antiques shops.** A guide to dozens of area antiques shops is available from the information center on Route 1. Besides Bethany Beach and Fenwick Island, the brochure's map also includes other antiquing sites as far north as Lewes and as far west as Route 113.

◆ **Japanesque.** This store stocks traditional Japanese items, including masks, cards, pottery, teapots, kimonos, jewelry, tea boxes, and women's apparel and accessories. *16 Pennsylvania*

Ave., Bethany Beach, DE 19930; tel. 302-539-2311. Open daily.

BEST FOOD SHOPS

SANDWICHES: ◆ **Di Febo's Cafe & Deli.** *789 Garfield Pkwy., Bethany Beach, DE 19930; tel. 302-539-4914. Open daily. Follow Garfield Pkwy. west from Rte. 1; it's on the right.*

SEAFOOD: ◆ **South Bethany Seafood Market.** *Rte. 1, Bethany Beach, DE 19930; tel. 302-537-1332. Open daily. Just south of Sea Colony in the Seaside Village Shopping Center.*

FRESH PRODUCE: ◆ **Bridgeside Produce.** *RD 1, Box 123, Ocean View, DE 19970; tel. 302-539-3004. Open daily Jun.-Nov. From Rte. 1, go west on Rte. 26 to the Rte. 26 bridge, just before Ocean View.*

BAKERY: ◆ **Touch of Italy.** *Rte. 26, Millville, DE 19970; tel. 302-539-1355. Open daily mid-Jun.-Labor Day; weekends Sep.-May. On Rte. 26 about 3 1/2 mi. west of Rte. 1.*

ICE CREAM: ◆ **Candy Kitchen Shoppes.** *123 Garfield Pkwy., Bethany Beach, DE 19930; tel. 302-539-8525. Open daily Apr.-Nov.*

BEVERAGES: ◆ **Shore Foods.** *115 Garfield Pkwy., Bethany Beach, DE 19930; tel. 302-539-6252. Open daily.*

WINE: ◆ **Beach Package Store.** *Ocean Hwy. S., Bethany Beach, DE 19930; tel. 302-539-7400. Closed Sun. On Rte. 1 south of Garfield Pkwy.*

SPORTS

Swimming, fishing, and volleyball are the big sports in Bethany, although other water sports are available on the bayside, including sailing, windsurfing, and boating.

FISHING

Fishing charters depart from the Indian River Inlet marina. Permits for surf fishing (off-road vehicles only) can be obtained at the chamber of commerce information center on Route 1 between Bethany Beach and Fenwick Island.

◆ **Harry's Tackle Shop.** Crabbing bait, supplies, and fishing tips. *201 Central Blvd., Bethany Beach, DE 19930; tel. 302-539-6244. Open daily. At Pennsylvania Ave.*

BOATING

◆ **Bay Sports.** Watercraft-rental concession at Fenwick Island

State Park offers catamarans, Windsurfers, kayaks, daysailers, and Waverunners. Sailing and windsurfing lessons. *Rte. 1, Fenwick Island, DE 19970; tel. 302-226-2677. Open daily late May-early Sep. On the bay side of Rte. 1, across from the main entrance to the park.*

◆ **Bayshore Water Skiing.** Waterskiing and instruction. *19 Hasselle Ave., Bay View Park, DE 19930; tel. 302-539-0481. Marina open Apr.-Oct. At Beaston's Marina, 1 mi. south of Sea Colony.*

◆ **Holts Landing State Park.** Bay access for sailing, fishing, and waterskiing. *Box 76, Millville, DE 19970; tel. 302-539-9060. Open daily. Admission in summer. From Bethany Beach, take Rte. 26 west to Rte. 347 north, then Rte. 346 north.*

SURFING

Designated surfing sites are at Fenwick Island State Park and north of Bethany Beach at the Indian River Inlet area of Delaware Seashore State Park.

◆ **Fenwick Island Surf Shop.** *Rte. 1 and Virginia Ave., Fenwick Island, DE 19944; tel. 302-539-5800. Open daily 9 a.m.-10 p.m. late May-early Sep.; Mon.-Fri. 11-5 and Sat.-Sun. 10-6 late Sep.-early May.*

BICYCLING

◆ **Bethany Cycle & Fitness.** Rentals, service, and accessories. *778 Garfield Pkwy., Ocean View, DE 19970; tel. 302-537-9982. Open daily. In Rte. 26 Mall, 1/2 mi. west of Rte. 1.*

GOLF

Besides a few southern Delaware golf courses and driving ranges, more than half a dozen public courses are just south in the Ocean City, Maryland, area.

◆ **Salt Pond Golf Club.** It has 18 holes, driving range, putting green, and pro shop. *300 Ocean View Pkwy., Bethany Beach, DE 19930; tel. 302-539-7528. Admission. From Rte. 1, go west on Rte. 26 or Rte. 360 to Cedar Neck Rd.*

TENNIS

Tennis is a big sport around Bethany Beach, but most of the

courts belong to resort properties and are not open to the public.

◆ **Bethany Tennis Club.** Offers short-term memberships. Eight Har-Tru courts. *Box 848, Bethany Beach, DE 19930; tel. 302-539-5111. Open daily May-Oct. Admission. On Cedar Neck Rd.*

◆ **Lord Baltimore Elementary School Tennis Courts.** Two public courts; first-come, first-served. *Box 21, Ocean View, DE 19970; tel. 302-537-2700. Open daily. From Rte. 1, go west on Rte. 26 about 2 1/2 mi. to the school on left.*

NATURE

◆ **Assawoman Wildlife Area.** More than 1,000 acres, including nature trails, bird-watching, fishing, canoeing, crabbing, and picnicking. There's also a self-guided auto tour. *Rte. 364, Ocean View, DE 19970; tel. 302-539-9820. From Rte. 1, go west on Rte. 26 and follow signs to Camp Barnes.*

◆ **Fenwick Island State Park.** Its 344 acres of ocean and bay shoreline include dune and marsh and shelter a wide variety of birds: gulls, terns, osprey, loons, herons, plovers, ducks, and geese. *c/o Holts Landing State Park, Box 76, Millville, DE 19970; tel. 302-539-9060, 302-539-1055. Open daily 8-sunset. Admission. On Rte. 1, about 3 1/2 mi. south of Bethany Beach.*

TOURIST INFORMATION

◆ **Bethany-Fenwick Area Chamber of Commerce.** The chamber has offices and a spacious visitors center serving both communities. *Box 1450, Bethany Beach, DE 19930; tel. 302-539-2100, 800-962-7873. Open Mon.-Fri. 9-5 and Sat.-Sun. 10-4. On Rte. 1, about 4 1/2 mi. south of Rte. 26 (Garfield Pkwy., Bethany Beach), at the north edge of Fenwick Island.*

CHAPTER 23

Ocean City, MD

Beauty	B
Swimming	A
Sand	A
Hotels/Inns/B&Bs	A
House rentals	B
Restaurants	A
Nightlife	A
Attractions	A
Shopping	A
Sports	A
Nature	B

Ocean City rises along ten miles of wide beach front like a muscular and benevolent giant, singular in purpose and confident of giving visitors what they want. And they want it all—surf, sport, nightlife, dining, variety. There is no pretense of quiet vacationland here, no heritage as a religious retreat as in some beach towns up the coast.

Hotels, motels, and condo towers line the ocean—

some mammoth, others just a couple stories above the sand. There's a boardwalk that's long and wide and has a life of its own, complete with trams that in summer run late into the night. The crush is enough to banish skateboarders to the skateboard park at Third Street and St. Louis Avenue.

The area wasn't always such a hopping place. Hunters and fishermen were the first to embrace it in the mid-1800s, and the city's reputation survives as the "white marlin fishing capital."

In 1875, the same year the city was incorporated, the Atlantic Hotel was constructed. An amusement park opened at the south end of town, which still operates as Trimpers Rides. A few years later, a rail line spurred development, and the first permanent boardwalk, five blocks long, was built in 1910.

With nearby population centers like Baltimore, Washington, and Philadelphia, the miles of sandy ocean front became a magnet for the masses. Today the city has nearly 10,000 motel rooms and 13,000 condo units for rent. In summer the average population is 300,000—quite a surge for a town of 7,500 year-round residents.

The layout on the narrow barrier island is simple. To one side is the Atlantic Ocean, to the other the bays. Down the middle, the Coastal Highway runs for 145 blocks. Six lanes at its widest point, it can be jammed with traffic on busy weekends.

HOW TO GET THERE

◆ From Washington, DC, take Rte. 50 east across the Bay Bridge and into Ocean City for 1st through 33rd Sts. For more northern addresses, follow Rte. 50 to Salisbury, then take Maryland Rte. 90 east across the bay into Ocean City at 62nd St.

◆ From Philadelphia or New York, take I-95 south past Wilmington, DE, to DE Rte. 1/U.S. Rte. 13. Follow Rte. 13 to Salisbury, MD, to U.S. 50 east.Then take Rte. 50 into Ocean City or switch to MD Rte. 90 for the last leg.

One long block to the east of Ocean Highway is the beach, the southern two-and-a-half miles of it bordered by the boardwalk. At the south end is downtown and the Ocean City Inlet—a waterway torn into existence by a hurricane in 1933.

Charter fishing and tour boats carry thousands of people into the bays and out to sea. Golf is a growing attraction, with seven courses in the area and several others on the drawing board. And within half an hour is Assateague Island National Seashore, a soothing coast that, with its undeveloped shoreline, grass-topped dunes, and wild ponies wandering freely, is in many ways the antithesis of Ocean City.

BEACHES
OCEAN CITY BEACH

This sprawling beach is so broad and long you can almost forgive all the development. If you keep your back to the motels and businesses and concentrate on the fine sand, huge ocean, and refreshing surf in front of you, the man-

Beauty	B+
Swimming	A
Sand	A
Amenities	A

made additions barely intrude on the natural setting. The southern end of the beach is the widest and most commercial, with a pier, an amusement park, and a boardwalk. Motels and condos continue to the less-crowded north, where the beach extends into Fenwick Island, Delaware. At the southern tip is the Ocean City Inlet, which provides a busy boating corridor into three big bays and separates Ocean City from Assateague Island.

Swimming: Clear, clean water with vigorous waves that aren't too intimidating. Lifeguard on duty.

Sand: Fine, light, and wide. The beach is groomed regularly.

Amenities: Plenty of places to rent beach equipment (including beach chairs for the disabled) and to buy food and drink at sand's edge. Boardwalk rest rooms at South Division, Caroline, Ninth, and 27th streets; the Worcester Street Bathhouses (for a fee) at Boardwalk and North First Street; the Sun & Beach Motel at 45th Street and the Coastal Highway; and at Philadelphia Avenue and Wicomico Street.

Sports: Frisbee, ball throwing, and other sports are prohibited 9

233

to 5:30 late May through mid-September. Kite-flying and body boarding are at the discretion of beach patrol. Surf fishing allowed 50 yards from swimmers. Surfing in designated areas. *Parking:* Plenty of on-street spaces. Several lots, especially downtown. Huge lots at 40th Street and Ocean Parkway and between the pier and the inlet at the south end.

ASSATEAGUE ISLAND BEACHES

Assateague is a 37-mile-long barrier island whose northern tip sits just south of Ocean City. This portion of the island has three bathhouse-equipped beach areas within a few minutes of each other, one at Assateague State Park and two at

Beauty	A+
Swimming	A
Sand	A
Amenities	B

Assateague Island National Seashore. There is also access to Sinepuxent Bay, although swimming is discouraged there because of unmarked drop-offs, broken shells, and murky water.

Wild horses, often called ponies because of their small stature, run free and can sometimes be spotted in the marshes as you cross the bridge onto the island, as well as along nearby roads. Feeding the animals is forbidden, but the horses have learned to kick over coolers in search of a meal and are said to be particularly fond of Hostess Twinkies. *From Ocean City, take Rte. 50 west over the Kelley bridge to the third light. Turn left onto Rte. 611 south for about 7 mi., to the Verrazano Bridge onto the island. Just before the bridge is the Barrier Island Visitors Center, where you can obtain maps and ask questions (tel. 410-641-1441).*

Assateague State Park

Nothing but wilderness in either direction. To the north is about five miles of beach that can be reached only on foot and beyond that, in the distance, on the other side of the inlet, Ocean City rises like a toy metropolis on the horizon. To the south is the national seashore, with an even longer stretch of sand accessible only by foot or off-road vehicle (permit needed). *Swimming:* The beach slopes gently to meet manageable waves. Lifeguard on duty. Some sandbars were washed away by 1995 storms, creating unusual seaward currents, but sandbars were expected to rebuild by summer of 1996.

Sand: Fine and light tan, with tiny flecks of black and white and an almost powdery consistency. Beach surface rolls, climbing to a six- to eight-foot grassless dune topped by a storm fence.

Amenities: Bathhouse with rest rooms, showers, snacks. Picnic tables and grills on bayside of the ocean dune. State campground nearby.

Sports: Body boarding, surf fishing.

Parking: Large parking lot next to the bathhouse.

National Seashore—North Ocean Beach

A boardwalk leads about 100 feet from the bathhouse, over the dune, revealing another splendid medium-width beach with a view contained only by the ocean and the dune. Electric fence is strung along the dune to discourage ponies from wandering.

Swimming: Clean water and robust waves that break perhaps 50 yards out and roll in on themselves three or four times before hitting the beach. Lifeguard on duty.

Sand: Fine and tan, mixed with some coarser brown sand, rising sharply from the water and sloping up to a high, grassy dune.

Amenities: Picnic tables and grills near bathhouse (rest rooms, showers, and snacks).

Sports: Body boarding, surf fishing. North of bathhouse is a road leading to a canoe- and bike-rental location on the bay (tel. 410-641-5029).

Parking: Large parking lot.

National Seashore—South Ocean Beach

The south beach seems extremely remote, with wind whipping and low dunes allowing a distant view. It's like standing at the edge of two vast plains—one the ocean and the other the sandy island. The beach extends in a straight line south; just beyond the swimming area is the beginning of an off-road-vehicle zone, so you may see surf fishing from four-wheel drives.

Swimming: Clean water and waves that break out a ways, then roll in low. Lifeguard on duty.

Sand: Fine and tan, rising uniformly to a low dune.

Amenities: Bathhouse with rest rooms, showers, and snacks.

Campground nearby.
Sports: Body boarding, surf fishing.
Parking: Large parking lot.

HOTELS/INNS/B&BS

◆ **Lighthouse Club Hotel** (very expensive). This luxury inn surrounded by water looks like the Thomas Point Lighthouse, with 23 well-appointed suites, including marble bathrooms, wet bar, terry robes, and decks. The eight upper-floor rooms have canopy beds, Jacuzzis, and fireplaces. The view over the bay is stellar. *56th St. in the Bay, Ocean City, MD 21842; tel. 410-723-6100, 800-767-6060. From Ocean Hwy., go north and turn right onto 60th St., which leads to the property jutting out into Isle of Wight Bay.*

◆ **Annabell's Bed & Breakfast** (expensive). This wicker-filled B&B right on the boardwalk has six rooms, three with private bath. The proprietor once owned a bakery, and her stuffed French toast is served on the front porch or, if you're in Room 2, on the private second-floor deck overlooking the beach and boardwalk. *1001 Atlantic Ave., Ocean City, MD 21842; tel. 410-289-8894. Closed Nov.-Mar. At 10th St. and the boardwalk.*

◆ **Coconut Malorie Hotel** (expensive). Larger sibling to the Lighthouse Club, this modern 85-suite hotel on Fager's Island has a Caribbean flavor, with elegant, spacious rooms, dark rattan furnishings, Jacuzzi, live plants. Check out the view from the hotel's tower, which has windows on all sides and is lined with colorful Haitian artwork. *59th St. in the Bay, Ocean City, MD 21842; tel. 410-723-6100, 800-767-6060. From Ocean Hwy., turn west on 60th St.*

◆ **Dunes Manor Hotel** (expensive). This 170-room hotel is known for good service, including complimentary afternoon tea traditionally served by owner Thelma Connor. All rooms are ocean front with private balconies, and rooms ending in 09 are suites with larger balconies. The hotel has Victorian public rooms; guest room decor is more modern. *2800 Baltimore, Ocean City, MD 21842; tel. 410-289-1100, 800-523-2888. Just beyond the boardwalk's north end, at 28th St. and the ocean front.*

◆ **Atlantic House** (moderate). This three-story Victorian has 11 guest rooms upstairs and a three-bedroom apartment downstairs, all individually decorated with a tasteful mix of antiques, white wicker, and garage-sale furniture, plus plenty of floral wallpaper and plants. Some of the private bathrooms are off the hall. Innkeepers Debi and Paul Cook can offer good advice—she's lived in Ocean City her whole life. *501 N. Baltimore Ave., Ocean City, MD 21842; tel. 410-289-2333. At 5th St., a block from the boardwalk.*

HOUSE RENTALS
◆ **Holiday Real Estate.** *7700 Coastal Hwy., Ocean City, MD 21842; tel. 410-524-7700, 800-638-2102; fax 410-524-7055. Open daily.*

◆ **O'Conor, Piper & Flynn Realtors.** *5200 Coastal Hwy., Ocean City, MD 21842; tel. 410-723-1000, 800-633-1000. Open daily.*

RESTAURANTS
◆ **Fager's Island Restaurant** (expensive). A classy casual atmosphere and excellent food. Indoor and outdoor deck seating on Assawoman Bay. Try the prime rib with fresh shaved horseradish or the Chesapeake seafood platter. If you're here for sunset, you'll savor the surprise ending. *60th St. in the Bay, Ocean City, MD 21842; tel. 410-723-6100, 800-767-6060. Open daily for lunch and dinner. Turn west onto 60th St. off the Coastal Hwy.*

◆ **Captain's Table Restaurant** (moderate). Many long-time Ocean City visitors consider this the best place for crab cakes. *15th St. and Baltimore Ave., Ocean City, MD 21842; tel. 410-289-7191, 800-237-4566. Open daily for lunch and dinner Apr.-mid-Oct. At the Santa Maria Motor Hotel.*

◆ **Galaxy Bar & Grille** (moderate). This fairly new eatery features such combos as baked artichokes in Mornay sauce and horseradish-crusted salmon. *66th St. and the Coastal Hwy., Ocean City, MD 21842; tel. 410-723-6762. Open daily for lunch and dinner.*

◆ **Phillips Crab House** (moderate). A classic crab house and part of the Phillips seafood empire, it's known for its crab feeds but also serves other fresh seafood, fried chicken, and steak in a sprawling space that can seat 1,100. All-you-can-eat buffet. *21st St. and the Coastal Hwy., Ocean City, MD 21842; tel. 410-289-6821, 410-289-7747 (for takeout). Open* *daily for lunch and dinner Apr.-Oct.*

◆ **Seacrets Bar & Grill** (moderate). One of Ocean City's most colorful dining and drinking spots, the Jamaican-themed restaurant sits at water's edge, where boaters can wade in. Four open-air bars, plus indoor dining on Jamaican specialties. Bathing-suit casual. *49th St. in the Bay, Ocean City, MD 21842; tel. 410-524-4900. Open daily for lunch and dinner.*

NIGHTLIFE

◆ **The Hurricane.** DJs spin pounding music for dancing fools; nautical theme. *68th and the Bay, Ocean City, MD 21842; tel. 410-524-2497. Open nightly at 8:30.*

◆ **The Ocean Club.** Reggae, calypso, and show bands. *49th St. and Ocean Hwy., Ocean City, MD 21842; tel. 410-524-7500. Open Wed.-Sun. in season.*

ATTRACTIONS

◆ **Frontier Town.** This western theme park includes an 1860s setting, Indian dancing, stagecoach rides, dancing girls, and a steam train. *Rte. 611, Ocean City, MD 21842; tel. 410-289-7877. Open daily 10-6 mid-Jun.-early Sep. Admission. From the Coastal Hwy., go west on Rte. 50 and then south on Rte. 611 for 3 1/2 mi.*

◆ **Jolly Roger Amusement Park.** Family-oriented amusement and water park, with rides and miniature golf. *30th St. and the Coastal Hwy., Ocean City, MD 21842; tel. 410-289-3477. Open daily 12-12 late May-early Sep.*

◆ **Life Saving Station Museum.** *Box 603, Ocean City, MD 21842; tel. 410-289-4991. Open daily 11-10 Jun.-Sep. and 11-4 May and Oct.; Sat.-Sun. 11-4 Nov.-Dec. and Apr. Closed Jan.-Mar. Boardwalk at the inlet.*

◆ **Trimpers Rides of Ocean City.** More than 100 rides and games at a park that grew up with the city. *Boardwalk and 1st St., Ocean City, MD 21842; tel. 410-289-8617. Open daily mid-Jun.-Sep. and Sat.-Sun. the rest of the year. At the south end of the boardwalk.*

SHOPPING

There's boardwalk and mall shopping, and nearby Berlin, Maryland, is an antiquing center.

◆ **45th Street Village.** More than 35 shops, including clothing, jewelry, gift, and specialty stores, plus restaurants and snack shops, a dinner theater, an arcade, and two nightclubs. *45th St. and the Coastal Hwy., Ocean City, MD 21842. Open daily.*

◆ **Ocean City Factory Outlets.** New outlet center includes about 30 stores, including Bass, Book Warehouse, Bugle Boy, Tommy Hilfiger, Van Heusen, Jockey, Geoffrey Beene, L'Eggs, Hanes, Bali, Playtex, Mikasa, and Nine West. *Rte. 50 and Golf Course Rd., Ocean City, MD 21842; tel. 800-625-6696 ext. 3365. Open daily. 1 mi. west of the Coastal Hwy.*

BEST FOOD SHOPS

SANDWICHES: ◆ **Mad Hatter's Cafe.** *104 25th St., Ocean City, MD 21842; tel. 410-289-6267. Open daily Mar.-Oct. Between Baltimore and Philadelphia Aves.*

SEAFOOD: ◆ **Waterman's Seafood.** *12505 Ocean Gateway, Ocean City, MD 21842; tel. 410-213-1020. Open daily. From the Coastal Hwy., go west across bridge and turn right at Keyser Point Rd.*

FRESH PRODUCE: ◆ **Birch's Produce.** *Rte. 611, W. Ocean City, MD 21842; tel. 410-213-0917. Open daily May-late Sep. From the Coastal Hwy., go west on Rte. 50 and turn left onto Rte. 611. Drive 2 mi.; stand is on the right.*

ICE CREAM: ◆ **Dumser's Dairyland.** Other locations on 49th Street and on the boardwalk. *124th St. and the Coastal Hwy., Ocean City, MD 21842; tel. 410-250-5543. Open daily. Boardwalk store open May-Oct.*

BEVERAGES: ◆ **Food Lion.** *119th St. and Ocean Pkwy., Ocean City, MD 21842; tel. 410-524-9039. Open daily.*

WINE: ◆ **94th Street Beer, Wine & Deli.** *9301 Coastal Hwy., Ocean City, MD 21842; tel. 410-524-7037. Open daily.*

SPORTS
FISHING

Public fishing piers are located at Inlet Park and bayside at Third, Ninth, 40th, and 125th streets.

◆ **Ocean City Fishing Center.** Large marina with charter fleet, boat rentals, bait-and-tackle shop. *Box 940, Ocean City, MD 21842; tel. 410-213-1121, 800-322-3065. Open May-Oct. From the Coastal*

Hwy., cross Rte. 50 bridge and make first left onto Shantytown Rd.

◆ **Talbot Street Pier.** Headboats and charter boats. *311 Talbot St. and the Bay, Ocean City, MD 21842; tel. 410-289-9125. Open May-Oct.*

BOATING

◆ **Advanced Marina.** Pontoon boats, ski boats, runabouts, and fishing boats. *66th St. and the Bay, Ocean City, MD 21842; tel. 410-723-2124. Open daily mid-May-Oct. On the bay between 66th and 67th Sts.*

◆ **Sailing, Etc.** Windsurfers and sailboats for rent; Rollerblade rentals and lessons. *54th St. and the Coastal Hwy., Ocean City, MD 21842; tel. 410-723-1144. Open daily 9 a.m.-10 p.m. late May-late Sep. and 10-6 Oct.-May.*

SURFING

Ocean City has more reliable surfing waves than most Middle Atlantic locations. Popular surfing spots are Eighth St., the Ocean City Inlet, and 48th Street, but when lifeguards are on duty, surfers must use one of two officially designated "surfing beaches" announced daily on local radio stations.

◆ **Malibu's.** Full range of surfboards, wet suits, Boogie boards, clothing; up-to-date surfing conditions. *713 Atlantic Ave., Ocean City, MD 21842; tel. 410-289-3000. Open daily. On the boardwalk at 8th St.*

BICYCLING

Many bike-rental outlets are located along the boardwalk.

◆ **Bike World.** Main store on Caroline Street, with other rental locations on the boardwalk at 15th, 17th, and 23rd streets. *6 Caroline St., Ocean City, MD 21842; tel. 410-289-2587. Caroline Street location ospen daily. A block south of 1st St. at the boardwalk.*

GOLF

More than half a dozen public courses are located on the Maryland mainland within half an hour of the Route 50 bridge leading west out of Ocean City. The local golf association offers package deals (tel. 410-723-5207, 800-462-4653).

◆ **Ocean City Golf & Yacht Club.** Two 18-hole courses (one seaside, one bayside). *11401 Country Club Dr., Berlin, MD 21811; tel. 410-641-1779, 410-641-1778. Open daily. Admission. From the Coastal Hwy., go west across Rte. 50 bridge to third light. Turn left onto Rte. 611 and go about 6 mi., then bear right at the fork onto South Point Rd. for 1 mi.*

TENNIS

◆ **Public tennis courts.** Bayside at 41st, 94th, and 136th streets and at 61st Street and Ocean Highway. Call for reservations. *Ocean City, MD 21842; tel. 410-524-8337. Open daily. Admission.*

NATURE

◆ **Assateague Island National Seashore.** Nature trails, picnic areas, fishing, boating, swimming, and camping. *7206 National Seashore Lane, Berlin, MD 21811; tel. 410-641-1441, 410-641-3030 (campground reservations). Open daily. From the Coastal Hwy., take Rte. 50 west. Turn left onto Rte. 611.*

◆ **Assateague State Park.** Fishing, canoeing, picnic area, ocean front. *7307 Stephen Decatur Hwy., Berlin, MD 21811; tel. 410-641-2120. Closed mid-Oct.-mid-Apr. From the Coastal Hwy., take Rte. 50 west and turn left onto Rte. 611.*

◆ **O. C. Princess.** Nature cruises. *Shantytown Village, Ocean City, MD 21842; tel. 410-213-0926, 800-457-6650. Departures Tue.-Sun. 4-7 May-Oct. Admission. Rte. 50 and Shantytown Rd.*

SAFETY TIPS

In summer it's a big city with a transient population, so keep cars locked, belongings out of sight, and valuables in motel safes. While the beach has a reputation for safe swimming, it's worth noting that in summer 1995—a summer of extraordinary storm activity that spawned rip currents—at least six people drowned, most of them when lifeguards were not on duty. On Assateague Island, beware of the mosquitoes and ticks.

TOURIST INFORMATION

◆ **Ocean City Visitors Bureau.** The information center is in the Convention Center. *4001 Coastal Hwy., Ocean City, MD 21842;*

tel. 410-289-2800, 800-626-2326. Open Mon.-Fri. 8-5 and Sat.-Sun. 9-5; extended hours in summer.

◆ **Worcester County Tourism Office.** The area west of Ocean City, including Berlin, Snow Hill, and Pocomoke City, is in Worcester County. *105 Pearl St., Snow Hill, MD 21863; tel. 410-632-3617, 800-852-0335. Open Mon.-Fri. 8-4:30. Snow Hill is southwest of Ocean City on Rte. 113.*

CHAPTER 24

Chincoteague

Beauty	A
Swimming	A
Sand	B
Hotels/Inns/B&Bs	A
House rentals	B
Restaurants	B
Nightlife	C
Attractions	B
Shopping	C
Sports	B
Nature	A

ross the long causeway from mainland Virginia to Chincoteague Island and the unspoiled, oyster-rich tidal bays and lush marshlands foreshadow the magic of this little corner. Cross another bridge and you're minutes from Assateague Island National Seashore, where the Atlantic Ocean comes crashing in on ten miles of unspoiled beach, and life's abrasions fade with each cleansing wave.

Nature and tradition take charge here.

Chincoteague National Wildlife Refuge shelters hundreds of bird species and, as everywhere in this marshy domain, shellfish galore. There are Jet Ski rentals, to be sure, but the prevailing currents in this watery realm run toward the serene. Fishing is no mere tourist attraction—it's a way of life.

The temperament is a far cry from the bustle of Ocean City, Maryland, not much more than an hour to the north. Seven miles long, Chincoteague Island spoons into the southern end of 37-mile-long Assateague Island. From the air, the islands and their attendant marshes and swamps swirl around each other like a finger painting. By land, there is only one way in: Virginia Route 175,

HOW TO GET THERE

◆ Chincoteague is about 3 1/2 hr. from Washington, D.C., and Philadelphia, and 1 1/4 hr. from Ocean City, MD.

◆ From Washington, take U.S. Rte. 50 to Annapolis and cross the Bay Bridge, following Rte. 50 south to Salisbury, MD, where it intersects Rte. 13. Take Rte. 13 south into VA until it intersects VA Rte. 175. Follow Rte. 175 east into Chincoteague.

◆ From Philadelphia, take I-95 south to Delaware Rte. 1 south; at Dover, take Rte. 13 south all the way into VA, until it intersects VA Rte. 175. Follow Rte. 175 east into Chincoteague.

◆ From Ocean City, take U.S. Rte. 50 west to Rte. 113; go south through Berlin, MD, to MD Rte. 12 south; follow Rte. 12 to Rte. 679 south, which intersects Rte. 175. Go east on Rte. 175 into Chincoteague. (Warning: Rte. 175 may not be posted at Rte. 679; look for Coffin's Market on the southeast corner.)

which ushers visitors smack into downtown Chincoteague, a quaint village of one- and two-story businesses where seafood is king.

Most of the lodgings and restaurants are on Main Street, which parallels the Chincoteague Channel, and Maddox Boulevard, which becomes Beach Road and leads to Assateague's wildlife areas and seashore. The state government wants to route traffic straight onto Maddox, bypassing the old bridge, but many residents are resisting that plan. On Chincoteague Island's east side, near Memorial Park, are more accommodations—primarily motels— along the Assateague Channel between the two islands.

A great time to visit Chincoteague is the third week in July. The Chincoteague volunteer fire company rounds up Assateague's wild ponies on the third Wednesday and Thursday of the month and swims them across the channel. In 1995, an estimated 40,000 people attended the roundup and an auction to benefit the fire company. At other times, the stocky horses can be hard to find, although they are often spotted in the Wash Flats area on wildlife tours organized through the refuge's visitors center. Far less elusive are the herons, egrets, oystercatchers, shore birds, and migrating species that vary widely by season. The area has earned an extraordinary reputation among bird-watchers. Other wildlife includes the diminutive sika deer and the bushy-tailed Delmarva squirrel, the size of a big rabbit.

Assateague Seashore is the only beach resort in northern Virginia, and the parking lots fill up on summer holiday weekends and during the pony penning. Arrive early to get a parking space, or you risk getting stuck in a one-car-out, one-car-in drill. Sometimes shuttles are offered, as well. Once at the beach, you can outdistance the crowds by walking north as far as necessary.

BEACHES
BATHHOUSE NO. 1

Climb the steps to the bathhouse and cross to the wooden platform atop the dune and a magnificent view unfolds.

Beyond the dune, the churning ocean and a medium-width beach extend to the north as far as the eye can

Beauty	A
Swimming	A
Sand	B
Amenities	B

see. To the south, the beach and dune curl away into what becomes Sandy Hook, the gnarled tip of the island. The dune's dense, blowing grass gives it a downy appearance. In back of the parking lot, serene Toms Cove sweeps to the other side of the island, and all around is dense green vegetation, marsh grass, and short, wind-swept bushes and trees.

From beach level, the parking lot, visitors center, and the remainder of the island disappear behind the dune. The beach is wild and undeveloped, with the only food concession being that provided to sandpipers by retreating waves. The setting feels very remote, especially in view of the miles of beach to the north that can be reached only on foot.

Swimming: Constant wave action makes for fresh, clean water. In summer the surf is considered manageable for swimmers, although signs warn of the possibility of seaward currents. Lifeguard on duty near the bathhouse.

Sand: Tan, fine, and clean, building to a substantial dune.

Amenities: Bathhouse has rest rooms and showers, but there is no food concession.

Sports: No organized sports.

Parking: Large lot; parking included in the $4-per-vehicle user fee good for 7 days.

BATHHOUSE NO. 2

A road leading south from the traffic circle continues to another large parking lot at Bathhouse No. 2, less than half a mile away. Near this bathhouse, the dune has deteriorated and the beach gives way to the lot. There is a stretch

Beauty	A-
Swimming	A
Sand	B-
Amenities	B

of a few hundred yards with no dune at all, which eliminates the secluded atmosphere. Still, the beach is excellent, and farther south the dune resumes. Looking north from that point, the beach has a rise in it that cuts off the view up the coast.

Three-quarters of a mile down the road is another parking lot but with no amenities. Oversand vehicles with permits can enter the beach here. This narrow throat of island begins the Sandy Hook section, which from mid-March to mid-August is off limits because of nesting piping plovers. The hook forms Toms Cove, and the tidal flats there are good clamming spots.

This throat or overwash area is where the action of wind and surf determine the island's shape as the sand "rolls over" on itself, moving from oceanside to bayside.

Swimming: Constant wave action. Lifeguard on duty.

Sand: Tan, fine, and clean.

Amenities: Bathhouse has rest rooms and showers, but there is no food concession.

Sports: No organized sports. Surf fishing to the south.

Parking: Large lot; parking included in the $4-per-vehicle user fee good for 7 days.

HOTELS/INNS/B&BS

Chincoteague has about 800 hotel rooms, some luxurious, some basic, and the majority in between. It also has a handful of good B&Bs. Since the island is surrounded by water, many rooms have scenic views, and it's worth asking for one. Prices range from under $50 to $150 a night.

◆ **Island Motor Inn** (expensive). Sixty of the best rooms in town, including 12 in a new section completed in 1995, with exercise room and indoor pool. Rooms are spacious and well-appointed. Room 301 has windows on two sides for fine views of the bay and causeway. The inn has its own 700-foot boardwalk and Japanese garden. A third-floor Jacuzzi (in the exercise room) is situated for sunset soaking. *4391 Main St., Chincoteague, VA 23336; tel. 804-336-3141; fax 804-336-1483.*

◆ **Assateague Inn** (moderate). The 24 rooms, some standard and some suites, are furnished in a neat but basic style, with sliding-glass doors opening onto a common front deck. The inn is set off from the roadway, tucked between pines and marshland, with boardwalk leading to a wooden pier along a saltwater creek. *Box 1038, Chincoteague, VA 23336; tel. 804-336-3738; fax 804-336-1179. At 6570 Chicken City Rd., near its intersection with Maddox Blvd.*

◆ **Driftwood Motor Lodge** (moderate). For beachgoers, this lodging is about the closest you can get to the national seashore. Waterfowl art adorns the walls of the 52 rooms, which come equipped with refrigerators. Ask for second- and third-floor east-end rooms for the best balcony views of the Assateague refuge and nearby lighthouse. Room 343 is a good choice. *7105 Maddox Blvd., Chincoteague, VA 23336; tel. 804-336-6557, 800-553-6117. Just before the bridge onto Assateague Island.*

◆ **Island Manor House** (moderate). This B&B in a house built in 1848 by the island's first doctor has six rooms with private bath, two with shared, and enough antiques to fill a museum, including impressive four-poster beds and Gibraltarlike bureaus. The Mark Twain Room has a water view, and the writer's framed signature is on display; it shares a hallway with another bedroom, and together they make a family suite. Public areas exquisitely furnished. *4160 Main St., Chincoteague, VA 23336; tel. 804-336-5436, 800-852-1505.*

◆ **The Watson House** (moderate). Restored Victorian with six comfortable rooms. All have delicately flowered wallpaper, high-back headboards, and private bathrooms. The Bay View Room has a bay window and sitting alcove. Stellar breakfast and afternoon tea, plus amenities like bikes, binoculars, and beach coolers. First-rate friendliness. An adjacent four-room sister property opened in spring 1996. *4240 Main St., Chincoteague, VA 23336; tel. 804-336-1564, 800-336-6787. Closed Thanksgiving-Easter. Across from Landmark Plaza.*

◆ **Waterside Motor Inn** (moderate). All 45 pleasant rooms have wooden balconies overlooking Chincoteague Channel. Various combinations of king, queen, and double beds. "Diplomat" rooms, with sofas and views on two sides, are at the end of each floor. Room 315 has an especially sweeping view (of the bay, causeway, and the hotel's wooden pier) and is near the pool. *3761 S. Main St., Chincoteague, VA 23336; tel. 804-336-3434; fax 804-336-1878.*

HOUSE RENTALS

Chincoteague Island has about 800 rental units, including cottages and houses, with weekly rates ranging from about $300 for a one-bedroom to $1,000 for a five-bedroom waterfront property. Assateague Island, which is all protected land, has no accommodations at the Chincoteague end of the island.

◆ **Chincoteague Island Vacation Cottages.** *6282 Maddox Blvd.,*

Chincoteague, VA 23336; tel. 804-336-3720, 800-457-6643. Open Mon.-Sat.

◆ **Coastal Realty.** *6497 Maddox Blvd., Box 385, Chincoteague, VA 23336; tel. 804-336-3716, 800-336-3716; fax 804-336-5846. Open Mon.-Sat.*

RESTAURANTS

◆ **Landmark Crab House & Waterfront Lounge** (moderate). One of the island's most colorful eateries, set on the water and full of nautical atmosphere, including ship-hatch tabletops, an outdoor deck, and a bar said to have been salvaged from an old Chicago haunt of Al Capone's. Among noteworthy entrées are crab imperial, crabmeat with Smithfield ham, soft-shell crabs, and steak. There's also a large salad bar. *6162 Landmark Plaza, Chincoteague, VA 23336; tel. 804-336-5552. Open daily for dinner. Closed late Nov.-late Mar. Landmark Plaza is on N. Main St.*

◆ **The Beachway Restaurant** (moderate). Perhaps the island's best and most diverse restaurant, it offers breakfast specialties such as seafood crepe St. James and oysters Benedict and dinner choices like Beachway Spanish paella and Chincoteague bouill-abaisse for two. Rack of lamb also is a favorite. Tasteful dining room. Reservations recommended. *6455 Maddox Blvd., Chincoteague, VA 23336; tel. 804-336-5590, 800-619-1694; fax 804-336-1826. Open daily for breakfast, lunch, and dinner. After Labor Day, open Fri.-Mon. Closed Dec.-Mar.*

◆ **The Village Restaurant** (moderate). A local favorite, it has a comfortable dining room and a casual bar-side dining section. Try the Chincoteague oysters—fried, steamed, stewed, or on the half shell. The crab imperial also gets raves. *6576 Maddox Blvd., Chincoteague, VA 23336; tel. 804-336-5120. Open daily for dinner. Closed Sun. after Columbus Day. Closed Jan.*

◆ **Barbara's Little New York** (inexpensive). For a break from the seafood routine, Italian subs, pizza, and pasta do the trick. Barbara Arena, a native New Yorker, makes it all from scratch, using family recipes. *4069 Main St., Chincoteague, VA 23336; tel. 804-336-3125. Open daily for lunch and dinner mid-May–mid-Sep.*

◆ **Memories** (inexpensive). Fun, dinerlike atmosphere at an east-side location that got its start in 1957 as Floyd's Drive-In. Grab a booth and order the pork barbeque or the oyster fritters. *3441 Ridge Rd., Chincoteague, VA 23336; tel. 804-336-3412. Open daily for breakfast, lunch, and dinner.*

◆ **Shucking House Cafe on the Bay** (inexpensive). Fine setting for breakfast or a quick lunch, with windows the length of the restaurant looking out on Chincoteague Bay. Chowders, stews, crab-cake sandwiches, and other light fare, prepared in the same kitchen used by the adjacent Landmark Crab House. *6162 Landmark Plaza, Chincoteague, VA 23336; tel. 804-336-5145. Open daily for breakfast and lunch. Breakfast buffet and fruit bar Memorial Day-Labor Day. Lunch buffet on Sun. Closed in Dec.*

NIGHTLIFE

◆ **Chattie's Lounge.** Live music weekends; DJs at other times. *4113 Main St., Chincoteague, VA 23336; tel. 804-336-9730. Open daily. Upstairs at Don's Seafood Restaurant.*

◆ **Landmark Crab House.** A marble-top grand piano in the bar; additional live music at the deck end of the restaurant. *6162 Landmark Plaza, Chincoteague, VA 23336; tel. 804-336-5552. Entertainment Fri.-Sun. 5 p.m.-12 a.m.*

ATTRACTIONS

◆ **NASA Visitors Center.** Exhibits on the history of flight, early rocket launches, space travel, and the business of the Wallops Island facility, which is launching suborbital craft such as balloons and sounding rockets. During launches, the rockets roar overhead and can be seen for a few seconds before they disappear skyward. *Wallops Flight Facility, J17, Wallops Island, VA 23337; tel. 804-824-1344. Open daily early Jul.-Labor Day. Open Thu.-Mon. 10-4 Sep.-early Jul. Closed Dec.-Feb. On the right side of Rte. 175, just before you reach Chincoteague.*

◆ **Oyster and Maritime Museum.** Exhibits focus on the area's water life. Aquarium. *7125 Maddox Blvd., Chincoteague, VA 23336; tel. 804-336-6117. Open Mon.-Sat 10-5, Sun. 12-4. Admission.*

SHOPPING

The town's shopping district is concentrated on Main Street, just after you cross the bridge into town. Expect to see a lot of bird- and pony-related items.

◆ **Ben Franklin 5 & 10.** The small-town five and dime is alive here. Bring the kids to show them what it was like when every town had a store like this. *4094 Main St., Chincoteague, VA 23336; tel. 804-336-3302.*

◆ **Decoys, Decoys, Decoys.** Hand-carved birds, elevated to an art form. *4044 Main St., Chincoteague, VA 23336; tel. 804-336-1402. Open daily.*

◆ **The Corner Book Store.** No better place to find books about Chincoteague, the ponies, and Virginia's eastern shore. *4076 Main St., Chincoteague, VA 23336; tel. 804-336-6643. Open daily.*

BEST FOOD SHOPS

SANDWICHES: ◆ **Food & Foto.** *4080 Main St., Chincoteague, VA 23336; tel. 804-336-6600. Open daily.*

SEAFOOD: ◆ **Russell Fish Co.** *512 S. Main St., Chincoteague, VA 23336; tel. 804-336-6986, 804-336-5528. Open daily. Next to the U.S. Coast Guard station.*

BAKERY: ◆ **Sugarbakers Bakery & Cafe.** *Main St., Chincoteague, VA 23336; tel. 804-336-3712. Open daily.*

ICE CREAM: ◆ **Island Creamery.** *6251 Maddox Blvd., Chincoteague, VA 23336; tel. 804-336-6236. Open daily mid-Mar.-Nov.*

BEVERAGES: ◆ **Parks Market.** *6739 Maddox Blvd., Chincoteague, VA 23336; tel. 804-336-5323. Closed Sun.*

WINE: ◆ **The Grubstake.** Wines, cheeses, bakery, ice cream. *6149 Main St., Chincoteague, VA 23336; tel. 804-336-3166. Open daily.*

SPORTS
FISHING

◆ **Capt. Bob's.** Motor boat rentals, tackle, and bait. *2477 S. Main St., Chincoteague, VA 23336; tel. 804-336-6654. Open daily.*

◆ **East Side Rentals & Marina.** Fishing charters aboard the motor boat *Chincoteague View*, plus island tours and nature cruises. *7462 East Side Rd., Chincoteague, VA 23336; tel. 804-336-3409, 800-889-1525. Open daily.*

◆ **Snug Harbor.** Rental cottages, boats, Jet Skis. *7536 East Side Dr., Chincoteague, VA 23336; tel. 804-336-6176. Open daily May-mid-Oct.*

BICYCLING

◆ **Beach Road Bikes & Mopeds.** Beach cruiser bikes for children and adults. Bike repairs. *6444 Maddox Blvd., Chincoteague, VA 23336; tel. 804-336-6542. Open daily Mar.-Dec.*

GOLF

Chincoteague Island has no golf courses, but there are several in the Ocean City, MD, area (*see* Ocean City chapter). Others nearby are Captain's Cove Golf & Yacht Club in Greenbackville, VA (804-824-3465), and the Nassawango Country Club in Snow Hill, MD (410-957-2262).

TENNIS

◆ **Chincoteague Memorial Park.** Two outdoor courts, no reservations, 45-minute limit when others are waiting. Unlighted. *Memorial Park Dr., Chincoteague, VA 23336. Open daily. On the east side of the island on Memorial Park Dr., a loop that intersects Ridge Rd. and East Side Rd.*

NATURE

Chincoteague National Wildlife Area and Assateague Island National Seashore make up the officially designated nature areas. Adjacent to each other on the southern tip of Assateague Island, both are reached by the same road. Other nature excursions are offered on the channels, bays, and waterways surrounding the islands.

◆ **Assateague Island National Seashore.** The Toms Cove Visitor Center has exhibits and a staff to answer questions. *Box 38, Chincoteague, VA 23336; tel. 804-336-6577. Seashore open daily 5 a.m.-10 p.m. May-Sep.; 6 a.m.-8 p.m. Oct.-Nov. and Apr.; 6 a.m.-6 p.m. Dec.-Mar. Admission.*

◆ **Assateague Island Tours.** This company has a contract to conduct wildlife tours from the refuge visitors center. It's an hour-and-a-half, 15-mile, narrated trip that covers the wildlife, history, and ponies. A tram goes to areas off-limits to other vehicles. *Chincoteague, VA 23336; tel. 804-336-6155. Twice-daily tours Jun.-Aug., once daily in Sep. and Apr.-May, and 3 times a week through Nov.; by reservation only in*

Mar. Admission. Sign up for tours in the refuge visitors center.

◆ **Capt. Barry's Back Bay Cruises.** An enthusiastic Capt. Barry Frishman, transplanted from New York State, pilots his pontoon boat on bird-watching trips, moonlight excursions, fun cruises, and adventure trips, depending on his passengers' interests. Fishing, crabbing, shell-collecting, swimming. *4256 Anderton Ave., Chincoteague, VA 23336; tel. 804-336-6508. Open daily in season. Admission. At the boat docks by Landmark Plaza, across from the Landmark Crab House.*

◆ **Chincoteague National Wildlife Refuge.** Several trails for hiking and biking, including the wildlife loop and the woodland trail. Visitors center near the entrance to the refuge posts a schedule of programs for the day. Snow Goose Pool and Swan Cove are popular bird-watching areas. *Box 62, Chincoteague, VA 23336; tel. 804-336-6122. Visitors center open daily 9-4, other areas dawn-dusk. On some trails, vehicles are permitted after 3 p.m. From Main St., turn right onto Maddox Blvd. and follow it to the refuge.*

◆ **Tidewater Expeditions.** Kayak excursions of area coastlines and coves. Lessons and rentals. *7729 East Side Dr., Chincoteague, VA 23336; tel. 804-336-3159. Open daily in season. Admission.*

SAFETY TIPS

The ponies are wild and will bite and kick; officials urge visitors to stay away from them and other wildlife, even if the animals approach. Rabies has been recorded on the islands. Ticks that carry Lyme disease are also present. Be prepared for aggressive mosquitoes. Swimmers should beware of seaward currents. Recent storms have altered the sand banks, which can create rip currents. Avoid diving in shallow bay water.

TOURIST INFORMATION

◆ **Chincoteague Chamber of Commerce.** *Box 258, Chincoteague, VA 23336; tel. 804-336-6161. Open Mon.-Sat. 9-4:30, Sun. 12:30-4:30. Closed Sun. Oct.-May. Turn off Main St. onto Maddox Blvd., which runs into a traffic circle where the chamber is located.*

◆ **Town of Chincoteague.** *4026 Main St., Chincoteague, VA 23336; tel. 804-336-6519. Open Mon.-Fri. 8-5.*

CHAPTER 25

Virginia Beach

Beauty	A-
Swimming	A
Sand	A
Hotels/Inns/B&Bs	A
House rentals	B
Restaurants	A
Nightlife	A
Attractions	A
Shopping	B
Sports	B
Nature	A

A bird's-eye view of the Virginia Beach area illustrates the old saying "Geography is destiny." Poised on the Atlantic Ocean near the mouth of the Chesapeake Bay, the low-lying land is punctuated with ports that dispatch merchant ships and warships to all corners. Rivers, inlets, bays, and marshlands carve watery shapes into the land mass, and along 28 miles of Virginia Beach coastline, from the big bay, around

Cape Henry, and down the coast to North Carolina, extends a virtually unbroken ribbon of sand that entices millions of people each year.

Virginia Beach's shoreline, dining, and diversions have propelled it into the big time. It's the largest city in Virginia, but because its 400,000 people are spread over 310 square miles, it feels more suburban than urban—and even rural in places.

Near the resort strip, the ambience is pure beach town. It's dominated by a two-and-a-half-mile paved boardwalk along a classic vista of broad, foamy waves, sparkling beach, and resort hotels stacked far up the coast, beginning at First Street and running out of sight to the north. This boardwalk differs from most, with their mishmash of honky-tonk storefronts hawking jewelry, pizza, and funnel cakes. Here the grass is groomed right up to the bench-lined pavement, and there's not a video arcade in sight. Each beach block is well marked, and bulletin boards make sure everyone knows what's scheduled at the 24th Street stage, where entertainers perform nightly from Memorial Day to Labor Day. To the delight of children, larger-than-life statues of fiddler crabs and other sea life peek out playfully here and there.

Alongside the walk runs a bike path—a rarity in beach towns, most of which shoo cyclists away during peak periods.

HOW TO GET THERE

◆ From Washington, DC, take I-95 south, to I-295 east, to I-64 east, through the Hampton Rds. tunnel. Then take Exit 284 in Norfolk (Virginia Beach Expwy.) east to the beach. In smooth traffic the 210-mi. trip takes about 4 hr.

◆ Most people arriving by air fly into Norfolk International Airport, about 10 mi. from Virginia Beach's resort strip.

◆ Amtrak trains stop daily in Newport News, VA, and passengers are transferred by bus to Virginia Beach, a 1-hr. 40-min trip.

Not only are bicycles welcome here, but Rollerblades and even skateboards are allowed on the boardwalk.

For nearly 40 blocks the boardwalk stretches past the hotels of Atlantic Avenue, the main thoroughfare in a hotel district that's a simple gridwork of roads, with Atlantic the first street paralleling the ocean, followed by Pacific, Arctic, Baltic, and Mediterranean avenues. It's an easy city to get around in, with street signs large, legible, and sometimes even lighted.

Just off shore, large tankers and warships ply the lanes to the Navy bases and commercial ports of Norfolk, Newport News, and other cities in the region known collectively as Hampton Roads. Military installations dot the area, and fighter jets spiral regularly through the skies with a roar known locally as "the sound of freedom."

Conservatism exerts a strong influence. Pat Robertson's Christian Broadcasting Network calls Virginia Beach home. And perhaps nowhere else has a city so large so vigilantly maintained its reputation as a family-oriented resort. It's a place whose very nature attracts the young, yet it wages a constant battle against youthful excess. "Cruising"—a slow, ritual, driving back and forth on the main drags—with its gumming effect on traffic, has been combated by ordinances that now make it illegal.

Those efforts notwithstanding, the city goes to great lengths to guarantee a good time for all. Large festivals are staples of life in Virginia Beach. Events like the Beach Music Weekend, the Boardwalk Art Show, the Viva Elvis! Festival, the North American Fireworks Competition, and the Neptune Festival draw tens of thousands of people. From Memorial Day to Labor Day, hardly a day goes by without some special event or free entertainment somewhere on the boardwalk.

BEACHES
RESORT STRIP BEACH

The main beach along the boardwalk is a classic of its kind—a long, wide, inviting stretch whose waves beckon swimmers and foam refreshingly over the feet of shore strollers. It is groomed regularly and kept clean despite the large crowds.

Beauty	A
Swimming	A
Sand	A
Amenities	B

The boardwalk—just a step or two above the sand—is an extension of the beach, unlike many others that are high and arcade-lined and have their own life apart from their beaches. It runs from Third Street at the south end to about 39th, with the most crowding and general beach frenzy in the blocks around 20th Street. To get away from the crush, head for the north end of the boardwalk or continue farther on the beach toward Fort Story.

Swimming: Robust waves—usually not rough enough to be hazardous—constantly break along several lines and roll in with a crash. Early morning surf is usually gentler. Water is clear but olive tinged. Lifeguard on duty.

Sand: Fine and almost light enough to qualify as white. The beach is level and uniformly wide—perhaps 50 yards—for the entire length of the boardwalk.

Amenities: Changing facility with rest rooms at First Street and Atlantic Avenue. Boardwalk rest rooms at 30th, 24th, and 17th streets. Many cafés and rental concessions along the boardwalk; rentals also on Atlantic Avenue.

Sports: Body boarding; volleyball and surfing at south end; fishing on rocks at Rudee Inlet.

Parking: Motels provide guest parking; elsewhere it can be tight in peak periods. Street parking, both metered and unmetered, fills up fast. Municipal lots at Fourth Street and Atlantic Avenue, 19th Street and Pacific Avenue, and 25th Street and Pacific Avenue. Private lots here and there, including at 21st Street and Arctic Avenue and at 29th Street and Pacific Avenue.

North Beaches
SEASHORE STATE PARK BEACH

Despite its name, Seashore State Park is not mainly a beach-front park. Most of its 2,770 acres are away from the water, and its main attraction is walking trails. The campground section, however, has a one-mile stretch of beach near the mouth of the Chesapeake Bay.

Beauty	B
Swimming	C
Sand	B
Amenities	D

From Memorial Day to Labor Day the beach is open only to people registered at one of the 233 campsites. The beach is fairly narrow, but the limit on who goes there means it's not usually crowded. The campground fills up only on weekends or holidays (reservations: tel. 800-933-7275).

The beach offers a sweeping view of the 14-mile-wide mouth of the bay, the Chesapeake Bay Bridge-Tunnel, and merchant ships anchored or passing in the distance. *From central Virginia Beach, follow Atlantic Ave. north to Rte. 60, and continue past Rte. 305. Turn right at the campground sign. (Going left takes you into the main park.)*

Swimming: Clear water with gentle waves a foot or two high that break at the shoreline. Lifeguard on duty.

Sand: Fine, light tan, with pine needles, shells, pebbles, and other washed-up natural debris. Narrow, backed by a long, low dune heavily vegetated with grass and small shrubs.

Amenities: Camp store, laundromat, snack bar, rest rooms.

Sports: None.

Parking: Large parking lot, with four boardwalks leading over the dunes to the beach.

FORT STORY BEACH

Fort Story is a U.S. Army base with several miles of ocean front, including a section of public beach open daily from Memorial Day to Labor Day and Friday through Monday during warm periods other times of the year. It's one of the few

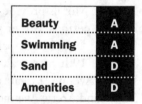

Beauty	A
Swimming	A
Sand	D
Amenities	D

public beaches where automatic-weapons fire can be heard above the cry of seagulls.

To one side of the main beach, only dunes and a few military antennae are visible, giving the place an undeveloped atmosphere. In the other direction, Virginia Beach hotels rise prominently. It is possible to walk the whole distance on the beach.

Besides the main public beach on base, there are several unmarked beach accesses, although parking isn't as convenient. The main road through the base is Atlantic Avenue (Route 305), and many of the roads leading off it toward the beach are restricted to base personnel. *From the Virginia Beach strip, follow Atlantic Ave. north about 3 mi. to the base's east gate (information: tel. 804-422-7975).*

Swimming: Strong waves crashing in, with the occasional loud slap rising impressively above the general roar. Lifeguard on duty.
Sand: Fine and light tan, a moderately wide stretch leading back to a long boardwalk that passes through a big cut in the dune.
Amenities: The base has a few stores within driving distance.
Sports: Fishing, surfing.
Parking: Two lots can hold more than 300 cars.

CHESAPEAKE BEACH

Chesapeake Beach (aka Chic's or Chick's Beach) is a long and narrow strip of sand overlooking the Chesapeake Bay Bridge-Tunnel and the bay. It's in a residential area and attracts mainly locals, but it's not far from Lynnhaven Inlet

Beauty	B-
Swimming	C
Sand	D
Amenities	D

marina and restaurants. Middle-class homes and a few businesses hug the coastline above the beach, so it does not have a sweeping or remote feel, but it's a calm alternative to the tourist strip. *From the strip, follow Shore Dr. (Rte. 60) north around Cape Henry, and continue west over the Lynnhaven Inlet bridge. Go about 2 mi. and make a right onto Pleasure House Rd., then a right onto Lookout Rd. Turn left at Chick's Beach Cafe onto Fentress Ave.*
Swimming: Small waves break constantly at the shoreline, providing more-than-average wave action for a bay beach. No lifeguard.
Sand: Fine, light tan, in a narrow strip averaging perhaps 10 yards wide.
Amenities: None. A few local restaurants have rest rooms for customers, including Alexander's on the Bay and Chick's Beach Cafe.
Sports: Fishing.
Parking: Residential street parking available. Alexander's on the Bay at the end of Fentress Avenue has parking for a fee.

LITTLE ISLAND PARK

Undiscovered Little Island Park has space for hundreds of cars and is located at a former Coast Guard station. Locals must be saving this beach for themselves.

Beauty	A
Swimming	A
Sand	A
Amenities	A

Part of a city park whose beach abuts a federal wildlife area, this beach has a remote character, even if you *can* see the lights of Virginia Beach to the north and the old Coast Guard buildings still standing here. There's also a long fishing pier—called the 3800 Block of Sandpiper Road Fishing Pier, to distinguish it from the pier downtown. *From Sandbridge, go south on Sandpiper Rd. for almost 4 mi. (information: tel. 804-426-7200).*

Swimming: Low waves roll into the beach in several tiers. Lifeguard on duty.

Sand: Fine, light, with tiny shells washed up by the waves. The beach is wide, slightly inclined, and backed by jagged dunes, some hearty with grass, others beaten down and eroded.

Amenities: Full range of services, including rest rooms, snack bar, and tennis and basketball courts.

Sports: Surfing, fishing.

Parking: Large lot for hundreds of cars. Per-car charge from Memorial Day to Labor Day: weekdays, $3; Sat.-Sun., $4.

HOTELS/INNS/B&BS

The city has 11,000 rooms to let, many in hotels and motels concentrated along the boardwalk. Many other lodgings, generally less expensive, are on the opposite side of Atlantic, as well as on Pacific Avenue, all within easy walking distance of the beach. For those who wish to avoid the boardwalk scene, several resorts are north of the boardwalk and even a few are farther north, near Cape Henry and the Lynnhaven Inlet.

◆ **Holiday Inn SunSpree Resort** (expensive). This appealing hotel at the north end of the boardwalk has 266 rooms, more than half of them ocean front and most others with ocean views, including standard rooms, junior suites, and efficiencies. Ask for one of the four Jacuzzi rooms. Typical decor is modern, Caribbean-style watercolors, and lots of light from the sliding-door onto the balcony. Junior suites are larger, with king-size bed and sleep sofa, plus a tiny sink, microwave, and refrigerator. *39th St. and Atlantic Ave., Virginia Beach, VA 23451; tel. 804-428-1711, 800-942-3224.*

◆ **Sheraton Oceanfront Hotel** (expensive). This recently renovated hotel has 204 rooms, 88 of them ocean front and 21 poolside facing the ocean. There's also one VIP suite. Seven rooms have Jacuzzis. A big indoor pool looks out on Atlantic Avenue.

Rooms have two double beds or, for a more spacious feel, one king-size bed and a sofa bed, floral spreads, and dark-wood furniture and headboards. *36th St. and Atlantic Ave., Virginia Beach, VA 23451; tel. 804-425-9000, 800-521-5635. On the ocean front.*

◆ **Thunderbird Motor Lodge** (moderate). This older motel at the north end of the boardwalk is less expensive than the slicker new properties and has ambience to boot. The T-Bird Cafe offers indoor or outdoor seating. Tropical murals around the pool. Guest rooms have ocean-front balconies and a 1950s look, just right for a place called the Thunderbird. Laminated imitation-oak furnishings, refrigerator, tile bathrooms. *35th St. and Atlantic Ave., Virginia Beach, VA 23451; tel. 804-428-3024, 800-633-6669. On the ocean front.*

◆ **Barclay Cottage Bed & Breakfast** (inexpensive). This historic B&B has six guest rooms in a two-story, veranda-wrapped beach cottage that is the last of its kind in Virginia Beach, preserved thanks to the teacher who refused to sell the property. Owners Peter and Claire Catanese have furnished the rooms individually, with many antiques, old photographs and art, and trunks refurbished by Peter. The Red, White & Blue Room is modern. The bed in the Sleigh Bed Room dates to 1810. *400 16th St., Virginia Beach, VA 23451; tel. 804-422-1956. Closed Nov.-mid-Mar. Two blocks from the beach at 16th St. and Arctic Ave.*

◆ **Comfort Inn Oceanfront.** This 83-unit hotel, less than ten years old and recently renovated, is a good value. In these two-room ocean-front suites, the sofa bed/TV area opens onto a 12-foot-wide balcony, and a polished tile hallway leads to the windowless bedroom, away from boardwalk noise but subject to hallway clatter. Decor is modern, with colorful floral curtains, muted walls, artificial plants, two-burner stove, sink, refrigerator. There's a three-room VIP suite. Avoid rooms 303 and 304, across from the housekeeping office. Pool looks out on the beach. *2015 Atlantic Ave., Virginia Beach, VA 23451; tel. 804-425-8200, 800-443-4733.*

HOUSE RENTALS

Virginia Beach is hotel-oriented, but it does have several hundred "cottage" rentals available. They're concentrated in two areas:

north of the boardwalk, between 40th and 79th streets, and half an hour south in the Sandbridge community. Most of the Sandbridge homes are largish and on stilts. Weekly house rentals range from $500 to $3,900, depending on location and size.

◆ **Atkinson Realty.** Weekly rentals in summer between 42nd and 89th streets. *5307 Atlantic Ave., Virginia Beach, VA 23451; tel. 804-428-4441. Open daily.*

◆ **Sandbridge Real Estate.** *3713 S. Sandpiper Rd., Virginia Beach, VA 23451; tel. 804-426-6262. Open daily late May-early Sep. Closed Sun. early Sep.-late May.*

RESTAURANTS

◆ **Lynnhaven Fish House Restaurant** (expensive). Regarded by many as the city's best seafood restaurant, it overlooks the Chesapeake Bay at the Lynnhaven Pier and packs 'em in for fresh catches of flounder, salmon, and orange roughy. There's also a cocktail lounge. *2350 Starfish Rd., Virginia Beach, VA 23451; tel. 804-481-0003. Open daily for lunch and dinner. From the tourist strip, take Laskin Rd. (31st St.) west to Colonial Rd. Go north to Great Neck Rd., then north to Shore Dr. (Rte. 60). Turn left and go about 1/2 mi., then turn right on Starfish.*

◆ **501 City Grill** (moderate). Inviting atmosphere with high tin ceiling and long wooden bar, a sweeping mural of wine country in the main dining room, and natural wood tables and chairs. The signature appetizer is Michelob shrimp. Popular entreés are the Cajun bourbon shrimp and scallops with penne and the Angus T-bone steak with red chili, onion rings, and cabernet sauce. Excellent wine list, including up to ten wines by the glass daily. *501 N. Birdneck Rd., Virginia Beach, VA 23451; tel. 804-425-7195. Open daily for dinner and for brunch on Sun. Just north of Rte. 44, at the end of the Birdneck Shoppes.*

◆ **Cafe Society** (moderate). Glass walls give this contemporary restaurant an open, airy feel. Starched white tablecloths, a black-and-white motif, an open kitchen, and a small stone-topped bar round out the Euro-café scene. Top dishes include the pan-sautéed crab and shrimp cakes with pineapple remoulade and wild rice, the grilled yellowfin tuna, and the Cafe combo (a fish tostada and a crab and lobster cake with rice and vegetables). Pasta and seafood specials daily. *1807 Mediterranean Ave., Virginia Beach, VA 23451; tel. 804-422-8774. Open Mon.-Fri. for lunch, daily for dinner, and Sun. for brunch.*

◆ **Rockafellers Restaurant** (moderate). This restaurant wrapped in windows and decks sits on the Rudee Inlet marina, with good views for both indoor and outdoor diners. Popular dishes are the Caesar salad, crab cakes, barbecued shrimp, and New York strip steak. Thursday night there's a Maine lobster special. *308 Mediterranean Ave., Virginia Beach, VA 23451; tel. 804-422-5654. Open daily for lunch and dinner and Sun. brunch. At Fifth St.*

NIGHTLIFE

The city's nightlife caters to the younger set, with nightclubs and restaurants offering DJs, dancing, and live entertainment. During summer, many hotels and resorts offer lounge shows.

◆ **H2O.** This restaurant/club has a high-tech look, with overhead TV screens, black floor and ceiling, a dance floor, a stage for live music a couple nights a week, and Master Choo's Rock & Roll Sushi Bar. *1069 19th St., Virginia Beach, VA 23451; tel. 804-425-5684. Open daily.*

◆ **Heartbreak Cafe.** Two-level dance floor with DJs playing Top 40 music and disco favorites. *800 Baker Rd., Virginia Beach, VA 23451; tel. 804-473-9746. Open Wed.-Sat. Take Rte. 44 to Newtown Rd. north; go left on Baker Rd. for 1 mi.*

◆ **Kokoamos Bar, Grill & Yacht Club.** Water-front night spot with a downstairs bar and upstairs "yacht club," each offering live music some nights. *2100 Marina Shores Dr., Virginia Beach, VA 23451; tel. 804-481-3781. Open daily. Follow Shore Dr. to N. Great Neck Rd. at Marina Shores.*

◆ **The Jewish Mother.** This casual deli-restaurant with a stage presents jazz, blues, and folk by regional and national performers. Large selection of beers and desserts. *3108 Pacific Ave., Virginia Beach, VA 23451; tel. 804-422-5430. Open daily. At Laskin Rd.*

ATTRACTIONS

◆ **A.R.E. Visitors Center.** The Association for Research and Enlightenment is devoted to the work of Edgar Cayce, known as the father of holistic medicine, whose psychic talents allowed him to make medical diagnoses. The visitors center offers tours, a 30-minute movie, ESP testing, lectures, a bookstore, and exhibits on Cayce and the association's work. *Box 595, Virginia Beach, VA 23451; tel. 804-428-3588. Open Mon.-Sat 9-8, Sun. 11-8. At 67th St. and Atlantic Ave.*

◆ **Cape Henry Lighthouse.** Walk up the 83 steps of this cut-stone lighthouse, first lit in 1792, for a sweeping view of Cape Henry, Virginia Beach, and environs. On a clear day you can see the whole length of the 17-mile Chesapeake Bay Bridge-Tunnel. At the top of the stairway, you must climb two short ladders, then squeeze through the small opening to the lamp house. *Fort Story Army Base, Virginia Beach, VA 23451; tel. 804-422-9421. Open daily 10-5 mid-Mar.-Oct. Admission. From the strip, follow Atlantic Ave. north to the army base.*

◆ **Christian Broadcasting Network Center.** Home of Pat Robertson and the 700 Club broadcast, it offers guided tours of some of the most advanced TV studios in the country, plus the chance to take part in the 700 Club live audience at 10 a.m. weekdays. (CBN also runs a nearby 249-room hotel, the Founders Inn; tel. 800-926-4466.) *977 Centerville Tpke., Virginia Beach, VA 23463; tel. 804-579-2745. Open Mon.-Fri. 8-5; tours Mon.-Fri. at 11:30 and 2. From the tourist strip, take Rte. 44 west to I-64 east to Exit 286-B.*

◆ **Life-Saving Museum of Virginia.** Housed in the decommissioned Virginia Beach Lifeboat Station, the museum's exhibits explore the history of the Coast Guard lifesaving service. *Box 24, Virginia Beach, VA 23458; tel. 804-422-1587. Open Mon.-Sat. 10-5, Sun. 12-5. Closed Mon. Oct.-May. Admission. On the boardwalk at 24th St.*

◆ **Mount Trashmore.** At 68 feet high, it was once a garbage heap—until the city turned it into a 162-acre park for biking, picnicking, and lakeside relaxing. A similar but larger project, City View Park, is scheduled for partial opening in 1996 near the Virginia Beach-Chesapeake City line. *300 Edwin Dr., Virginia Beach, VA 23451; tel. 804-473-5251. Open daily 7:30-sunset. From the strip, take Rte. 44 west to Independence Blvd. south, then make a quick left onto South Blvd. and a right onto Expressway Dr.*

◆ **Virginia Beach Center for the Arts.** The city's premier art museum, in its new home since 1989, includes a main gallery with contemporary art, students' exhibits, an auditorium, and regular tours. *2200 Parks Ave., Virginia Beach, VA 23451; tel. 804-425-0000. Open Tue.-Fri. 10-5:30, Sat. 10-4, Sun. 12-4.*

◆ **Virginia Marine Science Center.** This first-class museum is packed with marine life exhibits, including hands-on activities and a touch tank. It will remain open while undergoing a major expansion. *717 General Booth Blvd., Virginia Beach, VA 23451; tel. 804-437-4949. Open Mon.-Sat. 9-9 and Sun. 9-5 mid-Jun.-Labor Day; otherwise daily 9-5. Admission. From the tourist strip, take Pacific Ave. over the Rudee Inlet Bridge to General Booth Blvd.*

SHOPPING

Most stores close to the ocean-front strip are the standard beach shops: clothes, body boards, and saltwater taffy. For more serious shopping, there are several spots in Virginia Beach, Norfolk, and surrounding cities.

◆ **Hilltop Shopping Center.** More than 100 shops make up this big complex that is divided into north, east, and west sections. Among stores are the Kitchen Barn, Dan Ryan for Men, Travel House, Birkenstock Footprints, and Maternity Boutique. *Laskin and First Colonial Rds., Virginia Beach, VA 23451. Open daily. From the ocean front, take Laskin west to First Colonial.*

◆ **La Promenade.** More than two dozen distinctive shops, including NYFO Boutique, Kids Kids Kids, Dakota, Jos. A. Banks Clothiers, Pappagallo, Talbots, and Williams-Sonoma. *1860 Laskin Rd., Virginia Beach, VA 23451; tel. 804-422-8839. Open daily. From ocean front, go 3 mi. west on Laskin Rd.*

◆ **Loehmann's Plaza.** About 30 stores, including Lillian Vernon Outlet Store, Linens 'N Things, Baby Superstore, Marc Lance Menswear, and Off Broadway Shoes. *4000 Virginia Beach Blvd., Virginia Beach, VA 23451. Open daily. From the ocean front, take Laskin Rd. (which becomes Virginia Beach Blvd.) 8 mi. west.*

◆ **Pembroke Mall.** More than 100 stores, including Sears, Uptons, Stein Mart, Proffitt's. *Virginia Beach and Independence Blvds., Virginia Beach, VA 23451; tel. 804-497-6255. Open daily.*

BEST FOOD SHOPS

SANDWICHES: ◆ **Zero's Sub Shop.** *2106 Pacific Ave., Virginia Beach, VA 23451; tel. 804-491-2355. Open daily 10 a.m. to 1 a.m.*

SEAFOOD: ◆ **Virginia Beach Seafood.** *1706 Mediterranean Ave., Virginia Beach, VA 23451; tel. 804-428-4844. Open daily.*

FRESH PRODUCE: ◆ **Davis Farm Produce.** *Princess Anne and Sandbridge Rds., Virginia Beach, VA 23451; tel. 804-426-7553. Open daily May-late Oct. From the south end of the strip, go south on General Booth Blvd. and make a left onto Princess Anne Rd.*

BAKERY: ◆ **Sugar Plum Bakery.** *1352 Laskin Rd., Virginia Beach, VA 23451; tel. 804-422-3913. Open Tue.-Sat. 7:30-6 and Sun. 8-3. Closed Mon. From the strip, go west on Laskin Rd. past Birdneck Rd. It's on the left.*

ICE CREAM: ◆ **Uncle Harry's Cones & Cream.** *37th St. and Pacific Ave., Virginia Beach, VA 23451; tel. 804-425-8195. Open daily.*

WINE: ◆ **Taste Unlimited.** Good wine selection and a broad range of gourmet foods, desserts, sandwiches. *36th St. and Pacific Ave., Virginia Beach, VA 23451; tel. 804-422-3399. Open daily.*

SPORTS
FISHING
Dozens of charter fishing boats and headboats (which charge per person) operate from marinas at Rudee and Lynnhaven inlets. Freshwater fishing licenses can be bought at bait-and-tackle shops. A saltwater fishing license is required in the Chesapeake Bay and its tributaries unless you're fishing on a licensed pier, licensed charter boat, or licensed private boat.

◆ **Virginia Beach Fishing Center.** Deep-sea fishing, with two half-day trips daily, plus night fishing in the summer. *Rudee Inlet, Virginia Beach, VA 23451; tel. 804-422-5700. Open daily. On Rudee Inlet at Fifth St. and Pacific Ave.*

SURFING
It thrives here, especially between Fourth Street and Rudee Inlet, at Sandbridge Beach, and on the ocean edge of Cape Henry and the fishing piers at 15th Street and Little Island Park. From Memorial Day to Labor Day, surfing is not allowed along most of the main beach when lifeguards are on duty. To ask about a particular area, call the police department (804-428-9133). The East Coast Surfing

Championship attracts hundreds of surfers to the ocean front between Second and 11th streets for five days in August.

◆ **Wave Riding Vehicles.** Surfboards, surf reports, and fashions. *1900 Cypress Ave., Virginia Beach, VA 23451; tel. 804-422-8823. Open daily. At the corner of Cypress Ave. and 19th St.*

DIVING

The area's big diving attraction is shipwrecks. Some were caused by nature's treachery, others by German U-boats that prowled the area during World War II.

◆ **Undersea Adventures.** Scuba, snorkeling, and private charters to local wrecks in the Atlantic. Educational field trips conducted by Old Dominion University. *1294 Ketch Point, Virginia Beach, VA 23454; tel. 804-481-3688. Open Mar.-Dec. Operates out of Rudee Inlet, 200 Winston Salem Ave.*

BICYCLING

Many hotels offer bike rentals to guests, as do a number of bike shops. The six-mile Cape Henry Trail in Seashore State Park is open to bikers, as are Fort Story and Mount Trashmore Park.

◆ **Oceanfront Bikes.** Beach cruisers and mountain bikes. *616 Norfolk Ave., Virginia Beach, VA 23451; tel. 804-425-5120. Open Mon.-Sat. Sep.-May and daily Jun.-Aug. From Ninth St. and Atlantic Ave., go west 5 blocks on Ninth, which becomes Norfolk Ave.*

GOLF

Virginia Beach has nine public courses. One of them, Bow Creek Municipal Golf Course, was to be closed at least for the first half of 1996 for construction of a drainage canal.

◆ **Hell's Point Golf Club.** This par-72 course designed by Rees Jones includes 61 sand traps. *2700 Atwoodtown Rd., Virginia Beach, VA 23451; tel. 804-721-3400. Open daily. Admission. Near Sandbridge. From the resort strip, take General Booth Blvd. south, turn left onto Princess Anne Rd., and then left onto Sandbridge Rd.*

◆ **Honey Bee Golf Club.** This 18-hole, par-70 course designed by Rees Jones is home to the Virginia Beach Open. *5016 S. Independence Blvd., Virginia Beach, VA 23456; tel. 804-471-2768. Open daily. Admission. 5 mi. south of Rte. 44.*

◆ **Owl's Creek Golf Center.** This 18-hole, par-62 course designed by Brook Park goes along 40-foot sand dunes. *411 S. Birdneck Rd., Virginia Beach, VA 23451; tel. 804-428-2800. Open daily. Admission.*

TENNIS

The city has 210 public tennis courts scattered far and wide, but the biggest cluster is the Owl's Creek complex.

◆ **Owl's Creek Municipal Tennis Center.** Has 14 outdoor, lighted courts. Very reasonable. *928 S. Birdneck Rd., Virginia Beach, VA 23451; tel. 804-437-4804. Open daily 9 a.m.-10 p.m. Mar.-mid-Dec. and 9-5 mid-Dec.-Feb. Admission. From Fifth St. and Pacific Ave., go south on General Booth Blvd., then turn right on Birdneck Rd.*

NATURE

◆ **Seashore State Park & Natural Area.** This 2,770-acre park has nine trails for self-guided walks ranging from one-half to six miles long, including the two-mile Bald Cypress Trail, which cuts through a cypress swamp. The visitors center has schedules for interpreted nature hikes and beach walks. *2500 Shore Dr., Virginia Beach, VA 23451; tel. 804-481-2131. Visitors center open daily 9-6 early Apr.-late Oct. Admission. About 6 mi. north of the tourist strip.*

◆ **Virginia Marine Science Museum.** Sponsors whale-watching trips January to February, dolphin-watching trips June to October, and ocean-collection trips June to August. All depart from Rudee Inlet. *717 General Booth Blvd., Virginia Beach, VA 23451; tel. 804-437-4949. Open daily 9-5. Admission.*

SAFETY TIPS

Virginia Beach is a low-crime destination, but being a big city and a tourist hot spot, it is subject to petty theft. Keep belongings out of sight, lock car doors, and put valuables in hotel safes.

TOURIST INFORMATION

◆ **Virginia Beach Visitor Information.** *2100 Parks Ave., Virginia Beach, VA 23451; tel. 804-437-4700, 800-446-8038. Open daily 9-5. The main tourist information center is on Rte. 44. Information booths open on the boardwalk Memorial Day-Labor Day.*